The Annals of
DUBLIN
~ FAIR CITY ~

Dedication

To Frank Browne sj
my co-author in spirit

Others have been here and known
Griefs we thought our special own
    — Patrick Kavanagh

THE ANNALS OF
DUBLIN
~ FAIR CITY ~

E E O'Donnell SJ

with photographs from
The Francis Browne, SJ Collection

WOLFHOUND PRESS

First published 1987 by
WOLFHOUND PRESS
68 Mountjoy Square, Dublin 1.

© 1987 E E O'Donnell

Photographs copyright © Fr Francis Browne, sj Collection

British Library Cataloguing in Publication Data
O'Donnell, E E
The annals of Dublin ~ fair city ~.
1. Dublin (Dublin) —— History
I. Title
941.8'35   DA995.D75

ISBN 0 86327 149 9 HB
ISBN 0 86327 163 4 LIMITED EDITION

Cover illustration: 'A Bird's Eye View of Dublin'
by H W Brewer, A Supplement to *The Graphic*, 27 December 1890
courtesy of the Neptune Gallery, Dublin.

Cover design by Jan de Fouw
Typesetting by Redsetter Limited
Printed by Richard Clay Limited

CONTENTS

APPENDICES

'ELSEWHERE' — COMPARATIVE DATES

LIST OF MAPS, CHARTS ETC.

Front and rear endpapers: The City of Dublin: No. 1 of a Series of Views of the Principal Capitals of Europe: *London Illustrated News* (original size 900 x 330 mm) courtesy of the Neptune Gallery.

LIST OF PHOTOGRAPHS

The photographer, Francis Browne, was born in Cork in 1880. He went to school in Dublin, first attending Belvedere College – the alma mater of James Joyce – and then boarding at Castleknock. He joined the Jesuits in 1897 and was ordained a priest in 1915 by his uncle, Robert Browne, Bishop of Cloyne. He died in Dublin at the age of eighty having spent most of his life giving missions and retreats and working as an army chaplain. During the First World War he served in the Irish Guards. For outstanding bravery, he was awarded the Military Cross and the Belgian Croix de Guerre. His work brought Fr Browne all around the world, always with his camera at the ready. The only Continent he never saw was America – although he was heading for the United States on one memorable occasion, aboard the *Titanic*. As fortune (or his Superior) would have it, he disembarked at Queenstown (now Cobh) but his photographs of that tragic maiden voyage earned him an international reputation for photo-journalism. What is not so well known is that Frank Browne went on taking photographs of ships and trains and planes and people. He left behind him a record of how men, women and (especially) children lived between 1910 and 1950. His collection contains no less than 40,000 photographs, including nearly 3,600 of Dublin. The sheer volume and the artistic excellence of these meant that many agonizing choices had to be made in selecting the illustrations for this book. They have been chosen to complement and supplement the text as we trace the history of Dublin down the decades.

ACKNOWLEDGEMENTS

A sincere word of thanks to the following for reading all or part of my manuscript and for making many helpful suggestions, corrections and additions: Howard B Clarke (University College Dublin), Maurice Craig, Gordon Herries Davies (Trinity College Dublin), F X Martin (University College Dublin), Breandán Ó Riordáin (Director, National Museum of Ireland) and Tony White (National Council for Educational Awards). Any mistakes that remain are my own: I shall be grateful to hear about these so that they may be corrected in the second of numerous editions of this work!

Thanks, too, to my publisher, Seamus Cashman, and his associates at the Wolfhound Press for their encouragement, diligence and kindness manifested throughout the course of my publication. Further encouragement came from Ms Grace Perrott, Ms Pat Seager and Mr David Neary of Dublin Corporation: for this I am grateful.

For the use of copyright material, it gives me pleasure to make the following acknowledgements: to Liam de Paor and to Hutchinson for permission to reproduce the map of the Battle of Rathmines (1649), to Michael O'brien of The O'Brien Press for permission to reproduce the map of Viking Dublin; to Mrs Catherine Kavanagh for permission to quote from two of Patrick Kavanagh's poems.

During the years of reading that went into this book, the librarians of the Dublin Public Libraries (especially those at the Pembroke Branch and the ILAC Centre) and at the National Library of Ireland have been most obliging. I would likke to single out Ms Paula Howard of the Gilbert Library in Pearse Street for her constant attention and advice.

Next, I want to express my gratitude to the Jesuit Order for alllowing me to use the photographs of Fr Browne. Any correspondence regarding his Collection should be addressed to me.

Finally, but most importantly, I would like to say thanks to Ms Ursula Doyle of Irish Messenger Publications for typing and processing the words of my text.

E E O'Donnell, SJ
Gonzaga College
Dublin 6

The publisher wishes to acknowledge with thanks all those who have assisted in the production of this book — including Jan de Fouw for his design and advice; Nuala and Raymond Gunn for typesetting and layout; Jacobus Van Hespen for photographic prints for pages 66, 74, 123, 176, 178, 179 left, 182 top; and in particular thanks to Elizabeth Ryan for her extensive work on the photographs and maps for this book.

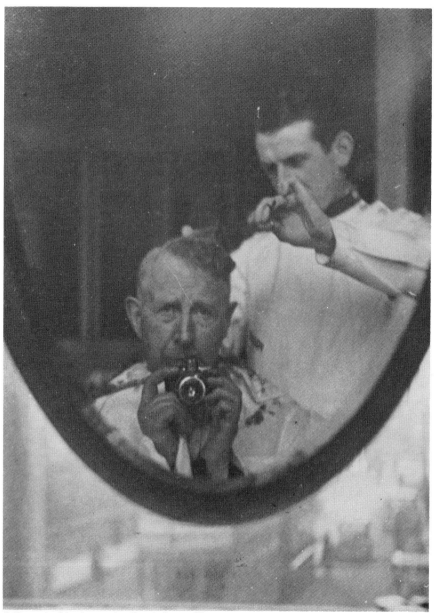

Self-portrait of the photographer, Francis Browne SJ.

INTRODUCTION

Is there any logic to Dublin at all? Is there any reason why it is always out-of-step with the rest of Ireland? Can anyone besides James Joyce make sense of what, by provincial Irish standards, is a vast, urban sprawl?

Answers: yes, yes and yes.

Start with the numbers of the Dublin buses. Is there any logic to them? There is, actually. To understand them, you have to go back to the days of the horse-drawn trams like the one that toppled into the canal-lock at Portobello Bridge in Rathmines leaving a permanent sense of doom about that place. The trams ran from the centre of the city, radiating clockwise from south to north. Number 1 went to the Pigeon House at Ringsend; Numbers 2 and 3 by different routes to Sándymount; 4 to Ballsbridge; 5-8 to Blackrock, Kingstown (Dún Laoghaire) and Dalkey; 9 and 10 to Donnybrook; 11 to Clonskeagh, etc.

The Dublin buses retain this basic logic. You can alight from most of them in the centre of the city (*An Lár*) and easily find a good bookshop. If you do this, you will see so many books on Dublin that you will be bound to ask: why another?

This book is different in that it tries to present all the important facts about Dublin in one volume – and brightens these up by throwing in some unimportant ones as well. Some recent (good) books on the city treat it thematically or geographically. This one does so chronologically in the belief that the addition of this fourth dimension will help to develop a truer picture of the city. It is too long since the annalists have been at work; the time is ripe for a new analyst to start probing.

This work is different, too, insofar as it gives a year-by-year account of the findings of the latest historical and archaeological enquiries. It is hard to keep abreast of all of these, but a genuine effort has been made to include the most recent historians' views on, say, the Battle of Clontarf and to report on the latest archaeological evidence found at the Viking site on Wood Quay. Unfortunately, even the newest histories disagree on dates. As regards buildings, the year when work *began* has been given but it has been very difficult to be consistent in this matter; architects names – when known – are given in brackets.

Confucius said that one image is worth a thousand words. Fr Frank Browne, SJ has posthumously added many thousands of words to my text. These hitherto unpublished photographs (from a private collection in the Jesuit archives which has been described by the photographic archivist, George Morrison, as 'the finest of its kind in the country, the Lawrence Collection not excepted') provide an added justification for this book.

Some hints on *how* to read the book might be in order. Shakespeare held that 'the evil that men do lives after them'. One could truly assert that the *good* they do, rather than being 'interred with their bones', lives after them as well. I do not just mean that, for example, we ought to be grateful to Lord Chesterfield for laying out the Phoenix Park so delightfully for us. I mean that little Dublin women (e.g. Molly Malone), as well as great Dublin women (e.g. Peg Woffington), little men (e.g. 'Bang-Bang'), as well as great men (e.g. James Joyce) have left footprints on the streets of Dublin that are still vibrant. Dublin has very special vibrations. A walk through the Liberties with any old Dubliner will put this rather mystical assertion beyond doubt.

Read this book imaginatively. Let it conjure up the past for you in the most vivid possible way. Stand where the Dodder enters the Liffey and watch Cromwell's men unload the first cabbages to be introduced to Ireland. See them dig the Cabbage Patch near St Patrick's Cathedral. Listen to their language – and to that of the children there to-day. After all, 1649 is not that long ago.

There is another way of reading this book: let time seem short. Picture a famous person who was born in 1838 and lived to sixty-five. There are old people alive to-day who can remember meeting that man long ago, can remember especially his stories of the Great Famine. So, in a way it is not long since the Hunger was upon us. It is really not so long ago that the GPO in Dublin was built (1814). 1814, in this way, was just before the Famine and just after the Act of Union when College Green lost its Parliament on New Year's Day 1801. The ghost of the Speaker of the Irish House of Commons still lingers in Foster Place.

While reading this book, keep this question at the back of your mind: *how* has Dublin evolved? Its evolution, you will discover, has been far from straightforward. What is progress anyway? Liam de Paor throws some startling light on this question in his recent book on *The Peoples of Ireland*. Having described the thatched houses of our stone-age ancestors, he concludes: 'In early Victorian Ireland hundreds of thousands of people were worse off than their forebears of 5,000 years ago.'

I do not mean to suggest that Dublin has always gone from bad to worse. There have been notable improvements in housing, health and a host of other areas. But watch how many steps back we took for each, say, three steps forward. To help you do this realistically, I have tried to paint a picture of the city 'warts and all'. Dublin had the first purpose-built maternity hospital in the world; at the same time, the infant mortality rate at the South Dublin Union was a staggering 17,253 out of 25,352 in a twelve-year period. Dublin grew to become the second-largest and one of the most beautiful cities of the British Empire: yet a cross-channel visitor had this to say in 1834:

> In walking through the streets of Dublin, strange and striking contrasts are presented between grandeur and poverty. In Merrion Square, St Stephen's Green and elsewhere, the ragged wretches that are sitting on the steps contrast strongly with the splendour of the houses and the magnificent equipages that wait without.

Striking contrasts still prevail. It is my hope that this book might motivate a few opinion-leaders to set about the task of rendering these contrasts less stark. Decision-makers in Dublin Corporation please note.

For whom is this book written? I had Dublin's citizens – whether old-timers or newcomers – primarily in mind, intending to give them a greater sense of belonging by reminding them of Dublin's past. As a spin-off, the citizenry might take a more active part in preserving what is worth preserving of the city – even if this entails taking to the streets in protest against ignorant pseudo-

development.

Secondarily, it is written for people from the rest of Ireland: to help explain *why* Dublin is different and to give them a greater appreciation of what is, after all, *their* capital city too.

Willy-nilly, the book is bound to be of practical use to the constantly-growing number of *aficionados* of James Joyce. This chronicle should help foreign as well as Irish readers of *Ulysses* and *Finnegans Wake*; it will tell them, for instance, when the National Museyroom was opened in Kildare Street and when the 'overgrown milestone' was erected in Phoenix Park.

Since this work is more of an exercise in communication than an academic history, enterprising teachers should find it serves their purpose; the more enlightened ones might even use it as a supplementary school text. To facilitate the work of teachers, I have tried to keep the spelling of Irish names in line with the principles laid down in *A New History of Ireland* (Moody, Martin and Byrne, eds.). Thus, King Brian's name is spelled Bóruma, not Boru.

Finally, for both adults and children, the book can be used as a guide. The specially devised index and the street-maps of historic sections of Dublin should make it an easy city to visit – whether you come from Kentucky or Kenmare, from Camden Town or Camden Street.

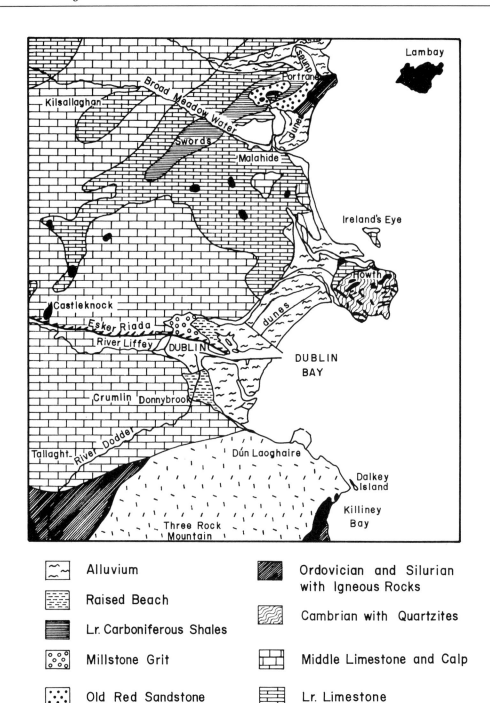

Fig. 1   Geological Map of Dublin.

GEOLOGICAL PREAMBLE

Dublin was not always the capital city of Ireland. It was not always a city – nor even a town. To make dates like AD 1014 seem recent, let us begin by taking a look at the site of Dublin before there were any people around at all. In a certain sense, it can be said that Dublin is 'as old as the hills'. But how old are its hills? The logic of geologists helps us answer this question.

BC

4,500,000,000	Formation of the earth's crust. Where Ireland stands now is all sea (see 70 million below).
2,000,000,000	Lowest form of life appears – *not* Dubliners!
600,000,000	Formation of the oldest rocks in the Dublin region: e.g. rocks of the Great Sugarloaf are made of quartzite of the Cambrian period.
360,000,000	Formation of more recent Dublin rocks: e.g. Kippure is made of granite from the Caledonian period. Dublin granite will be used in the city's finest public buildings and will be exported to build the Thames Embankment, London.
300,000,000	Formation of most recent Dublin rocks: e.g. Feltrim Hill is made of limestone of the middle carboniferous type; in its present form it is a feature produced by circumdenudation over the last few million years.
200,000,000	Interesting old fossils are embedded in rocks around Dublin coast. A good place to see them is between Malahide and Portmarnock.
70,000,000	Ireland emerges permanently from the sea. It had its head above water many times before this.
1,000,000	Great Ice Age begins: Ireland is 'buried' in ice for thousands of years. There were many – not just two – glaciations within this Great Ice Age.
30,000	'Modern Man' evolves, probably in Africa; not for another 25,000 years will human beings reach Ireland.
20,000	Second Ice Age beginning to end. 'The Scalp' gorge is formed by melt-waters flowing under glacial ice. Fifty-eight different minerals have been found in the Dublin area. They include gold and silver; the lead and barytes mined at

Ballycorus; the stontianite quarried at Golden Bridge; the zinc mined at Clontarf; the garnets gathered at Killiney.

12,000 The glaciation of the Midlands ends about this time. The village of Esker, near Lucan in County Dublin, takes its name from the eastern extremity of this phenomenon.

9,000 'Esker Riada' formed: a single ridge of gravel is supposed to run from Dublin to Galway but this is one of the myths of Irish geomorphology. In fact the ridge is composed of many eskers. There is more about the Dublin end of this ridge on page 31.

ELSEWHERE: Earliest known rocks are deposited in Zimbabwe and Manitoba, Canada (3,000 million years BC). First large-scale occurrence of fossils (600 million BC). Early ape fossils deposited in East Africa (20 million BC) and in Italy (10 million BC). Earliest known pre-human beings: *Australopithecus*, South Africa (500 thousand BC). More advanced pre-humans move to Western Europe: the Heidelberg Jaw (400 thousand BC). Neanderthal man inhabits the Rhineland (100 thousand BC). *Homo sapiens*: Cro-Magnon artists leave cave-drawings at Dordogne, France (30 thousand BC). Great flowering of palaeolithic art (18 thousand BC). First immigrants from Asia cross the Behring Straits into North America (10 thousand BC). In Java, the descendants of Solo Man are represented by the Wadjak people (probably dating from before 8 thousand BC).

DUBLIN'S RIVERS

8500   About this time, the Second Ice Age has come to an end. Glaciers have gradually slithered into the sea. In the great thaw, many of them turned into rivers. Some of Dublin's rivers have since disappeared; others have been channelled underground.

    The great mud-flat exposed in the bay at low tide helps to explain why Dublin is not the earliest part of Ireland to be inhabited: docking facilities for immigrant ships are poor.

    Some interesting details emerge when we take a look at these rivers one by one.

The **Tolka**, with its tributary **Pinkeen**, deposited an alluvial bank (later called Mud Island) near Ballybough Bridge at the entrance to Dublin Bay.

The **Bradogue**, now dry, flowed from Cabra down what is now Constitution Hill, ran across North Brunswick Street (formerly called Channel Row), turned at a right-angle south past St Mary's Abbey and went into the Liffey at Chancery Place (formerly a harbour known as The Pill).

The **Liffey** looked as if she was going to head south, met with tougher rock and swung in a circle to form a great mud-flat at her mouth. Places like Trinity College and Merrion Square stand on reclaimed land. The **Rye Water** joins the Liffey at Leixlip.

The **Camac** still flows parallel to Tyrconnell Road in Inchicore, cuts through the valley at Kilmainham, goes under Heuston Railway Station and enters the Liffey just to the west of Old Kingsbridge. The first village upstream, Rowserstown, still has its old mills and still deals in hand-woven cloth.

The **Poddle**, with its tributary river **Coombe**, was once the main supplier of Dublin's domestic water-mains. It can still be seen at Templeogue, Kimmage and Mount Argus. From there it runs underground beneath Patrick Street and Bride Street to join the Liffey (through a grille) a little to the east of Capel Street Bridge. A detailed map of the city water-course can be seen in the Civic Museum, South William Street. **Colman's Brook**, an artificially constructed tributary which ran into the Liffey near the church on Merchant's Quay, formed part of the old town's water supply. The Poddle, until recently, was thought to have filled the moat at Dublin Castle. Excavations there in 1986 tend to disprove this. Beside the Castle, at the foot of Cork Hill, it did form a black pool, or Dubh Linn, which gave the city its English name.

The **Steine** has now dried up. It used to flow down Earlsfort Terrace, along the south and west sides of St Stephen's Green, through College Green to the Liffey at what is now D'Olier Street. It took its name from the 'Steine', a standing-stone erected (as in other estuaries) by the Vikings. Some civic-minded Dubliners will place a replica on the spot, near Pearse Street Garda Station, in 1986.

The little **Swan** river has also disappeared. It flowed through Rathmines, Cullenswood (now Ranelagh), across Morehampton Road (where there is still a Swan Place) and entered the Dodder near London Bridge.

The **Dodder** and its tributary, **Owedoher**, are still going strong. Before it was artificially slowed down by weirs, the Dodder was a tempestuous and temperamental river in time of flood. Its tantrums will be recorded later, as the years roll by. In pre-historic times (and, indeed, up to the building of Sir John Rogerson's Quay in 1713), the Dodder left Ringsend high and dry. Geologists show that the Ringsend spit, formed of harder rock, was as narrow as two hundred yards in places.

Three small rivers, the **Santry**, the **Nanikin** and the **Holly Brook** flow into the north side of Dublin Bay.

The **Ward** rises in County Meath and flows through The Ward and Swords. A little further north, the **Broadmeadow** has an estuary famous for its swans just beyond Malahide.

Aerial view of the River Dodder.

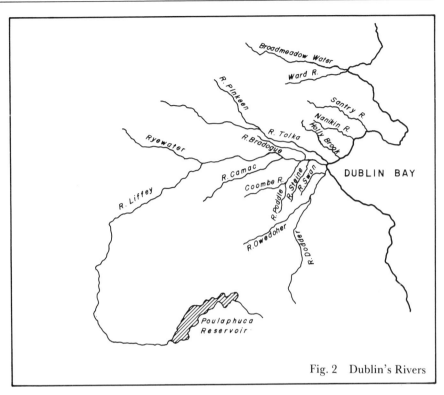

Fig. 2   Dublin's Rivers

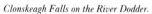

Clonskeagh Falls on the River Dodder.

Cromlech on Mount Venus.

Aideen's Grave, Howth.

THE FIRST DUBLINERS

8000 What with all that ice melting, the sea-level begins to rise. It is about this date (give or take a few hundred years) that Ireland becomes an island, severing its final physical link with Scotland. The mainland of Great Britain, incidentally, will remain attached to continental Europe for a few thousand years more.

5000 Mesolithic people hunt around the Dublin area. They hunt deer, catch fish and eat berries and nuts. They leave a midden behind them on Dalkey Island which, when excavated, will show that they were fishermen who burned oak, ash and holly-wood as charcoal to cook their catch.

4000 New arrivals from overseas, neolithic people, leave more substantial remains – e.g. stone axes, mainly at Sutton. They have domesticated animals and plants, so they are Dublin's first farmers. Although there is yet no sign of a village at Dublin, there is a hill-top cairn overlooking Dublin Bay on Tibradden Mountain.

3500 Portal graves are built on Larch Hill and **Mount Venus** and at Kilternan and Brennanstown. Some historians say the earliest village at Dublin dates to this time. It would have had about ten wooden huts where an extended family lived and farmed together. A visit to the stone-age village of Skara Brae on Orkney gives one a good idea of the technology of the time: cavity walls, indoor toilets with running water, central heating, etc. All of which makes the description of a Celtic house – coming shortly – seem anything but far-fetched.

3000 A more elaborate tomb, now known as **Aideen's Grave**, is built on the Hill of Howth. This is Dublin's first dolmen: the area was a 'late developer' in this type of construction. It is only now that people begin to settle in the Liffey valley in some numbers: they had been doing so on the Bann and the Boyne for centuries before this time.

2000 Besides the prehistoric fort on the north-side Bailey promontory, and the gallery graves at Ballyedmonduff and Kilmashogue on the south-side hills, there are many stone-age remains in the Liffey basin itself. For example, in the grounds of the Zoological Gardens there is a small cromlech which was transplanted from its original site at Chapelizod.

1900 The Bronze Age hits Dublin. There are three Bronze Age sites within the present limits of Dublin city. These are:

1800 **The Phoenix Park Cists**. These will be discovered in 1838 near St Mary's Hospital (then the Hibernian Military School) under a tumulus forty yards in circumference and fifteen feet high. The four stone cists each contained an urn of baked clay with skulls, shells and other remains. One of these is preserved in the National Museum. The tomb consisted of seven stones set in an oval and supporting a large covering stone.

1500 **The Round Barrow at Drimnagh**. Once a prominent landmark, this large tumulus (twenty-four yards across and ten feet high) will be destroyed by gravel quarrying. It will be excavated in 1938. Its Bronze Age skeleton and its lavishly-decorated pottery bowl can be seen in the National Museum.

1300 **The Suffolk Street Find**. In 1857, workmen laying pipes will discover a tomb containing a skeleton and funerary urn. Three copper axe-heads about five inches long will also be found: they are preserved in the Ray Collection at the National Museum.

1000 The Plain of Moynalty which extends westwards from Howth, is said to have been cleared of forest by this date.

500 The Irish name for Tallaght is *Tamhleacht Muintir Parthalon* i.e. the plague-monument of the Parthalonians (pre-Celtic people who inhabited County Dublin). The present-day 'travelling people' of Ireland are said to be the descendants of these ancient invaders.

ELSEWHERE: Weaving and metallurgy developed at Jericho (7000 BC). Ox-drawn plough and wheeled cart invented (before 6000 BC). Britain becomes an island (5000 BC). Earliest settlements in Egypt and Mesopotamia (5000 BC). Sumerian civilization flourishes; cuneiform writing (3500 BC). Hieratic writing perfected in Egypt (3000 BC). First settlements at Troy (2870 BC). Golden Age of China begins (2850 BC). Great pyramids built in Egypt (2700 BC). Stonehenge (1860 BC). Hammurabi Code, Babylon (1700 BC) Zenith of Minoan civilization, Crete (1450 BC). Temple at Luxor built (1400 BC). Israelites held captive in Egypt by Ramases II (1300 BC) but eventually make their Exodus (1230 BC). Siege of Troy (1200 BC). In Jerusalem, King David reigns (1000 BC) and Solomon builds his temple (961 BC). Homer's epics (c. 900 BC) herald the rise of Greek culture. Foundation of Rome (753 BC). Babylon captured by Persians whose Emperor Cyrus rules most of middle East (538 BC). Athens proclaims democracy (508 BC). Etruscan civilization reaches its height in Italy (500 BC).

THE CELTS

BC

350 The Bronze Age in Ireland lasts until about this period: all Bronze Age remains found around Dublin are, therefore, pre-Celtic.

300 The Celts arrive in Ireland about this time, or possibly a little later. They have weapons of *iron*, so they have little difficulty in conquering the country.

250 Celtic people settle at the mouth of the Liffey although little is known about the Celtic village of Áth Cliath ('the Ford of the Hurdles') from which Dublin gets its Irish name (see the year 2 AD).

200 In the various ancient annals of Ireland, there is no record of any fighting around Dublin, so iron would have been used for plough-shares rather than swords.

100 This description of a Celt's house, taken from an ancient text, gives some idea of what the village of Dublin was like:

> All the furniture of his house is in its proper place – a cauldron with its spit and handles, a vat in which a measure of ale may be brewed, a cauldron for everyday use, small vessels: iron pots and kneading trough and wooden mugs, so that he has no need to borrow them; a washing trough and a bath, tubs, candlesticks, knives for cutting rushes; ropes, an adze, an auger, a pair of wooden shears, an axe; the work-tools for every season, every one unborrowed; a whetstone, a bill-hook, a hatchet, spears for slaughtering livestock; a fire always alive, a candle on the candlestick without fail; a full ploughing outfit with all its equipment . . . There are two vessels in his house always: a vessel of milk and a vessel of ale. He is a man of three snouts: the snout of a rooting boar that cleaves dishonour in every season, the snout of a flitch of bacon on the hook, the snout of a plough under the ground.
>
> From the *Crith Gablach* in the 'Ancient Laws of Ireland'
> (Rolls Series), vol iv, p. 298.

75 The Celts develop a sophisticated culture, building over 28,000 *raths* and *dúns* (forts) throughout Ireland. Many of these may be seen around Dublin. Under their *rí* (kings) the most important Celts were the *brehona* (judges) and *filí* (poets), jointly known as the *Aosdána*. The gold torc is the symbol of the position of *saoí*, the highest Celtic honour. (In AD 1986 the Dublin author, Samuel Beckett, will be granted this tribute.

50 Celtic place-names like Rathmines, Raheny and Rathfarnham date from this period. With its central position on the east coast, Dublin begins to grow in importance. The main roads now lead to Dublin.

DUBLIN'S ROADS

Slighe Mór ran along the Esker Riada from Dublin to Galway. At the Dublin end, it terminated with what is now High Street (which became the main street of the medieval city). In the second century AD, this road will divide Ireland into two kingdoms, the northern one of Conn of the Hundred Battles and the southern one of Mugha, from whom Munster gets its name.

Slighe Chualann ran from Tara down through Stony Batter across the old ford of Áth Cliath and on through County Wicklow. Part of an ancient paved road can still be seen at Glendalough.

Slighe Midhluachra was the Derry to Waterford road. It came into Dublin via Swords and Drumcondra, ran down the course of Dorset Street and Church Street to cross the ford and continue on south via the thoroughfare now named Clanbrassil Street.

Slighe Dála ran out through the Coombe and Cork Street to Naas, Roscrea and eventually Limerick. A side-road or *bóthar* joined Roscrea to Cork.

A ***bóthar*** was the width of two cows, one lengthways and the other athwart (e.g. Stony Bóthar now anglicised into Stony Batter). A *slighe* was sufficiently wide for chariots to pass. The Celts *did* drive chariots.

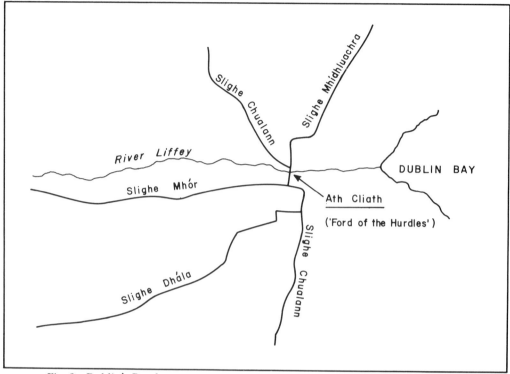

Fig. 3   Dublin's Roads

ELSEWHERE: Battle of Marathon (490 BC). Death of Confucius (479 BC). Building of the Parthenon begins at Athens (447 BC). Deaths of Euripides and Sophocles (406 BC). Socrates is executed (399 BC) and Plato dies (347 BC). The assassination of Philip of Macedon (336 BC) leads to the accession of Alexander the Great. Death of Aristotle (321 BC). First Punic War begins between Rome and Carthage (264 BC). Great Wall of China constructed (214 BC). Hannibal defeated by the Romans in Second Punic War (202 BC). Carthage destroyed by the Romans in Third Punic War (146 BC). Social War in Italy suppressed: Roman franchise granted to most Italians (88 BC). Belgian tribes invade Britain (75 BC). Julius Caesar begins his Gallic Wars (58 BC) and invades Britain (55 BC). Caesar defeats Pompey at Pharsalus (48 BC) but is murdered on the Ides of March (44 BC). Anthony and Cleopatra are defeated at Actium (31 BC) by Octavian who is granted the title Augustus (27 BC). Deaths of Virgil (19 BC) and Horace (8 BC). Birth of Christ (4 BC).

LEGENDS OF THE HEROES

AD

2   Death of **Cú Chulainn** in County Louth, according to legend, is avenged by his Ulster kinsman, Conall Carnach, who sends the poet Atharne to Dublin to demand tribute from the King of Leinster. Atharne demands a gift of one hundred and fifty ladies plus seven hundred white cows with red ears. A causeway of hurdles is thrown across the Liffey for the transit of this herd. From this the place took its name Áth Cliath – 'the Ford of the Hurdles'.

10   Another early chronicler disputes this story. He describes how the crossing of the river was first made when a monster, regurgitated from Newgrange on the Boyne, swept up to the Liffey and became wedged between both banks. Take your choice.

20   The court (*bruigne* in Irish) of a prince called Dá Derga becomes one of the six great 'Houses of Hospitality' in Ireland. The site of this court is near the source of the River Dodder; the name survives in Bohernabreena.

25   **King Crimthan** is said to have reigned over Leinster since the year that Jesus Christ was born. Some 'delightful adventures' occurred while he was on a foreign expedition. These are recounted in a poem ascribed to the King himself. He was brought by a fairy lady into her palace. She gave him a gilt chariot, a golden chess-board inlaid with transparent gems, a cloak of divers colours embroidered in gold, a sword ornamented with serpents, a shield embossed with silver. These and other treasures Crimthan brought home with him to his fort of Dún Crimthan (now Dungriffan) on the Hill of Howth.

'Cloch an Fear Mór' where Cú Chulainn died.
Standing stone in County Louth.

Ancient crosses County Dublin, (l to r) Cabinteely, Finglas, Tully.

BEFORE AND AFTER PATRICK

AD

70   The Roman general, Agricola, having mastered England, gathers information on Ireland with a view to invading the country; he decides against.

130   **Eblana** (Dublin) is named on map of the Alexandrian geographer, Ptolemy, who was using Agricola's information. Some historians maintain that Eblana was further north, in County Louth.

177   **Conn of the Hundred Battles** is said to have commenced his reign in this year. As mentioned earlier, he divided Ireland with King Mugha along the line of the Esker Riada.

254   **Cormac MacArt** becomes High King. During his reign, **Finn MacCumhal** and his warrior band, the Fianna, are supposed to have campaigned around Dublin. They hunt for Diarmuid and Gráine all over the Hill of Howth and have their winter quarters at Glen-na-Smól in the Dublin mountains.

280   The '**Uí Dercmaisig of Áth Cliath**' are the first recorded tribe of Dubliners.

291   **Duibhlinn** first mentioned in the *Annals of the Four Masters*. A battle at Dublin is won by Fiachra Srabhtine over the Leinstermen.

      Mac Giolla Mocholmog dispossesses the Uí Dercmaisig of the Lordship of Dublin.

300   The 'Coulter' plough, which brings great agricultural advances, is introduced from Roman Britain.

400   The Irish start attacking Britain, taking slaves such as Patrick.

450   **St Patrick** visits Dublin, according to legend. He is said to have converted the Dubliners and their leader, Alphin Mac Echold, to Christianity and to have baptized them in St Patrick's Well, now in the grounds of St Patrick's Cathedral, where a monument marks the spot. The original marker stands inside the Cathedral, at the west end of the nave.

      There were three other Wells of St Patrick in Dublin, one near the present Provost's Garden in Trinity College, another not far away in Nassau Place and the third near the junction of Camden Street and Camden Row, its exact site uncertain.

      On his way north, St Patrick is said to have stopped on Glasmanogue (Constitution Hill) and, looking back on Dublin, said: 'Although it's small and miserable now, there'll be a big town here in time to come. It will be spoken of far and near and will keep increasing until it becomes the chief town in the kingdom.'

      Though many of the stories about St Patrick are mere legends, we do know that he was a real person who had much influence on the early development of

Christianity in Dublin. As a former Dean of St Patrick's Cathedral (Rev J H Bernard, DD) puts it:

> It is to be borne in mind that, in Celtic times, churches were never dedicated to non-Scriptural saints except in the case of the actual founders. There is thus a *prima facie* presumption that St Patrick visited Dublin.

450-600 Although Dublin remained little more than a village until the arrival of the Vikings, many monasteries and schools were founded in its immediate vicinity during the early centuries of Irish Christianity. Glendalough, Glasnevin and Tallaght were particularly famous seats of learning. Aldhelm of Malmesbury (writing in 650) complained that English students were 'swarming like bees to be educated in Ireland' and the Venerable Bede, when describing the great plague which struck England in the year 664, wrote:

> Many of the nobility and of the lower ranks of the English nation went to Ireland at that time, forsaking their native land and retiring thither either for the sake of divine studies or of a more virtuous life . . . Some went around from one master's cell to another and the Irish willingly received them all and took care to supply them with food, to furnish them with books to read and to provide their teaching gratis.

Ruins of the following establishments survive, those marked with an asterisk being National Monuments:

*	St Áine	– Killiney	*	St Mac Cuilinn	– Lusk
	St Baróg	– Kilbarrack		St Máel Ruain	– Tallaght
*	St Begnet	– Dalkey Island		St Maignead	– Kilmainham
	St Broc	– Donnybrook		St Margaret	– St Margaret's
*	St Canice	– Finglas		St Marnoc	– Portmarnock
*	St Colum Cille	– Swords		St Mobhi	– Glasnevin
	St Damian	– Ballsbridge	*	St Mochua	– Clondalkin
	St Donagh	– Raheny		St Moling	– Kilmalin
*	St Doulagh	– Balgriffin		St Mosacra	– Saggart
	St Fintan	– Sutton		St Nathi	– Taney
	St Garbhan	– Kevin Street		St Nessan	– Ireland's Eye
	St Kevin	– Glendalough		St Sentan	– Bohernabreena

ELSEWHERE: Civil Service examination system established in China (6 AD). Death of Caesar Augustus (14). Crucifixion of Jesus Christ (c. 30). Romans occupy Britain (43). Great Fire of Rome (64) blamed on Christians by Emperor Nero (who dies in 68). Jerusalem destroyed by Romans (70). Colosseum completed in Rome (80). Hadrian's Wall built in England (122). Constantine proclaimed Roman Emperor in York (306) issues Edict of Milan in favour of Christianity (313). After the death of Emperor Theodosius, the Roman Empire is divided between East and West (395). Barbarian invasions begin with the capture of Spain by the Visigoths (415) and of N. Africa by the Vandals (429). Attila the Hun driven from Gaul (451). Clovis becomes king of the Franks (481) who eventually conquer Gaul. Birth of Mohammed (570). Gregory the Great becomes Pope (590) and sends St Augustine to convert Britain to Christianity (597).

PRE-VIKING CHURCHES

AD
600-800

Cill Céle Crist: built on the hill where Christ Church Cathedral stands today. Céle Crist was a saint once widely venerated in Leinster.

St Patrick's: small Celtic church, later replaced by St Patrick's Cathedral. The church is built on a small island in the River Poddle: hence its Latin suffix, *in insula*.

St Colum Cille's: built where St Audoen's (Protestant) Church now stands. Dublin's 'Lucky Stone' – a charm to which superstitious citizens attached magical powers – stood here for centuries. It is preserved in the porch of St Audoen's.

St Bride's: small church dedicated to St Brigid on Bride Street.

St Martin's: dedicated to 4th century saint, Martin of Tours, this is located at the end of St Martin's Lane (now Hoey's Court) off Werburgh Street, near the Castle steps.

St Mac Táil's: also known as *St Michael Le Pole* (or Poddle), this is the only Dublin church with a round tower. A wall-plaque on Ship Street marks the

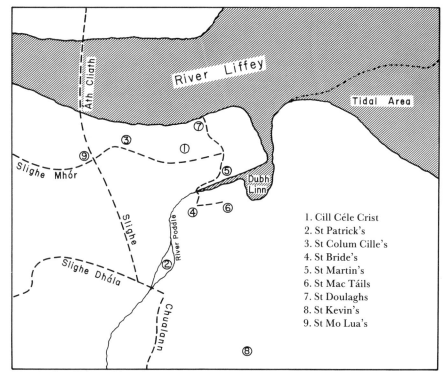

Fig. 4   Pre-Viking Churches.

spot. The ninety-foot tower – presumably added after the Vikings started raiding – will be demolished in 1778.

St Doulagh's: the 'city' church of the saint before moving out to the suburbs at Balgriffin, Malahide Road. Later it will become St Olave's, called after the Viking Saint Olaf. Its site is off Wood Quay, near the bottom of Fishamble Street.

St Kevin's: off Camden Street, behind Kevin Street College of Technology. Founded by St Garbhan, it is dedicated to St Kevin of Glendalough who died in 622 during St Garbhan's lifetime. Its ruins can still be seen from Camden Row.

St McLua's: near the Cornmarket, this old monastic establishment is built where the Slighe Mór (coming in from the west) joined the Slighe Chualann (coming up from the south).

SOME PRE-VIKING DATES

AD

496   Death of St Mac Cuilinn of Lusk.

544   Death of **St Mobhi of Glasnevin**: Saints Columba (founder of Derry, Swords, Iona etc.), Canice (founder of Kilkenny), Kieran (founder of Clonmacnois) and Comgall (founder of Bangor) are said to have been class-mates here under Mobhi.

590   A manuscript of the Psalms is written about this time, possibly by St Columba. Known as **An Cathach** (The Battler), it will be carried by The O'Donnell whenever he goes to war. (The oldest extant Irish manuscript, it is now in the library of the Royal Irish Academy in Dawson Street).

622   Death of **St Kevin of Glendalough**, one of the Patrons of Dublin.

660   St Wiro is consecrated Bishop of Dublin by the Pope about this year. Although Dublin itself is little more than a village, the diocese is sufficiently populous to warrant a bishopric.

664   The **Synod of Whitby** in England brings the Celtic Church into line with the Roman Church: liturgy and ritual are standardised and the date of Easter is fixed.

696   Death of St Moling.

764   Great snow in Dublin for nearly three months.

770   An army of Ulstermen (*Ciannachta Breg*) attacks Dublin; the soldiers are all drowned while crossing the Áth Cliath in a high tide.

775   St Rumold, Bishop of Dublin, is murdered in Mechlin, Belgium.

790   Death of Siadal (Sedulius), Bishop of Dublin.

792   Death of St Máel Ruain of Tallaght, where the famous **Stowe Missal** will be written, about the year 800. The monastic schools at Tallaght and Finglas become internationally famous centres of religious learning; they are known as 'the two eyes of Ireland'.

THE IRISH ABROAD

Before we attack the Vikings, something should be said about the overseas activity of the Celtic monks, many of whom were trained in Tallaght, Finglas, Glasnevin or Swords. Even before the time of St Columba, they had settled as hermits (called *papar* in the Sagas) in Iceland and Orkney.

St Columba, founder of the monastery at Swords, County Dublin, evangelized Scotland from his monastery on Iona which he founded in 563. A monk of Iona, St Aidan, brought Christianity to the north of England. Glastonbury was founded by Irishmen (*viri sanctissimi, praecipuis Hibernici*) who educated St Dunstan at that abbey.

'The Leinsterman', St Columbanus, went to France in 585 with twelve companions and founded the monasteries of Annegray, Luxeuil and Fontaine.

He died in 615 at his three-year-old foundation of Bobbio in Italy. One of his companions, St Gall, established the monastery of that name in what is now Switzerland.

In France, monasteries were established by St Fiacre at Meaux in 622 and by St Fursey at Legny in 646. Other Irish monks settled at Peronne, on the Marne, in 670. St Duncan taught at Rheims and left writings that are still extant.

In Italy, St Frigidian was Bishop of Lucca for twenty-eight years in the sixth century. St Molua also worked in Italy and St Donatius became Bishop of Fiesole near Florence. St Cathaldus became Bishop of Tarentum about 660; his brother, St Donatus, was Bishop of Lecce at the same time.

To complete the picture, various annals list the following Irishmen who helped to bring the Gospel to continental Europe: St Livinus suffered martyrdom in Flanders in 633 (his disciples settled in Mecklenburgh); St Arbogast, was consecrated Bishop of Strasbourg in 648; two saints Kilian: one martyred in Wurzburg in 689; his contemporary was abbot of Cologne; St Sedulius was consecrated Bishop of Gijon, Spain, in 721; St Virgilius became Bishop of Salzburg in 756; his Irish followers went as far as Vienna and Kiev.

ELSEWHERE: Arabia has become Moslem by the time of Mohammed's death (632). Moslems capture Jerusalem (638), Persia (641) and Alexandria (643). Synod of Whitby (663). Western advance of the Moslems halted at Tours by Charles Martel (732). Pepin becomes king of the Franks (751). Viking attacks on Britain begin with the sack of Lindisfarne (793).

'The Vikings' is the name commonly given to all the Scandinavians (or 'Ostmen' i.e. Men from the East) who left their native lands between the eighth and tenth centuries looking for loot and land. Different reasons are given for their migration: a population explosion or a famine at home; the spirit of adventure; younger sons being disinherited; remarkable advances in the methods of ship-building; the search for victims in a developing slave trade; poverty – and an attractive means of curing this ill at the expense of rich monastic settlements.

Sometimes called 'Norsemen', sometimes 'Danes', the raiders who settled around Dublin were of two types: Dark-haired Foreigners (Dubh Gaill) from which the name Doyle derives, and Fair-haired Foreigners (Fionn Gaill) who gave their name to Fingal, north County Dublin. The Danish historian, Johannes Brøndsted states:

That the Vikings in Ireland were mainly Norwegians is proved beyond question by the chronicles; but even if these were lacking, the evidence of place-names and archaeology would equally establish that conclusion. Ancient ninth- and tenth-century graves in Norway have been found to contain many objects and jewels of Irish origin: scarcely any similar finds have been made in Denmark and Sweden.

795   Vikings attack the monastery on **Lambay Island**, off Dublin. The Irish name for this island was Rahan; its port was Port-rahan, now Portrane. **Eyland** or **ey** was the Norse word for an island: e.g. Lamb Ey, Ireland's Ey, Dalk Ey.

807   The **Book of Kells**, that masterpiece of Celtic monastic art which is now in the library of Trinity College Dublin, is brought from Iona to Kells, County Meath, for safety.

837   A fleet of sixty Viking ships sails up the Liffey.

841   **Foundation of Dublin**: The Vikings establish their **longphort** on the Liffey. This will become the town of 'Dyflin', an important trading-post on the Viking shipping-lanes. Other Viking place-names from this period include Howth (Hoved), Harold's Cross, Baldoyle, Skerries, Lusk, Rush, Loughlinstown (*Baile na Lochlannaigh*, the Town of the Norse) and Bullock Harbour. The Vikings try to replace Christianity with the worship of Thor. From 841, until

the departure of the British in 1922, Dublin will remain mostly under foreign control. Viking laws are issued at the 'Thingmount', a flat-topped mound (40 feet high and 240 in circumference) near College Green – which used to be called Hoggen Green. This hill will be levelled in pre-Georgian times to provide a foundation for what is now Nassau Street. As on the banks of the Thames and the Seine, the Vikings erect a long-stone, called the 'Steine', on the Liffey shore (see 1985).

845   The Irish king, **Máel Sechnaill I**, plunders the new town. The Norsemen, however, soon regroup and recover the town.

851   Danish Vikings plunder the Norse settlement with the help of the Irish who take advantage of the current enmity between the Norwegians and the Danes.

853   **Olaf the White**, a mighty chieftain from Norway, reconquers Dublin. He is sometimes (wrongly) called the founder of the city. He rules over Dublin for nearly twenty years, sharing the kingship with Ivar I between 856 and 873. These difficult years for the Irish were described in the twelfth-century work, *Cogadh Gaedhel re Gallaibh*:

> If a hundred heads of hardened iron could grow on one neck, and if each head possessed a hundred sharp indestructible tongues of tempered metal, and if each tongue cried out incessantly with a hundred ineradicable loud voices, they would never be able to enumerate the griefs which the people of Ireland – men and women, laymen and priests, young and old – have suffered at the hands of these warlike ruthless barbarians.

871   Olaf and Ivar I return to Dublin from a joint expedition in Scotland, bringing back a large number of captives for the slave market.

873   Death in Dublin of Ivar, 'King of all the Norse of Ireland and Britain'. Olaf is presumed to have returned to Norway after Ivar's death, though this is mere hypothesis. We do know that his son, **Eystein**, reigned between 873 and 875.

875   **Halfdan**, who was probably a brother of Ivar, attempts to unite the kingdoms of Dublin and York. Confusion reigns in Dublin: not till 888 does Sitric I manage to gain a firm hold of the kingship. For the kingship during this period, see page 43.

880   **Cearbhall**, king of Ossory, captures Dublin briefly. He had sided with the Vikings and his grand-daughter had married a son of Olaf the White. Dublin did have Norse rulers in the 880s, though the succession is uncertain.

883   **Sichfrith** becomes king for five years.

888   **Sitric I**, son of Ivar, becomes king. He will be deposed in 893 but reinstated for a further two years in 894.

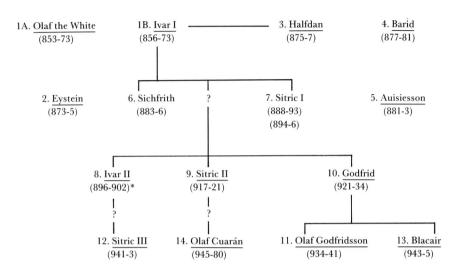

Fig. 5 Viking Kings of Dublin (853-980)

*The Vikings were expelled in 902 and did not return till 917.

896   Ivar II reigns for six years.

900   The Vikings bury their dead at **Islandbridge** from about this date. Their cemetery will be unearthed during the construction of the Phoenix Park railway tunnel in the nineteenth century. The Viking objects found at that time are on display in the National Museum.

902   The Vikings are expelled from Dublin by the men of Brega and Leinster. The Norse kingship will not be restored until 917.

917   **Sitric II** recaptures Dublin.
        About this time, timber and mud defences are built around Dublin. Remnants of these have been found on *Wood Quay*. Tenth and eleventh century houses, fences and foot-paths have been excavated nearby. All sorts of Viking artefacts (e.g. women's necklaces of amber beads and children's footwear) have been found there: they are now on view at the Annexe of the National Museum in Merrion Row.

919   **Battle of Islandbridge**: Sitric II defeats and kills the High King of Ireland, Niall Glúndub.

921   Sitric leaves for York, leaving his younger brother, Godfrid in charge of Dublin.

934   **Godfrid**, king of Dublin, dies. Succeeded by his son, Olaf.

936   Dublin burnt to the ground by Donnchad Donn, king of the Ua Néill.

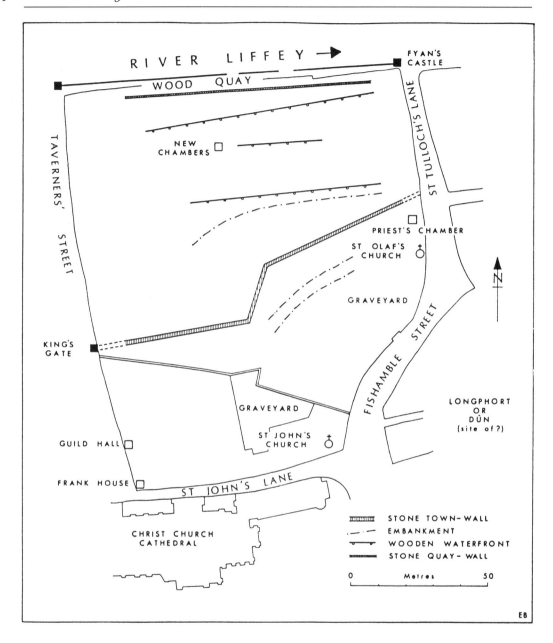

Fig. 6   Viking Site at Wood Quay. Reproduced from *Viking Dublin Exposed* by kind permission of the publisher The O'Brien Press Ltd., Dublin.

939   Dublin Vikings plunder Old Kilcullen: 'With the help of God and Saint Mac Táil', they are beaten off by Donnchad Donn and Muirchertach Mac Néill.

941   Olaf Godfridsson dies and is succeeded by **Sitric III** (of uncertain origin).

943   Olaf's younger brother, **Blacair**, becomes king for two years.

945   **Olaf Cuarán**, son of Sitric II, who had been driven out of York two years earlier, takes the kingship of Dublin from Blacair. Despite intermittent defeats – such as that suffered at the hands of the High King, Congalach, in 947 – he will reign over Dublin until the year 980. A P Smith says of him:

> A destroyer of Irish monasteries and kings, he began his career as an ardent heathen, feigned conversion to Christianity and quickly apostatized after being bullied into Baptism by King Edmund . . . . A disastrous defeat at Tara in Ireland at the end of a long fighting career decided him on finally abandoning his old gods and he died a penitent in Iona in 981.

945   Olaf Cuarán attacks York.

950   The Viking grave-yard at **Castleknock** dates back to about this year. It will be excavated in 1938.

952   Olaf Cuarán attacks Northumbria.

956   Olaf ambushes and kills the High King, Congalach.

970   The new High King, Donal Ua Néill, is defeated by the Irish of Brega 'with the help of Olaf Cuarán'.

980   The next High King, Máel Sechnaill II, defeats Dublin Norse at the Battle of Tara. Olaf Cuarán flees to Iona where he dies a year later.

ELSEWHERE: Coronation of Charlemagne as Holy Roman Emperor (800). Death of Charlemagne and division of his empire (814). Moslems invade Sicily (827) and S. Italy (840). France and Germany become separate states at Treaty of Verdun (843). Kingdom of Scotland begins with Kenneth Mac Alpin (844). Viking settlements established in Russia by Rurik, first at Novgorod, then at Kiev (862). Vikings capture Northumbria, East Anglia and Mercia (866), Iceland (874), Paris (885-6). Death of Alfred the Great (899). Monastic reform begins with foundation of Abbey of Cluny (910). Vikings capture Waterford (917) and settle in strength at Limerick (922). Fatimids establish their rule in Egypt (968).

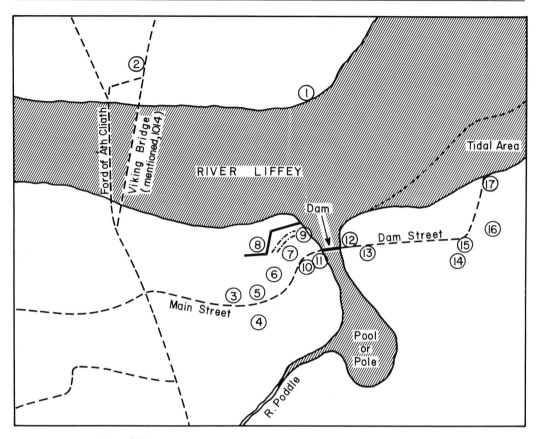

Fig. 7   Map of Hiberno-Norse Dublin.

1. St Mary's Abbey
2. St Michan's
3. St Michael's
4. St Nicholas (Within)
5. Christ Church Cathedral (Holy Trinity)
6. St John's
7. Earthen Ramparts (c.950)
8. Stone Wall (c.1100)
9. St Olaf's
10. Site of Viking Longphort?
11. St Paul's
12. St Mary's del Dam
13. St Andrew's
14. St Mary de Hogges
15. Thingmount
16. All Hallows
17. The Steine

HIBERNO-NORSE DUBLIN, 980-1169

By way of preamble, something should be said about the celebration of Dublin's 'Millennium' in 1988. The very reliable 15th century *Annals of Ulster* gave dates incorrectly (by one year) up to 1014. Knowing that the Battle of Clontarf took place in that year, the annalist decided to correct his dating from then on. To do this, he simply decided to have no entry for the year 1013. Therefore, his entries prior to that need to have one year added: e.g. the *Annals* give 840 as the date for the foundation of Dublin; the correct year is 841. What the annalist records for 988 actually happened in 989.

980   **Máel Sechnaill II** captures Dublin for the first time. Olaf Cuarán's son, Glúniarainn, soon expels him and becomes king for nine years.

989   Máel Sechnaill II captures the town again. He imposes an annual tax of one ounce of gold on each tenement (garth), i.e. on a Norse population that he clearly regards as still pagan. As the annalist puts it, 'he captures the town and makes it Irish'.

         Sitric IV ('Silkbeard') succeeds to the kingship when his brother, Glúniarainn is killed by a drunken slave. Sitric will reign for forty-seven years.

997   **First coins** minted by the Norsemen of Dublin. Samples can be seen in the National Museum.

1000   **Brian Bóruma**, King of Munster, helps the High King to capture Dublin and hold it for a fortnight. Two years later, Brian Bóruma will be acknowledged as High King by Máel Sechnaill; but he will still have to win the North.

1002   Sitric Silkbeard is allowed to retain the kingship of Dublin by Brian Bóruma who values the Norse trading links. Dublin, as we have seen, was an important port, servicing the Norse fleets en route to and from Normandy.

1006   Brian Boruma claims hostages from the North and becomes undisputed High King of Ireland.

1014   **Battle of Clontarf**. The king of Leinster, Máel Mórda, rises in arms against Brian Bóruma, the High King. Before fighting it out, both kings look for allies. Brian is joined by his own men of Munster, by the forces of Meath, by several chieftains from Connacht and by one Viking regiment from Northumbria; Máel Mórda persuades Sitric Silkbeard to enlist the help of the Vikings of Orkney, the Isle of Man and the Hebrides who arrive in strength under the leadership of Sigurd, Earl of Orkney.

   Brian Bóruma wins a crushing victory at Clontarf and, although he does not 'drive out the Danes' (as one used to be told), he succeeds in putting an end to Viking expansion in Ireland. Brian himself, however, is killed by a Viking chief, Brodar, towards the end of the battle. His son and grandson also die, as do Máel Mórda and many of his Viking allies.

   The site of the battle, according to some scholars, lies between present-day Summerhill and Ballybough. Other scholars say it took place around a weir at the mouth of the Tolka; still others locate it between Fairview and Clontarf proper. Since it was a long battle involving considerable numbers on each side, it is not unreasonable to suggest that fighting occurred all along this north-eastern shore of Dublin Bay and right up to the Áth Cliath where Dublin Bridge is mentioned for the first time.

   A common grave of the defeated Vikings will be found in 1763 when the Rotunda Gardens are being laid out. King Sitric, it must be remembered, took no part in the battle himself because of a row with Máel Mórda; he continued to reign in Dublin after 1014.

   Some excerpts from a single chapter of the *Orkneyinga Saga* (written about

Part of the site of the battle of Clontarf.

the year 1200) tell us about the build-up to the Battle of Clontarf and give a poignantly brief account of its outcome:

> Olaf Tryggvason (King of Norway) spent four years looting in the British Isles. Then he was baptized in the Scillies and from there sailed to England where he married Gyda, the sister of the King Kvaran (Ciaran) of Ireland. Next he spent a while in Dublin . . .
>
> Then Olaf sailed with five ships and didn't break his journey until he reached Orkney. There at Osmundwall he ran into Earl Sigurd, who had three ships and was setting out on a Viking expedition. Olaf sent a messenger to him, asking Sigurd to come over to his ship as he wanted a word with him.
>
> 'I want you and all your subjects to be baptized,' he said when they met. 'If you refuse, I'll have you killed on the spot . . . ' The Earl could see what kind of situation he was in and surrendered himself into Olaf's hands. He was baptized and Olaf took his son as a hostage and baptized him too . . . After that all Orkney embraced the faith . . . Earl Sigurd was married to the daughter of Malcolm, King of Scots, and their son was Earl Thorfinn . . . .
>
> Earl Sigurd went to Ireland in support of King Sigtrygg (Sitric) Silkbeard (but by the time he arrived Sitric had decided not to take part in the fight). He set out to fight King Brian of Ireland. The Battle took place on Good Friday. No one would carry the (cursed) raven banner (of Orkney), so the Earl had to do it himself and he was killed . . . Although King Brian won the victory, he lost his life.

As a postscript, it is interesting to note that Earl Sigurd's son, Thorfinn the Mighty, was responsible for the building of Christ Church Cathedral on the Brough of Birsay in Orkney.

1015   Great plague in Dublin. Opinions differ as to the precise nature of this disease.

1022   The Hiberno-Norse of Dublin are defeated in a sea battle by the King of Ulster, Niall mac Eochada.

1028   Sitric Silkbeard goes on pilgrimage to Rome – an indication that he is well in control of the situation at home.

Bishop Dúnán (Donatus) with the support of his friend, King Sitric, founds **Christ Church Cathedral** on the site of Cill Céle Crist. (Some historians give 1038 as the foundation-date but this is impossible since Sitric was deposed in 1036).

1032   Sitric is said to have founded **St Mary's Abbey, Howth**. In the late fifteenth century 'the College of Howth, housing four priests' will be built on this site – which supports the view that St Mary's was not an Abbey but a Collegiate Church.

1034 Prince Olaf of Dublin, Sitric's son, killed in England while going on pilgrimage to Rome.

1036 Sitric is deposed by Echmarcach, son of Ragnall who is himself deposed by **Ivar Haraldsson** two years later.

1046 Dubliners expel Ivar and restore Echmarcach to the kingship.

1052 Echmarcach is deposed again. **Diarmait mac Máel na mBó** captures Dublin and installs his son Murchad as king.

1054 Birth in Dublin of the great Gruffydd ap Cynan of Gwynedd who will later become King of All Wales.

1058 The Dublin fleet attacks Britain, helping Prince Magnus (son of King Harald Hardrada of Norway) to restore the earldom of Mercia to Aelfgar.

1067 Great outbreak of smallpox in Leinster.

1072 Diarmait killed at Odba (near Navan). **Gofraid I** becomes king.

1074 Gofraid I expelled by Toirrdelbach Ua Briain who installs his son Muirchertach as king.

Fig. 8   St Mary's Abbey, Dublin (see 1139).

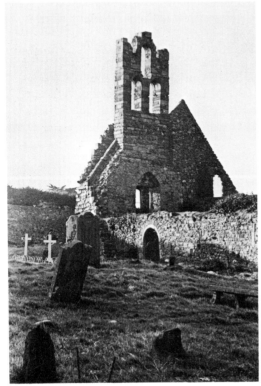

St Mary's Abbey, Howth.

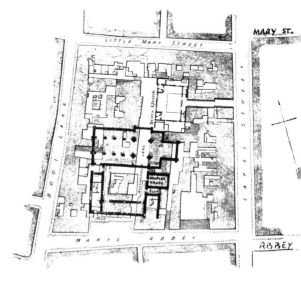

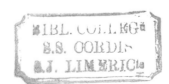

Bishop Dúnán dies. Succeeded by Gilla Pátraic who is duly consecrated by Lanfranc in Canterbury – not in Armagh (see 1097 below).

1086   **Donnchad mac Domnaill Remair** (who has replaced Muirchertach as King of Dublin) repulses a Brega (Meath) invasion at Battle of Clonliffe.

1089   **Muirchertach** kills Donnchad and regains kingship of Dublin.

1091   **Gofraid Méránach**, King of the Isle of Man, conquers Dublin.

1093   **St Michan's Church** is built near the Áth Cliath about this time. The dates 1095 and 1096 are also suggested. Probably named after a Norse bishop, it will be the only parish church on the north side of the city until 1697. Built mainly for the Viking community of Oxmantown (Ostman Town), the present building dates from 1685 and is renowned for its macabre vaults.

1094   Muirchertach Ua Briain, now called 'the High King with opposition', expels Gofraid Méránach from Dublin.

1095   Great plague devastates Dublin for two years. As with the 1015 epidemic, we are uncertain of the nature of this disease. The sixth-century pandemic had long since run its course and the next pandemic will not reach western Europe until 1347.

1097   **Bishop Samuel** of Dublin – consecrated at Canterbury in the previous year – claims church primacy, making St Michan's his seat instead of Christ Church. He will soon (in 1106) make peace with Ceallach, Archbishop of Armagh, and (in 1113) allow him to bring the *Bachall Ísu* (Staff of St Patrick) southwards. The famous relic will be kept at Ballyboghill (Baile an mBachaill) in north County Dublin as a symbol of Armagh's ecclesiastical supremacy over all Ireland, including the Norse See of Dublin.

1100   Samuel 'parades around Dublin like an Archbishop' although his See did not become an archdiocese for another 52 years (see 1152).

The first **stone wall** to be built around Dublin has been archaeologically dated to about this time.

1105   Muirchertach receives a present of a camel from King Edgar of Scotland.

1111   **Synod of Ráith Bressail** defines the boundaries of twenty-four Irish dioceses 'exclusive of the Hiberno-Norse bishopric of Dublin'.

1112   Second mention of a **bridge** across the Liffey, presumably on site of Áth Cliath. The first mention of such a bridge came in an account of the Battle of Clontarf, 1014.

1114   Muirchertach is deposed by his brother, **Diarmait Ua Briain**.

1120   **Domnall Ua Briain** (Muirchertach's son) succeeds to the throne. Called 'King of the Dublin Danes'.

1121   **Gréne (**Gregorius) becomes Bishop of Dublin; in 1152 he will become its first Archbishop.

1139   Foundation of Savigniac **Abbey of St Mary** (see 1147).

St Mary's Abbey was one of the finest buildings in Dublin. Figure 8 shows the plan of the building drawn by Thomas Drew, R.H.A. The Chapter House and 'slype' are all that remain. They can be seen, incredibly, underneath a warehouse in Meetinghouse Lane.

Visiting dignitaries to Dublin stayed in the Abbey's guesthouse which was the finest in the city. Besides the buildings, the monks owned extensive lands around the abbey. These were extended by Henry II when he visited Dublin in 1172 and gave St Mary's 'all the land of Clonlliffe as far as the Tolka'.

The abbey was suppressed by Henry VIII in 1539 but its statue of Our Lady of Dublin was saved. Hollowed-out and used as a cattle trough during the Penal Days, it was discovered in the eighteenth century in St Mary's Lane and now has a place of honour in the Carmelite church on Whitefriar Street.

It was in the Chapter House of this abbey that Silken Thomas began his ill-fated rebellion in 1534.

1141   Conchobar Ua Briain of Thomond succeeds to throne of Dublin.

1147   Savigniac Abbey of St Mary becomes Cistercian; it will become affiliated to Buildwas Abbey (Shropshire) in 1156. The remains of the abbey are now a National Monument, the key available on request.

1150   Toirrdelbach (Turlough) Ua Briain makes allies of the Dubliners under their Norse king, Brótar mac Torcaill. This king's name, incidentally, is an example of the hybrid surnames which became common and are still plentiful in Fingal, e.g. McKittrick (son of Sitric), MacAuliffe (son of Olaf).

1152   Synod of Kells makes Dublin an *arch*bishopric. **Bishop Gréne**, who had been Bishop of Dublin since 1121, becomes Archbishop. The Hiberno-Norse of Dublin were loath to accept the ecclesiastical supremacy of Armagh: when contact with Trondheim in Norway was severed, they had acknowledged the supremacy of Canterbury (see 1074 and 1172).

1154   **Muirchertach Mac Lochlainn** captures Dublin, but confirms Diarmait Mac Murchada as King of Leinster.

1155   The English Pope, Hadrian IV, in his bull *Laudabiliter*, authorises Henry II to take possession of Ireland. Henry does not act on this opportunity.

1156   Nunnery of **St Mary de Hogges** (Arroasian Nuns) founded near Hoggen Green (the old name for College Green).

1160   Probable date of **St Doulagh's Church**, Balgriffin, which is certainly pre-Norman. The Celtic church of St Doulagh (Fishamble Street) had been displaced by the Norse church of St Olaf.

1162   Diarmait Mac Murchada gains complete control of Dublin and grants the lands of Baldoyle to **All Hallows Priory** (Augustinian Canons) which he founded himself. It stood well outside the city walls of Dublin on the site now occupied by Trinity College.

1163   Archbishop **Laurence O'Toole** (Lorcán Ua Tuathail) replaces the secular clergy of Christ Church with a community of Augustinian Canons Regular. (Their priory was called Holy Trinity, which should not be confused with the university of that name nor with the Holy Trinity Friary founded in 1280).

St Doulagh's Church, Balgriffin.

1166   **Ruaidrí Ua Conchobair** becomes High King. Diarmait Mac Murchada, driven out of the Kingdom of Leinster, goes looking for foreign aid. Henry II (see 1155) allows him enlist an army (see 1170).

Hasculf mac Torcaill becomes the last Norseman to rule Dublin. His palace was beside Christ Church on the site that will be used for building St Michael's church at the top of St Michael's Hill.

Laurence O'Toole (canonized in 1225) is said to have built four Dublin churches:

St Paul's was the name of the chapel in the fortress thought to have stood on the same site as Dublin Castle. St Paul's was supposedly near the present church of the Holy Trinity (Chapel Royal).

St Andrew's was a parish church on Dame Street, nearly opposite the present Olympia Theatre. Dame Street (formerly Dame Lane) took its name from a dam on the river Poddle near Dublin Castle.

St Nicholas Within (the Walls). The lower part of this church (which was rebuilt in 1707) can be seen at the top of Nicholas Street, near Christ Church Place.

St Mary del Dam stood on the site of the present City Hall on Cork Hill at the Dam Gate. The crown from St Mary's statue in this church was used for the coronation of Lambert Simnel (see 1487). One of its old tombs can still be seen in the lobby of St Werburgh's Church.

ELSEWHERE: Discovery of Greenland by Vikings (982). Hugh Capet founds new dynasty in France (987). Vikings overrun Essex after Battle of Maldon (991). Leif Ericsson discovers N. America (1000). Coronation of Stephen of Hungary (1001). Svein Forkbeard captures England for the Danes (1013); Canute becomes king (1016). Under Robert Guiscard, Normans invade S. Italy (1046) and Sicily (1060). Under William the Conqueror they invade England (1066). Gregory VII (Hildebrand) becomes Pope (1073). *Domesday Book* compiled (1086). El Cid takes Valencia (1094). Pope Urban II preaches First Crusade at Council of Clermont (1095). Cistercian Order founded at Citeaux (1098). St Bernard founds monastery at Clairvaux (1115). Knights Templars founded (1119). Cormac's Chapel built at Cashel (1127-34). Second Crusade: failure to capture Damascus (1148). Frederick Barbarossa becomes Emperor (1152). Henry II becomes first Plantagenet king of England (1154). Mellifont Abbey founded by Cistercians (1157). Explosives used in Chinese war (1161).

ANGLO-NORMAN DUBLIN

The 'Normans' did not come from Normandy directly: they came from England and Wales, asked by their Angevin king (Henry II of England, who also ruled Normandy and other French provinces) to accept the invitation of Diarmait Mac Murchada to go to Ireland with him and win back the Kingdom of Leinster from which Diarmait had been ousted. In return, Diarmait promised to make Leinster subject to the King of England and to give his eldest daughter, Aoife, (and the right of succession to the throne of Leinster) to the leader of the Norman invaders. This leader was Richard FitzGilbert de Clare, Lord of Strigoil, better known as **Strongbow**.

1170   The Normans, who had reached Waterford the previous year, arrive outside the gates of Dublin. While the Archbishop, **Laurence O'Toole**, is negotiating with their leaders, two Norman knights, Raymond le Gros and Milo de Cogan capture the town with a handful of followers. With their suits of mail and expertise in archery this was no problem. King Hasculf flees and the rest of the Vikings are banished to Oxmantown. Thus begins 752 years of English rule in Dublin.

     Milo de Cogan becomes custodian (governor) of the town. One of Strongbow's closest friends, Walter de Rideleford, is granted extensive lands on the South Side, including the townland afterwards known as Baggotrath which stretched from Ballsbridge to Merrion Row.

1171   **Hasculf**, having collected a large army of Norsemen from overseas, attacks Dublin. He is defeated and beheaded. The Irish, under their High King, Ruaidrí Ua Conchobair, besiege Dublin. After two months, when the Normans are nearly starving, Strongbow attacks and defeats the Irish as Castleknock.

     St Audoen's Church built in High Street on site of St Colum Cille's. Called after the Norman Saint Ouen, from Rouen, for centuries its bells will be rung during storms to remind the citizens to pray for those at sea. Its present bells (1423) are the city's oldest. St Audoen's will be renovated in both the seventeenth and eighteenth centuries and have a 'face-lift' in 1984-5.

1172   **King Henry II** spends three months in Dublin. A willow-wood palace is built for him near the Thingmount (where St Andrew's Protestant church now stands in Andrew Street).

First Charter of Dublin: Henry gives the city as a present 'to my men of Bristol'. On his departure, he makes **Hugh de Lacy** his Bailiff, in reality first Viceroy. Strongbow, who became King of Leinster on the death of Dermot Mac Murrough in 1711, retains this kingdom as a vassal of Henry II.

The Irish bishops acknowledge Henry's overlordship at the **Synod of Cashel**.

Christ Church Cathedral is rebuilt by the Normans, influenced by Glastonbury and Wells (see 1028). Strongbow, FitzStephen and le Gros 'set about the rebuilding of the Cathedral with commendable promptitude and noble generosity'. In the years of the walled city, Parliament (whenever called) usually meets at Christ Church.

1173   Norman castle built by Hugh Tyrrell at **Castleknock**. Other castles soon follow at Dalkey, Clondalkin, Drimnagh etc.

St Michael's Church built on site of Hasculf's palace at the top of St Michael's Hill. (Only its tower remains: the rest of the structure will be rebuilt as the Church of Ireland Synod Hall).

St John's Church (afterwards amalgamated with St Michael's) stood at the top of Fishamble Street, on John's Lane East. Demolished, 1884. The fishmonger, Molly Malone, is buried in its adjoining grave-yard (see 1734).

1174   **St Thomas' Abbey** founded by Henry II in reparation for the murder of Thomas à Becket. It stood behind St Catherine's Church in Thomas Street. It was an abbey of Augustinian canons.

1175   **Priory of St John of Jerusalem** (Knights Templars) founded by Strongbow at Kilmainham. On the site of the present Royal Hospital, its lands included much of the Phoenix Park. Its Prior was always one of Dublin's most important citizens. When the Templars were suppressed, the buildings and lands were given to the Knights Hospitallers (see 1537).

> An aside on church/state relations will be in order here. Difficulties between church and state date back to the time of St Patrick (who is said to have lit a paschal fire on the Hill of Slane in defiance of the High King's at Tara). The Celtic monasteries were ravaged by Irish chieftains long before the advent of the Vikings. Disputes over the primacy of the Church have been mentioned already (see 1074, 1097, 1152). Grants of land to the Church were made by kings like Sitric (1025) and Diarmait Mac Murrough (1162) which resulted in some state control. The English Pope, Hadrian IV, specifically told Henry II to reform the Irish Church. This reform was started before the Synod of Cashel (1172) which Henry attended. The Normans' chief innovation, however, was the introduction of mendicant friars: Franciscans, Dominicans, Carmelites and Augustinians. Every preferment in church as well as state, was to be filled by Normans. The Dublin abbeys and priories thus became 'English strongholds'. After a hundred and fifty years' experience of this, The O'Neill

appealed to the Pope, saying: *The very clergy of the Englishmen assert that it is no more sin to kill an Irishman than a dog. The monks of the Cistercian Order at Inch, appearing publicly in arms, attack and slay the Irish, and yet celebrate their Masses notwithstanding.*

1176   Richard Talbot, given grant of land at **Malahide** by Henry II, builds the castle that is now open to the public.

1177   **Henry II** decides that his extensive dominions are to be divided up between his sons. Ireland is to go to his fourth son, John. Against the odds, John eventually becomes King of England – so a separate Ireland does not emerge.

Strongbow dies and is buried in Christ Church. His (supposed) tomb is in the nave. The small effigy nearby is said to be that of Strongbow's son who, according to popular tradition, was chopped in half for showing cowardice in battle.

First Synod of Dublin: Cardinal Vivian presides.

Howth Castle: Sir Amoricus (Almeric) Tristram is granted land here following his victory at 'the bridge of Evora', near Claremont Strand, on the 10th

Malahide Castle with Talbot tomb inset.

The old castle, Howth.

August, the feast of St Lawrence – whence, some say, the family name (see 1564). Howth Castle, over 800 years later, is still the family home.

1178   **St Werburgh's Church** is built, named after the saintly daughter of the King of Mercia. It will be rebuilt on the same site in Werburgh Street in 1715. Werburgh, Abbess of Chester, also had a church named after her in Bristol.

1179   **Knights Templars** established at Clontarf – where the Castle now stands.

1180   **St John's Hospital** (Ireland's first hospital) founded by Ailred the Palmer and his wife on their return from a pilgrimage to Jerusalem. It stood on Thomas Street, opposite 'John's Lane' Church, now the City Saw Mills. Ailred's community was of Augustinian hospitallers, brothers and nuns.

Death of Laurence O'Toole in Eu, Normandy, where his remains are still venerated (see 1225). His heart will later be brought back to Ireland and placed in Christ Church Cathedral. Henry II – exercising his feudal prerogative – names John Comyn as successor. For the next four centuries, the See is held by twenty-five archbishops who – despite the Synod of Cashel of 1172 – were 'born, bred and beneficed in England' with the exception of Archbishop FitzSimons (1484) who was a Palesman.

1181   **St George's Church**, on George's Lane (now Street). It will have to be rebuilt in 1213. Eventually, it will house the famous Guild of St George (founded 1474) to which the Mayor and Corporation belonged.

Decorative panel, Malahide Castle.

1184   **Swords** granted to Archbishop of Dublin: extensive ruins of his castle remain. (see 1317).

1185   **Prince John**, now the nineteen-year-old Lord of Ireland, visits Dublin for nine months. He behaves boorishly, according to his critic, Gerald of Wales, and 'leaves the realme a great deal worse than he found it'.

       Giraldus Cambrensis (Gerald of Wales) tours Ireland with Prince John and afterwards writes an unflattering history entitled *Expugnatio Hibernica*, published 1188.

1187   First Anglo-Norman geography-book of Ireland, *Topographia Hiberniae*, published by Giraldus.

1188   Pope Clement III gives great privileges to St John's hospital, thus creating **Dublin's first 'liberty'**: the Liberty of Ailred. (The 'liberties' gave people 'freedom from toll, passage, portage, lestage, pavage, quayage and carriage').

1189   **Little John**, one of Robin Hood's merry men, is said to have visited Dublin and fired an arrow 'from the Bridge to Oxmantown Green' – a prodigious distance.

1191   **St Patrick's Cathedral**. Building started by Archbishop John Comyn on site of old Celtic church. He raises it to collegiate status the following year, but it does not become a cathedral till 1219. Why a second cathedral? Because the Archbishop wanted to free himself from the monastic community at Christ Church by setting up his own Anglo-Irish diocesan chapter. In 1212, this will become known as the Archbishop's Liberty – as distinct from the Liberty of Christ Church (which was Dublin's smallest at one and a half acres). The north transcept of St Patrick's was the parish church of **St Nicholas Without** (the walls) until 1707.

1192   **Prince John's Charter** allows the citizens of Dublin 'to have all their reasonable Guilds'.

       Second Synod of Dublin: Papal Legate attends, his name unrecorded.

1195   **St Peter de Hulla Church** erected in Peter Street. In 1711 the French Huguenots will build a new church on the same spot.

1197   Dublin City is placed 'under interdict', i.e. excommunicated, because of quarrel between Prince John and the Pope.

1200   Shortly after he becomes King of England, John establishes the **Liberty of St Thomas** (see 1174). These 380 acres of land will become, in turn, the Liberty of Thomas Court, the Liberty of Thomas Court and Donore, and (after the suppression of the Abbey by Henry VIII) the Earl of Meath's Liberty.

1202   **Third Synod of Dublin**: John of Salerno represents the Pope.

1204   The construction of **Dublin Castle** and new city walls started by the viceroy, Meiler FitzHenry, by order of the Lord John at the expense of the citizens. To compensate them, the Lord of Ireland establishes **Donnybrook Fair** by Royal Charter. It will last until 1855.

Many other castles are built around the colonized area which will become known as 'the Pale' in the fifteenth century.

1207   John, who is now King of England as well as Lord of Ireland, grants another new charter to Dublin.

1209   **Black Monday**: on Easter Monday, 500 Normans are slaughtered in Cullen's Wood (Ranelagh) by the O'Byrnes and O'Tooles of Wicklow.

1210   **Norman Bridge** built over the Liffey, near the Áth Cliath. This will be the only bridge till 1670.

John visits Dublin for the second time, staying at Thomas Court (see 1174). This is the last Royal Visit to Dublin till 1394.

1212   Archbishop Henry of London succeeds John Comyn. He builds the Archbishop's **Palace of St Sepulchre** (now Kevin Street Police Station, where the seventeenth century gate-piers of the palace can still be seen) and sets up the Liberty of St Sepulchre. This Archbishop also had a hand in the building of Dublin Castle.

1213   John grants bishopric and abbey of **Glendalough** to Henry of London, Archbishop of Dublin.

1215   **Magna Carta** is signed by King John and his barons at Runnymede; the Charter is countersigned by Dublin's Archbishop, Henry of London.

1219   Collegiate Church of St Patrick is raised to **Cathedral** status.

1220   Hospitals for lepers: **St Stephen's** on site of the present Mercer's Hospital and **Lazaretto** on Lazar's Hill (now Townsend Street).

1222   Dublin imposes a tax on wines.

1224   **St Saviour's Priory** (Dominicans or Black Friars) founded on the site of the present Four Courts. Its extensive grounds reached to the corner of Cuckoo Lane and George's Hill. Under an outbuilding there in 1890 workmen found a tunnel 150 feet long heading for the Liffey. This was supposed to be an ancient passage which ran under the river to connect with the crypt of Christ Church. The story is still told of a soldier attending a state funeral in the Cathedral in the Middle Ages. Getting bored during the ceremony, he wandered down this tunnel to see where it led. When the sacristan had put away the ceremonial candlesticks used on big occasions, he unwittingly locked the soldier inside. Some months later his body was found gnawed to a skeleton. He still had his sword in hand and around him lay the corpses of over 200 rats which he had killed before the rest got to him.

1225   **St Francis' Friary** (Franciscans) established in Francis Street. The present RC church of St Nicholas of Myra is on the same site.

Canonization of Laurence O'Toole by Pope Honorius III.

1229   Henry III arranges for the annual election of 'a loyal and discreet **Mayor**'. Up to this time the title was 'Provost'; it will become 'Lord Mayor' in 1665.

1232   **Maurice FitzGerald** becomes Justiciar, the first of a long line of Geraldines to be head of the Administration.

1238   Requisition of all Irish exchequer moneys by King Henry III.

1240   **St Audoen's Arch**, Cook Street. It is the only remaining gate of Norman Dublin.

1243   New Hall added to **Dublin Castle**. The most elaborate building in Dublin to date, it gloried in a rose window and had running water.

1245   **John FitzGerald** succeeds Maurice FitzGerald as Justiciar.

1247   Henry III again requisitions moneys of Irish exchequer (see 1238).

1251   **Royal Mint** produces coins for Dublin (Henry III). Over £43,000 will be coined before this mint is closed in 1254.

1254   Dedication of St Patrick's Cathedral.

1260   The 'Cruciferi' (or 'Crutched Friars') take over St John's Hospital (see 1180). These hospitallers wear a red cross over their white robes; they enlarge the hospital to 155 beds.

1265   The Norman castle at **Balrothery** – named after the Irish, Baile na Ridirí, meaning 'the town of the knights'.

1266   Earthquake felt in Dublin.

1268   Thomas Smothe builds himself a large house near Donnybrook. Originally called Smothe's Court, the name will gradually be softened to Simmonscourt.

1270   **St Mary's Priory** (Carmelites or White Friars) founded near the present Carmelite church on Whitefriar Street.

1272   Edward I succeeds Henry III.

Balrothery Castle, 1265.

1280 **Holy Trinity Friary** (Augustinians) founded off Dame Street, behind the present Central Bank. Not to be confused with the Augustinian canons of the other Holy Trinity at Christ Church.

1281 **Royal Mint** reopens in Dublin. It will close again in 1283.

1283 A dreadful fire burns most of the city, including half of Christ Church.

1285 Dominican and Franciscan priests are denounced for 'making much of the Irish tongue'.

1291 Crown officials seize money of Italian merchant bankers in Dublin.

1293 Edward I gives safe conduct in Dublin to the merchants of Flanders.

1294 **Royal Mint** coins new Dublin money (Edward I).

Great storm destroys crops: famine and disease follow.

1296 Dublin merchants are allowed to export corn to Gascony.

ELSEWHERE: Murder of Thomas à Becket in Canterbury Cathedral (1170). Kamakura period of feudalism begins in Japan (1185). Capture of Jerusalem by Saladin (1187). Frederick Barbarossa, Philip of France and Richard the Lionheart lead the Third Crusade (1189) and capture Acre (1191). Fourth Crusade, diverted by Venetians, captures Constantinople (1204). Temujin the Mongol is proclaimed 'Genghiz Khan' (Mighty King) of Central Asia (1206). Children's Crusade (1212). *Magna Carta* signed at Runnymede (1215). New religious Orders: Dominicans (1215) and Franciscans (1223). King (later Saint) Louis of France captured while on Crusade (1250). Kublai Khan rules in China (1260) where Marco Polo travels to visit him (1270). Death of Thomas Aquinas (1274). Rising in Sicily, known as 'The Sicilian Vespers' (1282). Edward I completes his conquest of Wales (1284). Fall of Acre ends Crusades (1291).

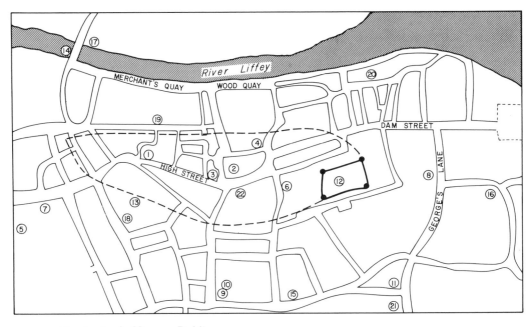

Fig. 9　Anglo-Norman Dublin.

1. St Audoen's (1171)	12. Dublin Castle (1204)
2. Christ Church Cathedral (rebuilt 1172)	13. City Wall (1204)
3. St Michael's (1173)	14. Dublin Bridge (1210)
4. St John's (1173)	15. Palace of St Sepulchre (1212)
5. St Thomas Court (1174)	16. St Stephen's (1220)
6. St Werburgh's (1178)	17. St Saviour's Priory (1224)
7. St John's Hospital (1180)	18. St Francis' Friary (1225)
8. St George's (1181)	19. St Audoen's Arch (1240)
9. St Patrick's (1191)	20. Holy Trinity Friary (1259)
10. St Nicholas Without (1191)	21. St Mary's Whitefriars (1270)
11. St Peter's (1195)	22. The Tholsel (1325)

'MORE IRISH THAN THE IRISH'

It was during the next century that the Normans (or the Old English as they are now generally called) were said to have become 'more Irish than the Irish themselves'. This expression must be taken with a grain of salt when applied to the Lords of Leinster. In County Dublin, especially, the link with England was considered to be crucial for trade and culture. The colonists continued to send their children to 'English' boarding-schools: the girls went to convents like Grace Dieu, near Swords, and the boys to places like St Wolstan's, near Celbridge.

1297   Parliament in Dublin has to tackle the problem of Norman integration with 'the mere Irish'. It enacts that the colonists should remain distinct from the native Irish. A policy of what we would now be tempted to call 'apartheid' bans the use of Irish dress and hair-style. These laws, however, will be increasingly ignored.

1300   Irish **wool taxed** at Bruges. Parliament at Dublin grants subsidy.

1302   **Royal Mint** is closed (see 1294).

1304   Fierce fire on the north side: much of St Mary's Abbey destroyed.

1305   **Public Lighting**: first mention of street-lights in city records (see 1616).

1307   The boundaries of **County Dublin** are fixed, as are those of eleven other counties: Kildare, Meath, Carlow, Louth, Waterford, Cork, Tipperary, Limerick, Kerry, Roscommon and 'Connacht'.

1308   **City Water Supply**: augmented with water from the Dodder at Templeogue, two thirds of the River Poddle is diverted through Thomas Court, down Thomas Street and High Street, to the City Basin outside St Audoen's Church. Citizens are allowed to run water from this into their houses provided their pipe is no wider than a goose's quill.

County Louth: the Bruce battlefield, 1318.

1310   **Edmund Butler** of the Ormond family becomes Justiciar.

The bakers of Dublin are drawn through the city on hurdles fastened to horses' tails, for using false weights and other frauds.

1312   **City Walls** extended north of the Liffey. No traces remain. South of the Liffey a substantial section of the Norman wall will be discovered at Wood Quay during the 1978-79 excavations but will be demolished by the Corporation to make way for their new office-blocks.

1313   First wooden bridge built over the River Tolka at Ballybough by John le Decer. The first flood will sweep it away. Soon rebuilt.

1315   Invasion of Edward Bruce. He lands at Larne with an army of Scots. Many Hiberno-Normans join him and he is crowned King of Ireland at Dundalk.

1316   Spire of St Patrick's Cathedral is blown off in a storm.

John FitzGerald is created first Earl of Kildare by Edward II.

1317   Advance of **Edward Bruce**: he camps with an army supposed to number 20,000 men near Tyrrell's Castle at Castleknock and bombards the Archbishop's castle at Swords (see 1327). To protect Dublin from Bruce's forces, St Saviour's Priory is demolished to build a new city wall along the Liffey at Merchant's Quay and Wood Quay. This makes Bruce abandon his attempt to capture Dublin. His brother, King Robert, comes to his aid but is repulsed at the Battle of Ratoath in County Meath and returns to Scotland.

1318   Edward Bruce defeated and slain at Faughart in County Louth. The Anglo-Irish in Dublin breathe a sigh of relief.

1320   **St Patrick's University** founded by Archbishop Alexander de Bicknor at the Cathedral. With the approval of Pope John XXII, public lectures are established but the lack of funding leads to gradual decay. The university will struggle on till the 1530s. Then it will be abolished.

1325   The **Tholsel** (or 'Toll Booth') erected in Christ Church Place. (The site is now fenced in for the impounding of motor-cars). The Royal Exchange and Excise Office, it will be rebult in 1680 and demolished in 1806.

1327   Archbishop Alexander de Bicknor, finding Swords uninhabitable, moves to a new castle at Tallaght. Magnificent walls still stand in Swords.

1328   **James Butler** created First Earl of Ormond by Edward III.

1329   **Paving of streets** begins. This is earlier than in most cities: for example, Bristol will have no paved streets till 1488.

Maurice FitzGerald created first Earl of Desmond.

1331   The O'Tooles of Wicklow raid Tallaght and steal 300 of the Archbishop's sheep.

Famine is relieved by 'a great shoal of fish, called Turlehydes, being cast on shore at the mouth of the Dodder'. Upwards of 200 of the 400-foot-long monsters (!) are caught by the starving Dubliners.

1334   The de Burgo (Burke, O Búrca) family 'goes native'. When the head of the house, Sir Richard, is murdered at Carrickfergus in this year, his heirs, Sir William and Sir Edmond become 'wholly independent Irish chieftains' and enemies of Dublin.

1337   Seven partridge land on roof of Christ Church: 'a portent which nobody could explain'.

1338   The Liffey is frozen solid for the first two months of the year. The citizens play football and light fires on the ice.

1339   **Royal Mint** reopens (see 1302).

1341   A law is passed excluding 'all but Englishmen beneficed in England' from holding office in Ireland.

1347   **The Black Death**: 14,000 Dubliners are said to have died in this plague between August and Christmas. This is an exaggeration, but many do die: possibly as many as one third of the population (i.e. 4,000 out of approximately 12,000 people). Until the worst ravages of the plague have passed, the richer citizens go to live with their friends in the country.

1351   **Great Council** at Dublin passes laws to curtail the hibernisation of the Anglo-Irish.

1361   Edward III sends his son, **Lionel, Duke of Clarence**, to Ireland as Lord Lieutenant.

1362   Nave of St Patrick's Cathedral is burnt down 'through negligence of John the Sexton'.

1366   **Statute of Kilkenny** decrees intermarriage with the Irish to be treason, that the colonists should remain separate from 'the Irish enemy', that they should speak English, renounce the Irish form of their names and desist from patronizing Irish poets or musicians. Even though Duke Lionel presides, this Statute of the Kilkenny Parliament will prove quite ineffective.

When the de Burgo family abjured the English lordship in 1334, the Butlers of Ormond were caught between the two Geraldine families of Kildare and Desmond. Of these two, the Earl of Desmond will become more and more Irish whereas the FitzGeralds of Kildare, on the boundary of the Pale, will become the connecting link between the English and the Irish. By the end of the fifteenth century, they will come to consider the office of Lord Deputy as their own by heredity. The Ormond family, to counterbalance this, will remain close to the King of England.

1370   **Archbishop Minot's Tower** is added to St Patrick's Cathedral. 147 feet high, it will be described in the nineteenth century as 'unrivalled in Ireland and unsurpassed as a belfry in the British Isles'.

1380   'The Pale' shrinks gradually as more colonists adopt Gaelic-Irish ways despite the wishes· of Dublin's rulers. Dublin citizens, including the Archbishop, Robert Wickeford, are now paying protection-money to avoid the ravages of the O'Byrnes, the O'Tooles and others.

1385   The Liffey Bridge collapses (see 1428).

1393   Richard II of England decides to take sterner measures. He assembles a large army and a well-equipped fleet to carry it to Waterford the following year.

1394   **Richard II** spends Christmas in Dublin. Using a policy of 'surrender and regrant, the king knights four Irish chieftains (O'Neill of Ulster, O'Conor of Connaught, O'Brien of Munster and Art Mac Murrough of Leinster) in Christ Church Cathedral. This gesture is not appreciated either by the colonists or by the Irish: The O'Donnell who, of course, had a vested interest, calls The O'Neill a traitor.

The king grants a tax of one penny per house to repair the Liffey Bridge.

1398   Recurrence of plague.

1399   Richard II has to visit Dublin again: he is the last English king to do so till 1689.

1400   Hybrid (English/Irish) names date back to around the turn of this century: e.g. Booterstown (the town of the Road), Ringsend (the end of the spit of land), Stonybatter (stony road).

1402   Thomas Cusack becomes the first Mayor of Dublin to have a gilt sword carried before him when he travels in public – following the London custom. With the Corporation, the Mayor 'rides the franchises' annually: i.e. he tours the city boundary and throws a javelin into the sea at Ringsend to denote the city limits.

The O'Byrnes of Wicklow are defeated by the citizens of Dublin with great slaughter. The Dubliners are led by their Mayor, John Drake.

1403   **Dunsany Castle**, originally built by Hugh de Lacy *c.*1200, passes by marriage to Sir Christopher Plunkett. In the 1780s, it will be restored and decorated by Michael Stapleton. Further additions and alterations will be carried out in the 1840s.

1411   **Birmingham Tower** is added to Dublin Castle.

1423   The present bells of St Audoen's ring for first time. (The tenor bell will have to be replaced in 1984).

1424   Another plague: Viceroy Mortimer among the many who die.

1428   Dublin Bridge – still the only one – is rebuilt by the Dominicans to serve their north-side priory. No other bridge will cross the Liffey till 1683.

1434   The Mayor and citizens do penance for abusing the abbot of St Mary's Abbey.

1439   Another plague: over 3,000 people die in Dublin.

1449   **Richard, Duke of York** arrives in Dublin as Lord Lieutenant. As heir presumptive to the English throne, he wins Ireland (except for Ormond) to the Yorkist side in what were to be known as The Wars of the Roses.

1452   Richard, Duke of York, returns to England to fight Lancastrians. Ormond becomes Lord Lieutenant.

The Liffey is entirely dry at Dublin 'for the space of two minutes'.

1454   Dublin Corporation issues a decree ordering

> all men and women of Irish blood whether nuns, clerics, journeymen, apprentices, servants, beggars etc. to quit the city within four weeks and anyone found within the city gates after that time shall forfeit their goods, chattels, etc. and be cast into prison and suffer other penalties.

The evicted people settle at **Irishtown**. The (now obsolete) Roman Catholic custom of bringing home 'Easter Water', for curative purposes, will be practised in Irishtown until the early twentieth century.

1457   'Irishmen' again banished from Dublin. Here is a quote from the *Dublin Assembly Roll* of the year:

> It was ordained by the said assembly from thenceforward no Irish men, no men with beards above the mouth, nor their horses nor their horseboys, shall be lodged within the wall of the city of Dublin. And whosoever lodges any of the aforementioned contrary to this ordinance, to pay 6s. 8d. as many times and as often as they be found guilty; and half thereof to the court and half to the town works.

1459   York, defeated in England, returns to Ireland. In the following year, he will hold a parliament at Drogheda which will declare that 'Ireland is and at all times has been corporated of itself'.

1460   York returns to England where he is defeated and killed. Ormond becomes Lord Lieutenant for the second time.

1461   **Edward IV**, son of York, becomes King of England. Ormond executed.

1462   **FitzGerald of Desmond** is made Lord Lieutenant. To the government in England he is too Irish by half; he is soon replaced by an Englishman, Sir John Tiptoft – quaintly known as 'The Butcher'. Desmond is officially beheaded at Drogheda without trial.

1474   Foundation of the **Guild of St George** to which the Mayor and Corporation belong.

1475   Bull for founding a university at Dublin issued by Pope Sixtus IV (see 1320).

1483   **Richard III** becomes king. He will leave little mark on Ireland before his death on Bosworth Field two years later.

1485   Beginning of the Tudor era with **Henry VII**. Reluctantly, he leaves the government of Ireland to Garret Mór FitzGerald, Earl of Kildare, whose Dublin residence, called 'The Carbrie', was in Castle Street. Henry VII was the king who uttered the famous words: 'Since all Ireland cannot rule this man, let this man rule all Ireland'. FitzGerald will join in the plan to overthrow Henry who had taken the crown by force.

Tarring the roads (see 1329).

Bringing home the Easter Water, Sandymount Church (see 1454).

1487   **Lambert Simnel**, a boy of ten years, described by Henry VII as a pretender but upheld by Margaret of Burgundy and other members of the English royal family as genuine, is crowned as King Edward VI in Christ Church Cathedral by Archbishop FitzSimons of Dublin with the support of most of the Anglo-Irish lords. Garret Mór FitzGerald's brother, Thomas, accompanies Simnel with an army to England. The army is routed at Stoke. Thomas FitzGerald is killed in the battle and Simnel is reduced to the rank of scullery-boy in Henry VII's kitchen.

1488   Stone bridge is built over the Tolka at Ballybough – to replace the wooden one of 1313.

1490   The first importation of claret into Dublin.

1492   **Perkin Warbeck** claims the throne. Declared – correctly in this case – to be a pretender, but accepted by FitzGerald Earl of Desmond as genuine, Warbeck is soon executed.

Fierce row in Dublin between the Earls of Kildare and Ormond. They fight it out in St Patrick's Cathedral, then shake hands through a hole chopped in a door to the Chapter House. The door is still on view in the south transept of the Cathedral.

1494   **Poynings Law**: the new Lord Deputy, at a meeting of the Irish Parliament in Drogheda, enacts that laws can only be made by the Irish Parliament after the king and council in England have given their approval.

1495   Garret Mór is attainted and taken to London for questioning. He is acquitted and returns the following year as Lord Deputy.

1497   The Mayor and Corporation of Dublin re-enact the ancient right of sanctuary for Christ Church.

1509   **Henry VIII** succeeds as King of England and Lord of Ireland (see 1541).

1512   Riots in Dublin due to poverty. For not stopping them soon enough, the Mayor is sentenced to walk barefoot through the city streets.

1513   **Garret Óg FitzGerald** succeeds his father, Garret Mór, both as Earl of Kildare and as Lord Deputy of Ireland.

1520   Plague in Dublin.

1528   A celebrated Passion Play is performed on a stage at Hoggen Green (now College Green).

1533   Garret Óg is summoned to London by Henry VIII (who has just broken with Rome after his marriage to Anne Boleyn). 'Silken' Thomas FitzGerald, Garret Óg's son, becomes deputy Lord Deputy.

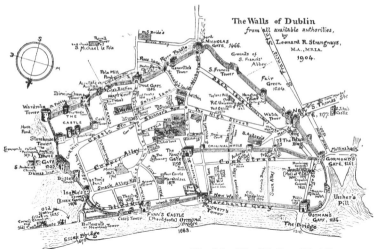

Fig. 10   The Walls of Dublin

'The Pale' shrinks in extent and Dublin becomes impoverished. A merchant writes: 'All the butchers in Dublin have not so much beef to sell as would make one mess of browse' – whatever that might be.

1534   **Revolt of Silken Thomas**. Believing that his father had been executed, Thomas flings down the sword of state in the Chapter House of St Mary's Abbey. When Archbishop John Allen makes remonstrances, Thomas tells his followers to 'get rid of the fool'. The Archbishop escapes and attempts to sail to England for safety. His ship is stranded at Clontarf and he seeks refuge at the house of his friend, Mr Hollywood of Artane. The Archbishop's hiding place is soon discovered and he is brutally murdered.

1535   Silken Thomas surrenders after fifteen months in rebellion. He will be brought to London and executed (along with his five uncles) at Tyburn two years later.

ELSEWHERE: 'Babylonian Captivity' of Pope in Avignon (1309-77). Robert Bruce defeats the English at Bannockburn (1314). Beginning of 100 Years War between England and France (1338). 'Black Death' reaches Europe (1346). Ming Dynasty begins in China (1368). Peasants' Revolt in England (1381). Death of Chaucer (1400). Battle of Agincourt (1415). Relief of Orleans by Joan of Arc (1429) who is burnt at stake (1431). Henry the Navigator rounds Cape Bojador (1433). Renaissance begins: invention of movable print (1454). Wars of the Roses begin (1455). Spain united by marriage of Ferdinand of Aragon with Isabella of Castile (1469). Bartholomew Diaz rounds Cape of Good Hope (1488), Christopher Columbus discovers West Indies (1492), John Cabot discovers Newfoundland (1497), Vasco da Gama finds sea route to India (1498), Amerigo Vespucci charts S. American coast (1499) and Pedro Cabral discovers Brazil (1500). Machiavelli's *The Prince* (1513). James IV of Scotland defeated by English at Flodden (1513). Luther's *Theses* (1517) ignite the Reformation. Charles V elected Holy Roman Emperor (1519). Magellan circumnavigates the world (1519). Death of Leonardo da Vinci (1519). Rise of Sulieman the Magnificent (1520). Ivan the Terrible becomes Czar of Russia (1533).

Wrenboys (see 1550)

REFORMATION DUBLIN

1535   Henry VIII, now self-appointed Head of the Church of England, decides to implement his new religious policy in Ireland. He appoints George Browne as Archbishop of Dublin and has him consecrated by Thomas Cranmer at Canterbury. Dr Browne becomes one of the 'King's Commissioners' for Ireland. In a letter to Thomas Cromwell, the English Lord Privy Seal, he writes:

> My most honoured lord, your humble servant, receiving your mandate as one of his highness's commissioners, hath endeavoured, almost to the danger and hazard of his temporal life, to procure the nobility and gentry of this nation in due obedience in owning of his highness their supreme head, as well spiritual as temporal, and do find much oppugning therein, especially my brother, Armagh, who had been the main oppugner, and so hath withdrawn most of his suffragans and clergy within his see and jurisdiction. He made a speech to them laying a curse on the people whosoever should own his highness's supremacy, saying that isle, as it is in their Irish chronicles 'insula sacra', belongs to none but the Bishop of Rome that gave it to the king's ancestors. Your lordship may inform his highness that it is convenient to call a parliament in this nation to pass the supremacy by act.

Four points to bear in mind regarding the Reformation in Ireland: (i) it was a gradual process of change, not something that happened overnight; (ii) Henry VIII was a Catholic who disliked the current Protestant theologies of continental Europe: in the Roman Church's view, he was a schismatic, not a heretic; (iii) Henry's writ did not run very far in Ireland so his 'reforms' were mostly confined to the Pale; (iv) even within the Pale, it was some of the nobility and gentry who 'conformed', not the mass of the people and not many of the clergy – so English clergymen had to be imported.

1536   Lord **Leonard Grey**, Henry's deputy in Dublin, calls a parliament which passes the Act of Supremacy. From now on, King Henry, not the Pope, is officially Head of the Church in Ireland. Some Lords of the Pale, remembering what had happened to Silken Thomas and his uncles, meekly submit.

1537   Henry VIII orders the **dissolution of the Irish monasteries**. Archbishop Browne and Sir Anthony St Leger preside over the disposal of the Dublin monasteries over the next few years.

St Mary de Hogges	*granted to*	James Sedgrave of Much Cabragh (His home is now the Dominican Convent in Cabra).
Whitefriars	*granted to*	Francis Aungier (developer of Aungier Street and environs).
St Mary's Abbey	*granted to*	James FitzGerald, Earl of Desmond, and Sir John Travers, Master of Ordnance, for storing artillery (see 1641 for further disposal).
St John's Hospital	*granted to*	Thomas Luttrell, Knight.

St Thomas' Court	*granted to*	William Brabazon, Earl of Meath.
St Francis'	*granted to*	William Hande, Gentleman.
St Saviour's	*granted to*	Lawers of the King's Inns.
All Hallows	*granted to*	The Mayor, Bailiffs, Commons, and citizens of Dublin, 'and their successors forever' – in thanks for resisting Silken Thomas (see 1591 for further developments).
Holy Trinity Friary	*granted to*	Walter Tyrrell in 1541 and later to Sir Thomas Luttrell.
St John's, Kilmainham		kept by the Crown as a residence for the Lord deputy.

1538 **Archbishop George Browne** (by now one of the more ardent Reformers) makes a large bonfire of Dublin's sacred relics – including the famous *Bachall Ísu* (see 1097) – in Christ Church Place.

1539 St Patrick's University is abolished by decree of Henry VIII.

1541 Henry VIII is declared '*King* of Ireland' by an Irish parliament: up to this, English monarchs had been only 'Lords' of Ireland.

1542 Counter-reformation begins: Pope Paul III sends two Jesuit legates to Ireland. (This has the distinction of being the first Jesuit Foreign Mission. St Ignatius Loyola, who had founded the Order two years earlier, wrote instructions for the legates as to 'The Manner of Dealing with the Irish Princes and People'. Unable to enter Dublin, the Jesuits returned to Rome after spending five weeks in Ulster).

1547 **Edward VI** – aged ten – succeeds Henry VIII. The Regent, Somerset, sends Sir Edward Bellingham, a physical-force man, to rule Ireland.

1548 Protestantism is declared the official religion of Ireland. Bellingham tries to bring in the same changes as are being introduced in England. Even within the Pale, these changes are rejected. Numerous revolts result. Bellingham is recalled to England, leaving Ireland in a state of war.

1550 St Patrick's Cathedral is reduced to status of a parish church.

Wren-boys, still popular today in the Fingal area of County Dublin, are said to have originated in the middle of the sixteenth century. The 'mummers', as they are sometimes called, have handed down their rhymes from generation to generation. For example, here are some of the words still recited by the Swords Mummers:

George: Here I come, Prince George, And afterwards I rode away.
Out of England I have fled. I've fought in England, France and Spain
I have fed my horse on oats and hay And now I'm here to fight again.
. . . .

What can you cure, doctor?

Doctor: I've got a little bottle
In my waistcoat pocket.
It's called 'hocus pocus medical pain'
Have a sup, Prince George, and
Rise up and fight your battle again.
It can cure the plague-go-in and the plague-go-out
The pipsy-popsy and the gout.
And if you don't believe me, all I say
Is enter in here Joe the butcher.

1551   **Book of Common Prayer** is the first book ever printed in Ireland. It comes from the press of Humphrey Powell in Dublin.

Edward VI transfers ecclesiastical Primacy from Armagh to Dublin.

1533   **Queen Mary** succeeds to throne. She restores the primacy to Armagh and Roman Catholicism to Ireland. No friend of the Gaelic Irish, Mary will carry out the first 'plantations' (in Laois and Offaly).

1554   Archbishop Browne is expelled from Dublin by the new Primate, George Dowdall, Archbishop of Armagh.

1555   **Hugh Curwin**, a Scotsman, is appointed Archbishop of Dublin by Queen Mary and Pope Paul IV.

Cathedral status is restored to St Patrick's.

1556   Despite her religious activities in England this year, Queen Mary burns no Protestants in Dublin.

ELSEWHERE: The Reformation sweeps through Europe. Thomas More and John Fisher are executed in England (1535). Emperor Charles V campaigns in North Africa with Admiral Andrea Doria (1535). Anne Boleyn (1536) and Katherine Howard (1542) executed. Erasmus dies (1536). Michelangelo paints *Last Judgement* in Sistine Chapel (1536-41) and designs dome of St Peter's, Rome (1546). 'Pilgrimage of Grace': popular rising in N. England (1536-7). Jesuit Order founded (1540). Council of Trent opens (1545) launching Counter-reformation. Moscow is destroyed by fire (1547). The Turks capture Tripoli (1551). Peace of Augsburg (1555). Charles V retires, leaving his empire to Philip II (1556). World's worst earthquake kills 830,000 at Shensi, China (1556).

Elizabethan-style houses, Leinster Market.

A public clock, Fleet Street (see 1560).

Trinity College (see 1592).

ELIZABETHAN DUBLIN

In spite of her religious persecutions, Elizabeth I did much for the material development of Dublin. Still mainly confined within its walls on the south side of the Liffey, Dublin was virtually re-built in the wooden-beamed houses of the Tudor period. One of these Elizabethan houses stood on the corner of Castle Street and Werburgh Street until 1813.

1558   On her accession to the throne, Elizabeth re-establishes the Anglican Church. Archbishop Curwin of Dublin 'accommodates his conduct and conscience to the policy of the new sovereign'.

1560   Parliament in Dublin declares Ireland officially Protestant once again.

Villages' grow up around Dublin: Donnybrook, Rathfarnham, Raheny. Drumcondra, etc.

Elizabeth I orders the city's first three **public clocks**: for Dublin Castle, the Tholsel (in Christ Church Place) and St Patrick's Cathedral.

1562   To facilitate communication, Elizabeth establishes an efficient **postal service**: Alderman Nichols Fitzsimon appointed first Postmaster of Dublin.

1564   **Howth Castle** (see 1177) is rebuilt by the twentieth Earl of Howth.

Adam Loftus, Archbishop of Armagh, becomes Dean of St Patrick's in Dublin as well.

1565   **Elizabethan Wars** in Ireland – to continue until 1603 – start in earnest. Sir Philip Sydney, a ruthless Lord Deputy, steps up the persecution of the Catholics.

1567   **David Wolfe S.J.** becomes the first Jesuit to set foot in Dublin. Immediately arrested, he spends five years as a prisoner in Dublin Castle.

Adam Loftus becomes Protestant Archbishop of Dublin. For his building of Rathfarnham Castle, see 1585.

1568   Unsuccessful attempt is made to revive St Patrick's University.

1571   First book in Gaelic printed in Dublin: John Kearney's *Aibidil Gaoidheilge & Caiticiosma* (Gaelic Alphabet & Catechism). The first work ever to be printed in Gaelic had been published earlier this year: it was a religious ballad of Pilib Mac Cuinn Chrosaigh, issued on a single sheet at Dublin.

1575   Plague. Dublin decimated. As happened during the Black Death (see 1347) the wealthier citizens leave the capital. Parliament moves to Drogheda.

1579   The 'shiring' of Ireland: the boundaries of County Dublin and of some other counties in Munster and Connacht had already been fixed (see 1307). In this year the other counties of Ireland are established. Based on the ancient Irish chiefdoms, 'O'Reilly's Country', for example, becomes 'County Cavan'.

1581   **Edmund Spenser**, the poet, becomes secretary to another ruthless Lord Deputy, Grey de Wilton. In Ireland, the 'gentle' Spenser wrote *The Fairie Queene* and a proposal for the extinction of the Irish race.

1584   **Sir John Perrott** becomes Lord Deputy and pursues the Wars with vigour.

1585   **Rathfarnham Castle**, built by Archbishop Loftus, then the Lord Chancellor. The original building will be beautifully renovated in Georgian times.

1586   Another unsuccessful attempt is made to revive St Patrick's University.

1587   **Red Hugh O'Donnell**, son and heir of The O'Donnell of Donegal, is captured by the English and imprisoned in Dublin Castle. (He will escape in 1590 but will be recaptured. The following year he will escape again, this time successfully.)

1592   **Trinity College** is founded by Queen Elizabeth on site of former Priory of All Hallows (see 1539). In a letter to her new Deputy, Lord Fitzwilliam, the Queen states the two reasons for founding the University: for the 'education, training and instruction of youths and students in the Arts and Faculties, so that they might be better assisted in the study of the liberal arts and in the cultivation of virtue and religion'; and to counteract the new practice of Catholics who are sending their sons 'into France, Italy and Spain, to get learning in such foreign universities, whereby they have been infected with Popery and other ill qualities, and so become evil subjects'.

'The Colledge' – as it was called – originally stood further back from College Green than at present. None of the Elizabethan buildings remain: the oldest parts of Trinity are now the 'rubrics', the lower storeys of which date back to the reign of Queen Anne.

Hugh O'Neill (Earl of Tyrone) and Red Hugh O'Donnell (Earl of Tyrconnell) hold the north of Ireland against Elizabeth's forces. They receive no support from Dublin. As the historian Meehan put it:

'The Catholic nobility of the Pale were ever foremost in maintaining English oppression, so long as it did not interfere with their temporal possessions.

Howth Castle, with interiors.

1593   **George Carew**, the new Lord Deputy, builds a hospital for 'poor, sick and maimed soldiers' on Dame Street, opposite the new 'college'. This building will become Chichester House in the time of the Lord Lieutenant of that name (1604-16). Parliaments will be held there even before the house is replaced by the new Parliament Buildings in 1729.

1596   Terrible gunpowder explosion in Winetavern Street. One hundred and twenty people are killed when a spark from a horse-shoe ignites several barrels of nitrate just unloaded from a ship.

1598   The **Jesuits** establish their first base in Dublin – a Mass House in Cook Street. Accused of dabbling in politics, the Jesuits are blamed for tampering with the loyalties of the principal Catholics of the Pale.

1599   Irish rebels burn Kilmainham and Crumlin. They also break into the bawn of St Patrick's Cathedral and steal the cattle.

   Elizabeth sends **Robert Devereux**, Earl of Essex, as Lord Lieutenant. Not a success and accused of collaborating with the Jesuits, he will be recalled to England after six months – to be beheaded after a rebellion. His Irish post is given to Charles Blount, Lord Mountjoy.

1601   **Mountjoy** marches from Dublin to defeat O'Neill and O'Donnell at the Battle of Kinsale. The Elizabethan Conquest is nearly complete.

1603   O'Neill finally surrenders to Mountjoy – not knowing that the Queen had died three days earlier.

   Dubliners, rejoicing that 'Jezabel is dead!', prepare to re-introduce the Mass. In a forceful Royal Proclamation of James I, they are told that 'no tolerance will be given to the Romish religion'.

ELSEWHERE: *Thirty-nine Articles* of Church of England (1563). Don John of Austria defeats the Turks at Lepanto (1571). St Bartholomew's Day massacre of Protestants in France (1572). Holinshed's *Chronicles* (1577). Gregorian calendar introduces New Style dating (1582). Execution of Mary Queen of Scots (1587). Defeat of Spanish Armada (1588). Henry IV of France says 'Paris is worth a Mass' – and becomes Catholic (1593). Edict of Nantes grants liberty of worship (1598). Hugh O'Neill repulses English advance on Ulster at Battle of the Yellow Ford (1598). English East India Company founded (1600). Death of Calderón de la Barca (1600). Union of Scottish and English crowns under James VI & I (1603). Shakespeare's *Hamlet* (1603).

JAMES I AND CHARLES I

The persecution of Roman Catholics continued under James I with one significant addition: the Catholic 'loyalists' of the Pale, although English in origin, were treated like 'the mere Irishe'. Fr Henry Fitzsimon, a 'distinguished' Jesuit of Dublin who was already a prisoner in Dublin Castle for six years, provides a good example of the changed policy. Son of Nicholas Fitzsimon, a Lord of the Pale who had remained a staunch Catholic and a loyal subject of the Queen (see 1562), Henry had tried to avoid politics but was jailed for his religious views. Still in prison when James I came to the throne, he wrote several letters from Dublin Castle to the Jesuit General in Rome. In one of these, dated 1604, he describes how 'all' the Catholics of Dublin were treated:

A sudden and violent storm burst upon the Catholics . . . Six of the principal churches of the city were prepared for the occasion, preachers were appointed, the parishioners were numbered and registered, members of the Privy Council and very many spies were on the watch in each of the churches in order to detect and report the absentees . . . Wherefore, although our chief citizens are kept in prison, no day ever dawned that was more glorious to us and more disastrous to our enemies who are now bewildered, and puzzled what to do, whether they should go on or go back . . . .

1604 **Sir Arthur Chichester** becomes Lord Deputy (till 1616), resides with the Loftus family at Rathfarnham Castle and lays plans for the overthrow of the Earls of Ulster.

1607 **Flight of the Earls** (O'Neill and O'Donnell) from Lough Swilly in Donegal. Chichester soon heads north to mastermind the Plantation of Ulster and win the title, Earl (later Marquis) of Donegall.

In a letter from Madrid (where he is English Ambassador), Sir Charles Cornwallis recommends the plantation of Ulster by Scotsmen. He puts his proposal colourfully:

The king my master, being possessed of Scotland, hath in that country near adjoining to the north part of Ireland, a people of their own fashion, diet and disposition, that can walk their bog as well as

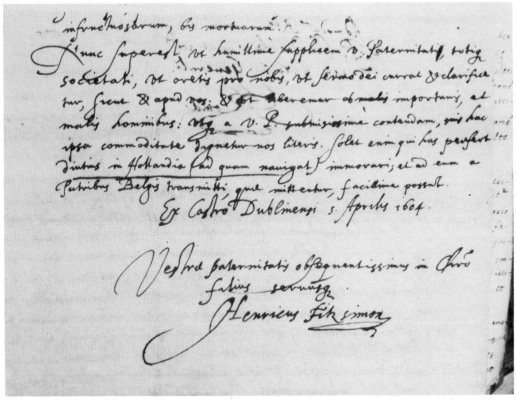

A letter from Fr Henry Fitzsimon, Dublin Castle.

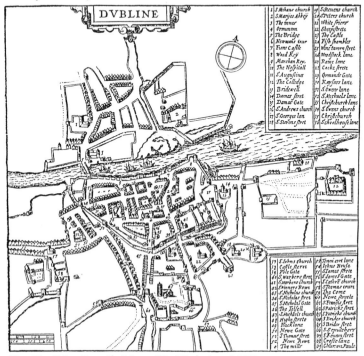

Fig. 11   John Speed's Map of Dublin's (see 1610).

themselves, live with their food and are so well practised and accustomed in their own country to the likes, as they are apt to pull them out of their dens and withdrawing places, as ferrets are to draw rabbits out of their burrows.

1610   **First map of the city of Dublin**, drawn by John Speed.

1611   During these decades, new alliances begin to form in Dublin. Under James I, the 'Old English' who are still Catholic begin to side with the Irish against the 'New English' Protestants.

Sir Edward Fisher builds **Phoenix House** on leased land at the present site of Magazine Fort. The Phoenix Park (see 1662) is called after this house.

1614   A deputation of 'Old English' Dubliners goes to see King James looking for a relaxation in his penal laws against Catholics. The king dismisses them contemptuously, describing them as 'half subjects', saying:

> You give your soul to the Pope and to me only the body – and even it,
> your bodily strength, you divide between me and the King of Spain.

Viscount Moore comes into possession of the lands of St Mary's Abbey (see 1537 and 1714).

1615   Further persecution of the Catholics of Dublin. The priests have a price on their heads but continue their ministry at secret Mass Houses in the back lanes. The Franciscans, for example, celebrate the liturgy in Adam and Eve's Tavern, off Merchants' Quay.

1616   **Public Lighting**: Corporation orders every fifth house in the city 'to have lanterne and candle-light set forth' (see 1305). Gas-light will come to the streets in 1825 and electricity in 1881.

1620   An English visitor, Luke Gernon, is impressed by the appearance of Dublin. 'The buildings', he tells us, 'are of timber and in the English form.'

1623   The Pope decides to retain the Irish hierarchy: this distinguishes Ireland from every other country ruled by Protestants (whose hierarchies are dissolved by the Pope).

1627   Jesuit college, chapel, and novitiate are built where Tailors' Hall stands to-day, with funds donated by the dowager Lady Kildare. The property, including the library, will be confiscated in 1629 and given as a present to Trinity College. Many religious orders establish houses in the Cook Street area at this time.

1628   'The Graces' granted by **Charles I**: These are concessions given to the 'Old English' (who had remained Catholic) in return for 'a large sum of money': £40,000 a year for three years, to be precise.

1629 Lord Dorchester reports: 'On St Stephen's Day, the Government suppressed by peaceful means several priests' and nuns' houses and seized some priests.' (see 1627 above).

1633 Sir Thomas ('Thorough') **Wentworth**, Earl of Strafford in 1640, becomes Lord Deputy for seven years. 'The Graces' were not withdrawn; Wentworth (see 1627) favours the Catholics more than the Presbyterian planters of the north.

1635 Sir William Brereton, the future Parliamentary general, writes:

> The City of Dublin is extending its bounds and limits very much . . . Here are divers commodities cried in Dublin as in London, which it doth more resemble than any town I have seen in the King of England's dominions'.

1638 Postal services are improved with the opening of the first GPO in Castle Street (see 1562). From here the GPO will move to High Street, Sycamore Alley, Fownes Street, Suffolk Street and College Green before the first purpose-built office is erected in Sackville (O'Connell) Street in 1814.

1639 **Black Oath** administered by Wentworth to all adult Presbyterians, forcing them to abjure the Scottish Covenant.

1640 Wentworth summoned to London: Parliament accuses him of ill-treating the Planters, being too lax on Catholics and of raising an army in Ireland for use in England.

1641 Wentworth is executed in England. **Insurrection** in Ireland. A plot to seize Dublin Castle is discovered. The Dean and Chapter of Christ Church flee to England: the Cathedral is taken over (till 1660) by Presbyterians and Anabaptists (see 1657). Withdrawal of 'The Graces' leads to revolt by Lords of the Pale.

1642 Confusion in Dublin due to English Civil War. The Catholics (both 'Old English' and Irish) set up their own government – the **Confederation of Kilkenny**.

The Confederates of the Pale defend Baldongan Castle, near Skerries, against the Parliamentary forces who besiege it under Col. Trafford whose secretary reports: 'On the next day they beat down the castle and put all to the sword, which were about 200. That day 26 priests were shipped for France, which deserve better to be hanged.'

1646 **Owen Roe O'Neill** and Thomas Preston besiege Dublin: Viceroy (Ormond) and Royalist citizens withstand the siege.

Ormond's 'Peace' proclaimed in Dublin.

1647 Colonel **Michael Jones**, with 2,000 Parliamentary troops, lands at Dublin.

Ormond surrenders the city to Jones, 'an uncouth and austere fanatic but a

St Francis Xavier's cross (see 1651).

Improved postal service (see 1638).

very brave and brilliant soldier'. Dublin Corporation gives Jones the freedom of the City and a present of **Donnycarney House**. This house was previously owned by John Bathe of Drumcondra Castle who was dispossessed for complicity in the rebellion of 1641.

1649   Charles I is executed. Ormond returns to attack Dublin; captures Rathfarnham Castle but is defeated by Jones at the **Battle of Rathmines**. For the following account of the battle, we are indebted to Liam de Paor (from his *The Peoples of Ireland* by kind permission):

Ormond, a slow and cautious commander, was besieging the more dashing and aggressive Jones in Dublin when he received word that Cromwell was about to sail for Ireland. At sunset on 1 August 1649 he sent Major-General Purcell with 1500 men to re-fortify Baggotrath castle by night, in order to deny Jones grazing for his horses east of Trinity College and to provide cover for batteries of guns to command the river approaches from Ringsend. Purcell was misled by his guides, went astray, and reached Baggotrath only an hour before daylight, to be expelled from the incomplete work by Jones's cavalry. Jones's centre advanced on foot from Dublin due south to Cullenswood. Meantime, his cavalry rode 3 km through Donnybrook to Milltown, wheeled north over the high ground above the Dodder, and struck Gifford's rear as Jones's foot engaged his front. By the end of 2 August, Ormond had been driven from the Dublin area. A good account of this battle was published by F E Ball in the *Journal of the Royal Society of Antiquaries of Ireland* for 1902, but this map is based on a re-examination of the evidence.

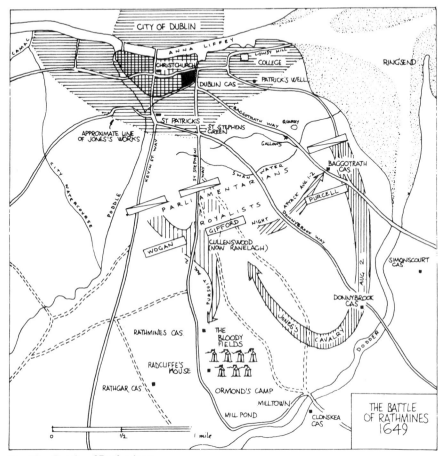

Fig 12.   Battle of Rathmines.

CROMWELLIAN DUBLIN

1649   **Oliver Cromwell** arrives at Ringsend with 12,000 troops and spends ten
        months creating havoc in Ireland. Cromwell's troops introduce cabbage for the
        first time into Ireland (see 1668).

        Cromwell's horses are stabled in St Patrick's Cathedral. The castles of
        Rathfarnham, Kimmage and Tallaght soon fall to Cromwell's forces: more
        stabling provided! Persecution of Catholics throughout Ireland which now
        becomes part of British Commonwealth with the devolved parliament
        suspended.

1650   **Ireton**, Cromwell's son-in-law, is left in charge of the army when the Protector
        returns to England in May.

1651   The Church of Ireland and its bishops are treated equally harshly: the Dissen-
        ters (Calvinists/Puritans) have their day. Fr Robert Nugent, Superior of the
        Jesuits, writes to Rome saying: 'We have lost all our property here for the
        moment'. One piece of Jesuit property was not lost at this time. A crucifix which
        belonged to St Francis Xavier was preserved all through the Penal Days.
        Subsequently venerated in St Michan's Church, Halston Street, it will be stolen
        from a glass-case there in 1983.

1652   **'Down Survey'** carried out by Dr William Petty (see 1661) as a prelude to the
        Cromwellian Settlement. He estimates that 850,000 people live in Ireland and
        that between fifteen and twenty per cent of them are Protestant. 15,582,487
        statute acres of land are confiscated from Catholics – who are told to get 'to Hell
        or to Connacht' – and given as payment to Cromwell's soldiers and supporters.
        In August, Parliament decrees that death is to be the penalty for Catholic
        landowners not transplanted by 1st May, 1654.

        Transplantation was the mildest punishment to which the Catholics were
        subjected. Death and forfeiture of all property was decreed for all who did not
        lay down their arms within twenty-eight days; for all who had hand, act or part
        in the Kilkenny Convention; for 'all Jesuits and other priests who had aided and
        abetted the rebellion'; and for Ormond, twenty-two other peers, one bishop and
        eighty knights and gentlemen mentioned by name.

1654   May 1st deadline is observed. General Charles Fleetwood, now in charge of
        army, is commissioned 'to spread the Gospel and the power of true religion and
        holiness'.

1655   **Henry Cromwell**, Oliver's fourth son, arrives as Commissioner and lives in
        Phoenix House (see 1611) on site of Magazine Fort. The steps near Bow Bridge
        over the River Camac are called 'Cromwell's Quarters' after him. He will
        receive the title of Lord Deputy two years later.

        Governor of Dublin Castle is ordered to deport all Catholic priests in his
        custody to Barbados (unless they are guilty of murder).

1657   'Act for convicting, discovering and repressing of popish recusants': this forces Catholics to take the oath of abjuration against the Pope and to deny the doctrine of transubstantiation on pain of sequestration of two-thirds of their property. Henry Cromwell himself was not anxious to persecute Cathlics, so the Act is only partially enforced.

1658   Death of Oliver Cromwell. **Richard Cromwell**, his third son, succeeds as Lord Protector. (His elder brothers, Robert and Oliver, had died young.)

1659   Parliament resolves that the government of Ireland shall be by commoners nominated and approved by parliament, and not by any one person. It is worth noting that the followers of Cromwell are the first to give Ireland democratic legislation - Papists apart.

Henry Cromwell leaves Ireland knowing that the Commonwealth's days are numbered.

Dublin Castle is seized by a party of officers favourable to the restoration of the monarchy.

ELSEWHERE: Charles I beheaded in London (1649). Oliver Cromwell sacks Drogheda and Wexford (1649). Hobbes' *Leviathan* (1651). Foundation of Cape Colony by the Dutch (1652). Cromwell dissolves Rump Parliament and becomes Lord Protector (1653). Isaac Walton's *The Compleat Angler* (1653). Rembrandt's *Jan Six* (1654) and *Titus Reading* (1656). Huygens discovers the satellites of Saturn (1656) and invents the pendulum clock (1658). Bernini designs the piazza of St Peter's, Rome (1656). Boyle's Law (*re* air pressure) stated by Robert Boyle, son of Richard, First Earl of Cork (1659). Peace of the Pyrenees signed between Spain and France (1659). Van Goyen paints his *View of Nimegen* and Velazquez his *Infanta Margarita Teresa* (1659).

RESTORATION DUBLIN

> At the end of the Cromwellian era, Dublin was in a sorry state. Its population had been drastically reduced and most of the larger buildings – including its two cathedrals – were in poor condition. Dublin Castle looked much as it did 400 years earlier, but most of the mediaeval structures (with the exception of St Mary's Chapter House, and St Audoen's) had disappeared.

1660   **The Restoration**: Charles II is called home and crowned King of England, Scotland and Ireland. One of his first acts of gratitude is to present a new chain of office to the Mayor of Dublin (see 1691).

Church of Ireland is restored as the established faith.

Catholics (who had taken the Royalist side in the Civil War) expect a restoration of their lands and expect Ormond to stand by the terms of the 'Peace' he had offered in 1646. Neither is granted. Dr J. G. Simms estimates that by 1671 just over *one* fifth of Irish land was in Catholic hands; the figure had been *three* fifths in 1641.

1661   William Petty is knighted and appointed Surveyor-general of Ireland (see 1672, 1682).

1662   **Ormond** returns (as Lord Lieutenant) from exile in Paris with big ideas on how to make Dublin a sparkling capital. His reception in Dublin 'was, for the splendour thereof, a kind of epitome of what had lately been seen at London upon His Majesty's happy restoration'. He starts by planning quays for the north side: Ormond Quay first, then Arran Quay (called after his son). Ormond serves two terms as Lord Lieutenant: 1662-69 and 1677-85. From this year on, he spells his name *Ormonde*.

Phoenix Park laid out by Ormonde (but its walls are not built for nine years).

St Stephen's Green is laid out by Dublin Corporation: the park, not the houses. Up to now it has been a grazing common. Gallows stand at Harcourt Street corner and in Gallows Row (now Merrion Row) near the end of Baggotrath Lane (now Baggot Street).

Smock Alley Theatre opened by John Ogilby, Master of the Revels. It is on Essex Street (where the Church of SS. Michael and John stands now). The Dublin actress, Peg Woffington, will make her name here.

1663 **Quakers**: First Dublin meeting of Society of Friends. Poorly received at first (e.g. Elizabeth Fletcher and Elizabeth Smith are imprisoned in Newgate), the Quakers will go on to become 'pillars of the community'.

In this year and in 1666 two Acts are passed prohibiting all imports of Irish cattle into England.

1665 The title 'Mayor of Dublin' becomes '**Lord** Mayor' (see 1229).

1666 Dublin sends 100,000 head of cattle for the relief of London after its Great Fire.

1667 Birth of **Jonathan Swift** in Hoey's Court, off Werburgh Street. (He will study Divinity at Trinity College and become Dean of St Patrick's in 1713).

College of Physicians is granted charter by Charles II (see 1692).

1668 **The Cabbage Patch**: Protestant graveyard is established opposite St Patrick's Deanery. Now a public park, it was here that Oliver Cromwell's troops planted their cabbages in 1649.

1670 **Blew-Coat School**, properly King's Hospital, founded by charter of Charles II. Before moving to Blackhall, Place, it stood on Queen Street at the edge of Oxmantown Green. Queen Street is named after Charles II's wife, Catherine of Braganza.

New **Chimes of Bells**: the six at Christ Church Cathedral ring for first time on 30th July; the eight at St Patrick's Cathedral on 23rd September.

1671 **Phoenix Park**: Walls built at the behest of Ormonde (who was swindled by the builder); deer and pheasants are imported from England so that the gentry can hunt in the Park. In spite of all Ormonde's 'improvements', Grafton Street, still a lane leading from Hoggen Green to St Stephen's Green, is said to be 'so foul that people could not walk in it'.

Great fire in **Dublin Castle**: Much of the building, with the exception of the Vice-regal quarters, destroyed (see 1684).

1672 **Arthur Capel**, Earl of Essex, becomes Lord Lieutenant (till 1677).

Richard Steele, the essayist, born in Dublin.

Land is reclaimed from the Liffey on the south side: new quays are built by **Aston** and **Hawkins**: Aston's Quay; South Wall.

Sir William Petty (see 1652) surveys Dublin and finds that there are:

> 3,300 houses of more than one smoak (i.e. chimney), that there are 1,180 ale-houses and 91 breweries.

1673 **Sir Bernard de Gomme** publishes his map of Dublin. It shows a huge 'Citadel' near Merrion Square – which was never built.

1674   Further development of north side quays: **Jonathan Amory** extends Ormond Quay after receiving the Amory Grant.

        Barrack Bridge built (of wood) across the Liffey at Watling Street. Dublin's second bridge, it became known as 'Bloody Bridge' because four people died in riots when it was opened. The riots were started by the ferrymen who were losing a living (see 1858).

        St Andrew's (P) Church (Dodson) built near its original namesake (see 1166). Popularly known as the Round Church, it is quite *avant-garde* in its time. Remodelled by F. Johnston in 1793, it will be burned down in 1860 and replaced by the present more conventional building.

1675   Development on south side by **Francis Aungier** (afterwards Lord Longford): Aungier Street, Cuffe Street, York Street, Longford Street and environs.

1676   **Essex Bridge** built at Capel Street by the developer, Sir Humphrey Jervis (who also builds Capel Street itself as well as Mary Street and Jervis Street). It will collapse after ten years, be rebuilt 1753-5 and again rebuilt 1874-5.

1677   Ormonde returns as Lord Lieutenant (till 1685).

1678   **Peter Talbot**, RC Archbishop of Dublin, is arrested after the English 'Popish Plot'. He dies in custody either in Dublin Castle or in Newgate Prison: authorities differ.

        Batchelours Walk is laid out, ending at Bagnio Slip, where a ferry crosses the Liffey to Aston's Quay.

1680   **Royal Hospital**, Kilmainham. On the site of the old Priory (1175), this building is designed by William Robinson – not by Christopher Wren as is often averred. It will be restored and opened to the public in 1985. It is the oldest surviving fully classical building in Ireland.

        St Mobhi's Church rebuilt in Glasnevin (behind the present Meteorological Office) on site of ancient monastery.

1681   Agitation in Dublin when **Oliver Plunkett**, RC Archbishop of Armagh, is executed at Tyburn.

1682   **Ellis Grant**: Further extensions of the North Quays by William Ellis. The Ellis family also owned the **Boot Inn** (still open) on the Naul Road at the back of Dublin Airport.

        Another **Petty** Survey (see 1672) puts the population of Dublin at 58,000: Maurice Craig finds this 'surprising, in that he [Petty] thought that ten years earlier the entire population of Ireland was not much over a million'.

1683   **Arran Bridge** built at Queen Street. Rebuilt and named after Charlotte of Mecklenburgh between 1764 and 1768, it is now dedicated to Queen Maev and is the oldest city bridge across the Liffey.

Ormonde Bridge built (between Essex Bridge and the Old Bridge). It will be swept away by a flood in 1806 and replaced by Richmond Bridge in 1813.

1684   Viceregal quarters in **Dublin Castle** destroyed by fire. Reconstruction plans are drawn up by William Robinson; completed by Molyneux in 1688.

Ormonde moves his residence from Phoenix House to 'The King's House', Chapelizod, where his successor, Lord Clarendon, will find the ground great for growing asparagus.

1685   Charles II, 'The Merry Monarch', dies and is succeeded by his Catholic brother, James II.

Richard Talbot – brother of the former RC Archbishop – is given command of the army in Ireland under the new (Protestant) Viceroy, Lord Clarendon.

Petty's **Atlas of Ireland** published.

Protestant influx: thousands of Huguenots take refuge in Dublin, fleeing from persecution in France after the revocation of the Edict of Nantes. Skilled in weaving, they settle in the south-west of Dublin: the Coombe, Weaver Square, etc. Front-gabled houses, called 'Dutch Billies', will survive in the Liberties until quite recently.

First newspaper in Ireland, *The Dublin Newsletter*, printed.

Outside St Stephen's Green (see 1662).

1686   **Phillipps' Map of Dublin** carefully drawn (see 1904).

Collins' Map of Dublin Bay gives an interesting plan of the city.

1687   Richard Talbot (who had been created Earl of Tyrconnell two years earlier) is sworn in as Lord Lieutenant in place of Clarendon.

Severe flooding in Dublin: coach and horses swept away while crossing Essex Bridge.

William Congreve writes his first play, *Incognita*, while a student at Trinity College.

1688   House of Benedictine Nuns opens in Ship Street.

Many Protestants begin to leave for England.

A son is born to James II, sparking off the 'Glorious Revolution'.

ELSEWHERE: Restoration of British monarchy (1660). Royal Society founded in London (1660). Building of Palace of Versailles begins (1662). Capture of New York by the British (1664) leads to three years of war with the Dutch. Great Fire of London (1666) recorded by Pepys in his *Diary*. Newton's Laws of Motion (1666). Milton's *Paradise Lost* (1667). Portuguese independence recognized by Spain (1668). Peasants and Cossacks revolt in Russia (1670). Great drama in France: Corneille's *Tite et Bérénice*, Molière's *Le Bourgeois Gentilhomme* and Racine's *Bérénice* (1670). Dutch recapture New York (1673) but hand it back to the British at Treaty of Westminster (1674). Christopher Wren begins rebuilding St Paul's Cathedral, London (1675). 'Popish Plot' in England (1678). Pennsylvania adopts a Constitution and Philadelphia is laid out (1682). Bunyan's *The Pilgrim's Progress* (1684). Monmouth's rebellion crushed at Sedgemoor by James II (1685). Revocation of Edict of Nantes (1685) leads to large-scale emigration by French Protestants. The Venetians bombard the Acropolis and wreck the Parthenon at Athens (1687).

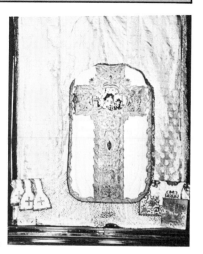

St Oliver Plunkett's vestments at Dunsany Castle (see 1681).

FROM BILLY TO GEORGE

1689 **James II** arrives in Dublin to the delight of his Catholic supporters, the Jacobites. Mass is celebrated in Christ Church. (The tabernacle and candlesticks which were used are now on view in the crypt). This is the first Royal Visit since Richard II came in 1399.

'Brass money' is turned out by the Royal Mint at 27 Capel Street.

Benedictine convent founded in North King Street.

Richard Talbot, Earl of Tyrconnell, is given more power than ever.

Patriot Parliament held in King's Hospital, the school on Queen Street.

Dublin Gazette first issued by James II. An official government periodical, it will be suppressed by William of Orange within a year – but will soon reappear (see 1705).

James decides to give Trinity College to the Jesuits – provided they are English. Six Jesuits arrive from England. So does William of Orange . . .

1690 King James rushes through Dublin after his defeat by William of Orange at the Boyne. Lady Tyrconnell jeers at him *en route*: when he accuses his 'cowardly Irish soldiers' of running away, she retorts: 'It appears that your Majesty has won the race'.

William of Orange attends thanksgiving service in St Patrick's. Protestants rejoice. His army camps at Finglas; hence 'King William's Ramparts' there.

1691 **William of Orange** presents new mayoral chain of office, to replace the original one (which was lost in 1688). Still in use, it was first worn by Bartholomew von Homrigh, father of Swift's 'Vanessa'.

New 'Penal Laws' follow on the broken Treaty of Limerick. (For earlier Penal Laws see 1615 and 1649.)

1692 Catholics, once again, are excluded from the Irish Parliament.

Quakers (Society of Friends) open a Meeting House on Eustace Street.

College of Physicians is granted new charter by William and Mary (see 1667 and 1890).

1695 Penal Laws begin to bite in Dublin: Protestants are barred from marrying Catholics; Catholics are barred from carrying arms, from entering the army or the legal profession, from establishing schools or colleges, from owning a horse worth more than five pounds, etc. These laws will not be relaxed till the second half of the following century. The penal system will be more or less completed under Queen Anne.

1696 Mail Boat sinks in storm off Howth Head: eighty passengers lost.

Dublin port (see 1708).

1697   The north side of the city has grown so much that two new parishes are established, the first since St Michan's (1095): **St Mary's** (Burgh) built on Mary Street (1702) and **St Paul's** (on North King Street near Blackhall Place). The latter will be rebuilt in 1827. Both churches are funded by a tax on the citizens.

1698   Irish woollen exports banned by act of London parliament: this will give rise to the linen industry of the north.

   The Case of Ireland Stated by **William Molyneux**. Because it advocated independence, it becomes the first Irish book to be burnt by the public hangman.

1700   The Liberties become more industrialized: brewing, poplin, silk etc. In this century, the population of Dublin grows from 40,000 to 172,000 while the population of Ireland rises from two to five and a quarter million.

   Brabazon House built by the Earl of Meath in Mill Street.

1701   **Royal Barracks** (now Collins Barracks) built to design of Thomas Burgh. (It is now the oldest inhabited barracks in the world; it used to have the largest barrack square in Europe). Burgh has succeeded William Robinson as Surveyor-general.

   Statue of William of Orange (by Grinling Gibbons) erected in College Green. (Mutilated frequently down the years, it will be definitively blown up in 1925).

1702   **Marsh's Library** (beside St Patrick's Cathedral) established by Archbishop Narcissus Marsh. Oldest public library in Ireland.

St Mary's Church (Burgh). It is now the oldest unaltered church in Dublin (see 1697).

City Workhouse built on James's Street. (This becomes in turn the site of the Foundling Hospital, the South Dublin Union, St Kevin's Hospital and St James's Hospital. See Appendix on Hospitals.)

1703   The new Queen Anne extends the Penal Laws to Presbyterians, excluding them from 'any office, civil or military, or receiving any pay or salary from the crown, or having command or place of trust from the sovereign'.

Pue's Occurrences, well-known Dublin newspaper, begins publication. It will be issued twice a week for just over seventy years.

1704   **St Matthew's Royal Chapel** opens at Ringsend. (Although rebuilt in 1878, the original tower still stands). With bigger ships being built, Ringsend becomes the port of Dublin, with 'Ringsend Cars' racing to the city – over the sand at low tide.

1705   *The Dublin Gazette* (see 1689) goes to press once again. (It has been published twice a week ever since: now named *Iris Oifigiuil*).

1706   **Tailors' Hall**: Dublin's oldest remaining guild hall is built on Back Lane. Although the Irish Georgian Society's *Records* for 1912 state that this building *is* the old Jesuit College of 1627, modern scholars say that the tailors built a new hall on the same site.

1707   **St Nicholas Within** rebuilt on Nicholas Street (see 1169).

(Old) **Custom House** (Burgh) built on the quays where the Clarence Hotel stands now. The city crane stood in front of it: hence Crane Lane, which still exists.

St Luke's built on the Coombe, mainly for Huguenots; it has since become the Church of St Nicholas Without and St Luke (recently closed).

1708   **Dublin Ballast Board** established; North and South Lotts reclaimed.

Joseph Addison, the essayist, is secretary to the Lord Lieutenant 1708-11 and 1714-15. There is a walk dedicated to him in the Botanic Gardens.

1710   **Mansion House** built by Joshua Dawson who is developing this area; it is immediately taken over by the Corporation as the official residence of the Lord Mayor. (The Round Room will be added for the Royal Visit of 1821).

Development of **Molesworth Fields** (belonging to Viscount Molesworth of Swords) and of adjacent 'city lands of Tib and Tom', now Grafton Street and South Anne Street area.

The Bleeding Horse Inn (now 'The Falcon') opens on Camden Street.

The Brazen Head Hotel is rebuilt on Bridge Street about this time; the original tavern here is said to have opened in 1198. Still open for business, this was a favourite meeting-place for Irish patriots.

1711 Infirmary added to the Royal Hospital at Kilmainham (see 1680) by Thomas Burgh.

St Peter's Church (see 1195) rebuilt on Aungier Street.

Molyneux House, one of the city's first large private residences, built in Peter Street. Demolished 1942.

Fire-engines invented: two of them can still be seen in the lobby of St Werburgh's church.

1712 **Trinity College Library** (Burgh). Originally, the ground floor was arcaded. The number of books grew so quickly that the arcades had to be walled in to provide more shelf space (see 1858).

1713 **Sir John Rogerson** (later Chief Justice) builds his quay – a business venture.

Sir John Rogerson's Quay.

Jonathan Swift becomes Dean of St Patrick's Cathedral. In *A Short View of the State of Ireland*, he writes:

> I would be glad to know by what secret method it is that we grow a Rich and flourishing People, without Liberty, Trade, Manufactures, Inhabitants, Money, or the privilege of Coining; without Industry, Labour or Improvements of Lands, and with more than half of the Rent and Profits of the whole Kingdom annually exported, for which we receive not a single Farthing. And to make up [for] all this, nothing worth mentioning, except the Linnen of the North, a Trade casual, corrupted and at Mercy, and some Butter from Cork. If we do flourish, it must be against every Law of Nature and Reason, like the Thorn at Glastonbury, that blossoms in the midst of Winter.

Besides the punitive trade restrictions, Dublin, like the rest of Ireland, now has to contend with the avaricious agents of absentee landlords. In a list published in Dublin in 1713, the income spent by 'Irish' landlords in England totals £621,499; by 1769 this figure will rise to £1,208,982.

ELSEWHERE: Siege of Derry (1689). Battle of Aughrim (1691). Treaty of Limerick (1691). Massacre of Glencoe MacDonalds in Scotland (1692). Sarsfield dies at Battle of Landen (1693). Freedom of the press established in England (1695). Dampier explores NW coast of Australia (1699). Deaths of Dryden (1700) and Locke (1704). Act of Settlement (1701) leads to Hanoverian succession in England. War of Spanish Succession begins (1701). St Petersburg founded (1703). Gibraltar captured by the British (1704). Marlborough wins battles at Blenheim (1704), Ramillies (1706), Oudenarde (1708) and Malplaquet (1709). Berkeley's *Principles of Human Knowledge* (1710). Handel's *Te Deum* and Pope's *The Rape of the Lock* (1712). England makes peace with France at Utrecht (1713).

GEORGIAN DUBLIN, PHASE I

Parliament Buildings, College Green (see 1729).

Apart from its cathedrals and older churches, the centre of
Dublin as we know it to-day was built during the reigns of
the four Georges (1714-1830). The Gardiners were the
family mainly responsible for the development of the
north side. Their family titles included Mountjoy and
Blessington, hence those street-names. The 'country'
house of the Gardiners was in the Phoenix Park, now the
Ordnance Survey Office.

1714   **Luke Gardiner** buys St Mary's Abbey lands, called the 'Drogheda estate' from Viscount Moore, now Earl of Drogheda (see 1614) hence Henry Street, Moore Street, North Earl Street, Off Lane and Drogheda Street called after Henry Moore, Earl of Drogheda. (Drogheda Street is now Lower O'Connell Street; Off Lane is now Henry Place.

    Peg Woffington, who will become London's leading actress, born in Dublin 'in humble circumstances'.

    Little St George's Church (Hill Street) built by Sir John Eccles for his tenants. Only the tower remains. Eccles developed the Temple Street/Eccles Street area.

    Mill's Map of Dublin shows the shipping approaches to the city, with the deepest channel of the Liffey skirting the grounds of Trinity College.

1716   **The Linen Hall** is built on Yarnhall Street (off Bolton Street). Only the gateway remains. Linen tycoons from the north of Ireland sell their fabric here: hence the streets named Coleraine, Lurgan, Lisburn, etc. which still survive – although Derry Street has disappeared. Between 1812 and 1816 the value of linen sold here will be £5,254,988.

1717   **Henty Luttrell**, who betrayed the Irish Jacobite cause in 1691, is shot dead in a sedan chair outside his house in Stafford Street.

1718   **Nathaniel Hone**, the Elder, painter, born in Dublin.

    Charitable Infirmary founded: see Appendix on Hospitals.

    Jewish burial ground dedicated at Fairview. The first Jews to come to Ireland were of Portuguese and Spanish origin. Within a few years, they were sufficiently numerous to establish a synagogue in Crane Lane, off Dame Street. In the Fairview area, they settled at Annadale. In 1857 they erected the building which still stands in front of the cemetery. An inscription on the wall reads: 'Built in the year 5618'. This was the Jewish year corresponding to 1857 in the Christian calendar.

1719   The **Sixth of George the First**: Act declaring right of English Parliament to legislate for Ireland 'in all causes whatsoever'.

    Spranger Barry, actor, born in Dublin. Garrick's great rival in London, he will found Crow Street Theatre (off Dame Street) in 1758.

1720   **Dr Steeven's Hospital** (Burgh) is built thanks to legacy left by Dr Richard Steevens to his sister Grissel. The hospital will open in 1733 and Grissel will live in an apartment there. (She was the victim of an unkind Dublin rumour that she was cursed by having the head of a pig. In fact she had no such deformity).

1722   **Delville**: 'stately' home built in Glasnevin (where the Bon Secours Hospital stands now) by Dr and Mrs Delany. Dean Swift was a frequent visitor but he wrote this satire on Delville's pretensions to grandeur:

A razor, though to say't I'm loth,
Might shave you and your meadow both . . .
A little rivulet seems to steal
Along a thing you call a vale,
Like tears adown a wrinkled cheek,
Like rain along a blade of leek,
And this you call your sweet meander,
Which might be sucked up by a gander,
Could he but force his rustling bill
To scoop the channel of the rill . . .
In short, in all your boasted seat
There's nothing but yourself is – great.

1723   The scandal of **Wood's Halfpence**: base money foisted on the Irish is attacked by Swift in his nationalistic *Drapier's Letters*. Despite the work of William Molyneux (1698) which appealed to the intelligentsia, Stephen Gwynn says that 'modern Irish history begins with the publication of those letters' – which won the hearts of the Dublin people.

1725   *The Dublin Journal*: serious newspaper founded by George Faulkner, Swift's publisher.

1728   **Brooking's Map of Dublin** shows the city as it was before its great expansion in the latter half of the eighteenth century (see 1983.)

1729   **Parliament Buildings**, College Green. Main (central) block designed by Edward Lovett Pearce. This replaces Chichester House (see 1593) and will later (see 1803) become the Bank of Ireland. Generally recognised as 'the earliest important public building in these islands to embody the full Burlingtonian ideals of correctness'.

Edmund Burke born at 12 Arran Quay.

St Mark's Church, Great Brunswick St (now Pearse St), where Oscar Wilde will be baptised.

Smuggling is on the increase at this time: 'On Sunday night were seized ten Ankers of Brandy, which were found hid in the sand between the Walls of North Strand' – *Dublin Gazette*, Feb 24th.

1730   **Henrietta Street** is developed by Luke Gardiner and called after the Viceroy's wife, Henrietta, Duchess of Grafton. Its huge houses (by Pearce, Cassels, etc.) make it the grandest street in the city. Popularly known as 'Primate's Hill' because the (Protestant) Archbishop of Armagh has his Dublin residence here. Luke Gardiner's grandson, Lord Mountjoy (see 1798) will live here, as will Lords O'Neill, Shannon, Dillon and Kingston, Sir Lucius O'Brien of Dromoland and Dr Duigenan, MP, a convert from Catholicism whose insane anti-Popish vehemence will come under Grattan's lash.

Frances Jennings dies at the Poor Clare Convent which she founded (1725) at

63 North King Street. She was the widow of Richard Talbot, Duke of Tyrconnell; her sister, **Sarah Jennings**, was Duchess of Marlborough.

1731　(Royal) **Dublin Society** founded (in the rooms of the Philosophical Society, Trinity College) to improve the condition of the country and promote agricultural research. Its first premises are in Mecklenburgh Street, then it will move to Shaw's Court off Dame Street and later, (via Grafton Street, Hawkins Street and Leinster House) to Ballsbridge (see 1814).

Stillorgan Obelisk (Pearce) erected on unusual rustic grotto.

1732　**Drumcondra House** (Pearce). Now All Hallows College.

1733　Aungier Street Theatre (Pearce).

1734　**Trinity College**: Dining Hall and Printing House (Cassels). The former will be rebuilt in the 1760s. The latter is still one of the city's architectural gems.

Student Riots: In this same year, there is less constructive activity at Trinity College. One of the Fellows of the College, Edward Ford, is assassinated by a group of students. In her history of the university, Constantia Maxwell states that 'there was a great deal of ill-feeling among the upper clases of Dublin over the affair.'

George Berkeley, the philosopher, is consecrated Church of Ireland Bishop of Cloyne in St Paul's Church, North King Street. A true patriot, he pleads for justice and reasonable government in Ireland.

Molly Malone, fishmonger, buried in St John's churchyard that is *if* the Ms Malone listed in St Werburgh's parish records as having died this year *is* the famous shell-fish dealer.

Mercer's Hospital built on site of St Stephen's.

Magazine Fort constructed in Phoenix Park. Dean Swift comments:

> Behold a proof of Irish sense,
> Here Irish wit is seen.
> When nothing's left that's worth defence
> They build a magazine.

1735　**La Touche's Bank** (Castle Street) – the ground-floor walls remain beside the main gate of Dublin Castle.

The Hell Fire Club is founded by Parsons, first Earl of Rosse, in the Eagle Tavern, Cork Hill. The club will hold meetings in Speaker Connolly's shooting-lodge on the top of Montpelier Hill.

1736　Smuggling: 'six car loads of tobacco were seized at Clontarf' – *The Dublin Newsletter*, March 5th.

Georgian ironwork, St Stephen's Green.

1737   **Newbridge House**, Donabate (probably by Cassels) built for Charles Cobbe, afterwards Archbishop of Dublin. Opened to the public in 1986.

1739   **Clanwilliam House** (Cassels) – Stephen's Green, next door to the present Newman House.

   Marshalsea Debtor's Prison, off Thomas Street. Isaac Butt will be jailed here. (Marshalsea Lane is still there, but the prison has been demolished).

   Hugh Douglas Hamilton, one of Ireland's best painters, born in Dublin.

1740   **Tyrone House** (Cassels) – on Marlborough Street, now the Department of Education, built for Lord Beresford.

   Bread riots in Dublin, May 31st – June 2nd.

1741   **Musick Hall** (Cassels) opens on Fishamble Street.

1742   Handel's *Messiah* is performed for the first time ever in Dublin's Musick Hall. A brass plaque on Kennan's engineering works in Fishamble Street marks the spot. The combined choirs of Christ Church and St Patrick's Cathedral participate and the composer pays the highest compliments to the Dublin musicians. (Incidentally, there was a second 'musick' hall in Fishamble Street at the time: the Philharmonic Room, opposite St John's Church at the top of the street, neither of which remain today).

1743   Publication of pamphlet by **Charles Lucas**: *A remonstrance against certain infringements on the rights and liberties of the commons and citizens of Dublin.*

1744   Mass-house in Pill Lane collapses, killing the priest and nine of the congregation. Pill Lane is now Chancery Street, near the Four Courts.

ELSEWHERE: Scottish Jacobite rising defeated (1715). Handel's *Water Music* (1715). Defoe's *Robinson Crusoe* (1719). Fahrenheit's thermometer (1720). 'South Sea Bubble' financial fiasco (1720). Peter the Great becomes Czar of All the Russias (1721). Bach's *Brandenburg Concertos* (1721). *New York Gazette* founded (1725). Methodists founded in Oxford by John Wesley (1729). Handley invents the mariner's quadrant (1731) and John Kay the flying-shuttle loom (1733). *Boston Evening Post* founded (1735). Highwayman Dick Turpin hanged (1739). Frederick the Great becomes King of Prussia (1740). Hume's *Moral and Political Essays* (1741). Garrick makes his début on the London stage (1741). Celsius invents another thermometer (1742). Fielding's *Joseph Andrews* (1742). The American Philosophical Society founded (1743).

GEORGIAN DUBLIN, PHASE II

> The man responsible for the south side becoming the posh one was James FitzGerald, Duke of Leinster. When asked whether he'd miss his peers on the north side, he said: 'They'll follow me wherever I go.' Lord Fitzwilliam of Merrion and Viscount Molesworth were important property developers, as were Joshua Dawson and Joseph Leeson.

1745   **Leinster House** (Cassels) built as a town house for the FitzGeralds. The Irish architect, James Hoban, was said to have taken his design for the White House in Washington from here but experts now think this unlikely.

           St Patrick's Hospital founded through the bequest of Dean Swift who qualifies his legacy with the supreme stab:

> He left the little wealth he had
> To build a house for fools and mad
> And showed by one satiric touch
> No nation wanted it so much.

           Crampton Court built off Dame Street (beside the Olympia Theatre). Once a busy commercial centre, it is now derelict.

1746   **State Apartments** (Dublin Castle) renovated. The architect, Joseph Jarratt, claims to have designed the new buildings, but it is probable that his work was based on designs by Pearce (see 1684).

1747   **Phoenix Park** (see 1662) opened to public by the Earl of Chesterfield who builds the Phoenix Monument *impensis suis* (by his own efforts). One of the most popular Viceroys, he was once warned to beware of Papists. He replied, 'The only dangerous Papist in Dublin is Miss Ambrose' – a local beauty.

           Oliver Goldsmith involved in a student riot at Trinity College. Having 'absented himself for some time', he will return to take his B.A. degree two years later.

           John O'Keeffe, dramatist, born in Dublin.

1748   **Gardiner's Mall** laid out by Luke Gardiner down the middle of Sackville Drogheda Street (Upper O'Connell Street) which will remain largely residential until Carlisle (O'Connell) Bridge is built in 1794.

1749   Spire, 101 feet high, added to St Patrick's Cathedral by George Semple.

        Drawing Schools open, later to become the Metropolitan School of Art and, later still, the National College of Art and Design (see 1971).

1750   **Lying-in Hospital** (Cassels) founded by Dr Bartholomew Mosse. Oldest maternity hospital in the world, it later (1767) will become known as the Rotunda (see Appendix on Hospitals).

1751   House built in Phoenix Park for ranger, Nathaniel Clements. Later (1801), this becomes the Vice-regal Lodge, now **Áras an Uachtaráin** (the Presidential Residence).

        Mespil House, 'with anonymous but quite outstanding ceilings', built by Dr Barry as his *country* residence! Now demolished to make way for Mespil Flats.

        Richard Brinsley Sheridan, dramatist, born at 12 Upper Dorset Street.

        Rutland Square (now Parnell Square) laid out. The houses on the east side of the Square (Ensor, Vierpyl and others) are the earliest. Note the episcopal crosses on the gate-posts of Number 4: Cardinal McCabe lived here. (Born in Engine Alley in the heart of the Liberties, Edward McCabe rose to become Archbishop of Dublin. He died here in 1885.)

        Trinity College: West Front designed by Theodore Jacobsen – despite statements to the contrary.

The Vice-regal Lodge (see 1751).

Dublin Castle: Genealogical Office and Bedford Tower. The original three-storey building was later reduced to two storeys. Many authors attribute this building to Thomas Ivory, but experts now consider this extremely unlikely.

Merrion Square laid out by Lord Fitzwilliam. The park became the property of the Catholic Archbishop of Dublin (see 1974).

1752 **Methodist Chapel** opens in Whitefriar Street. It will close in 1849.

Gregorian Calendar comes into operation. 3rd September (Old Style) becomes 14th September (New Style). This explains why, for instance, the Battle of the Boyne did not take place on 12th July, 1690. The actual date of the historic encounter was 1st July.

1753 **Essex Bridge** rebuilt (see 1676).

Moira House, built on Usher's Quay by Lord Moira. In 1826 it will become the Mendicity Institute. Lady Moira will hold famous soirees here in a superb octagonal room. The riverside from here to Kingsbridge is called Lord Galway's Walk.

Marathon at North Strand: 'To be run for by girls under the age of 25 years on Whitsun-Monday and Tuesday, next, each day, a good Irish Holland shift, a pair of Cambric Ruffles, and a set of Ribbons, from the Sign of the Salmon, North Strand, to Ballybough and back again. No less than three to start for same.' – *Dublin Gazette*, June 9th.

Views of Dublin drawn by **Joseph Tudor**.

Leeson Street (see top page 101).

1754   **Roque's Map of Dublin** shows how the city has grown. Foley Street (previously Montgomery Street of Joycean 'Monto' fame) is shown as 'World's End Lane'. John Roque also produces maps of the city in 1756 and 1757.

1756   **Roe's Distillery** opens, off James's Street. The premises will house the biggest windmill in Ireland, built around 1800. The windmill still stands, minus its sails, topped by its familiar onion-tower with the mitred figure of St Patrick. It is the tallest mill tower ever built in these islands.

1757   The **Wide Streets Commission** is established. Under its secretary, Thomas Sherrard, it is made responsible for widening streets and for opening many new ones (see 1769 and 1784). It begins its work with **Parliament Street**.

1758   **St Thomas' Church** (Smyth) built on Marlborough Street. Now demolished.

  Crow Street Theatre opens, off Dame Street. 'Spranger' Barry will become a celebrated actor here. The ownership of the theatre will pass to Frederick Jones in 1799.

  Marino Casino (Chambers) designed for Lord Charlemont. Not completed till 1776, this architectural gem is often said to be the most beautiful building in Ireland. It will be restored and opened to the public in 1982.

1759   **Guinness's Brewery** opens at St James's Gate. The original gate, depicted on bottles of stout, now stands parallel to James's Street.

  Trinity College: Provost's House built. Architect unknown, the house is the only one of its size in Ireland still in occupation as a house.

  Grand Canal reaches Dublin, terminating at the harbour to the back of James's Street. The connection with the Liffey will be added in 1790.

1760   **Black Dog** Debtor's Prison built (beside Green Street Court). The grim edifice can still be viewed from Halston Street.

  Meeting at the Elephant Tavern in Essex Street gives rise to first **Catholic Committee**.

  Saul's Court Academy, off Fishamble Street, is founded by John Austin, sj whose parents were told by Jonathan Swift to 'send him to the Jesuits; they'll make a man of him'. The school roll will include both primary and secondary students and eventually a wing will be added for boarders. In its first fifty years, more than three thousand boys will be educated here, including John O'Keefe (the painter-dramatist), Michael Blake (the Bishop of Dromore), Daniel Murray (the Archbishop of Dublin) and 'many other prominent Catholic and Protestant laymen'. Dr George Little in his monograph, *Rev. John Austin S.J.*, makes the point that Saul's Court was the predecessor of Belvedere College and educated its first Rector, Fr Peter Kenny, but he seems to be stretching the point when he says: 'It must be emphasised that Saul's Court was then and for long after the best classical school in Dublin'. **Samuel White's Grammar**

School in Grafton Street (where Richard Brinsley Sheridan and Thomas Moore were educated) and **St Bride's School** in Great Ship Street (which turned out Henry Grattan and John Fitzgibbon, Earl of Clare) have at least an equal claim to fame.

1761   First performance of an Italian opera in Dublin, at the Smock Alley Theatre: *La Cascina* by Giuseppe Scolari.

Publication of *The Trial of the Cause of the Roman Catholics* by **Henry Brooke**.

ELSEWHERE: Battle of Fontenoy (1745). 'Bonnie Prince Charlie' is defeated by the English at Culloden (1746). Benjamin Franklin's *Plain Truth* (1747). 'Blue-Stocking' ladies meet in London (1750). 'Capability' Brown introduces return-to-nature gardening in Britain (1750). Vol. I of Diderot's *Encyclopédie* published in France (1751). Voltaire's *Essay on Morals* (1753). 30,000 people perish in Lisbon earthquake (1755). British prisoners die in 'Black Hole' of Calcutta (1756). Birth of Mozart (1756). Clive conquers Bengal (1757) and Coote defeats the French at Wandewash, India (1760). Haydn composes four symphonies (1760).

On the Grand Canal (see 1759).

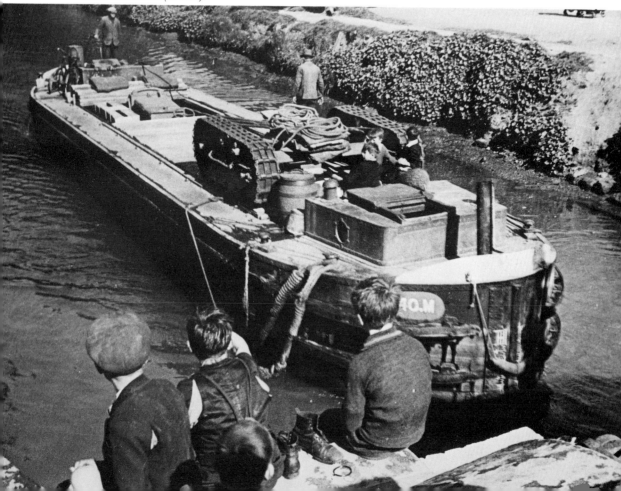

Elegant plasterwork, Mespil House 1751.

Buck Whaley's house, 86 St Stephen's Green, 1765.

French polisher at work.

THE GOLDEN YEARS

In the last forty years of the eighteenth century, Dublin reached the height of its glory. Most of its best buildings were built at this time when the city became the second largest in the British Empire and the fifth biggest in Europe. It was described as 'a triumph of elegance'.

1762   **Charlemont House** (Chambers) built for Lord Charlemont in Rutland (Parnell) Square. Now the Municipal Gallery (see 1933), this building gave the north side of the square the name **Palace Row**.

1763   Laying-out of the North and South Circular Roads.

First issue of *The Freeman's Journal*.

1764   **The Rotunda** (Ensor). Dublin's largest hall to date opens for fund-raising functions for the hospital. Now the Ambassador Cinema.

The rebuilding of Arran Bridge (Gen. Charles Vallancey) begins. Completed four years later, it is now the oldest Liffey bridge in Dublin (see 1683).

1765   **86 St Stephen's Green** (Robert West) is built for the father of Buck Whaley. Later it will house the Catholic University; it is now Newman House. Here Cardinal Newman presided, Gerard Manley Hopkins taught and James Joyce thought.

Two samples of Buck Whaley's exploits: he leapt out of a first-floor window of the present Newman House on St Stephen's Green into the carriage of a startled young lady; and he travelled all the way to Jerusalem and played handball against the ancient city walls in order to win a bet of £15,000.

City Assembly House, now the Civic Museum, built in South William Street.

24 Upper Merrion Street built for Lord Mornington. Birthplace of the Duke of Wellington and the town house of the Chief Secretary, Lord Castlereagh (see 1800). It now, ironically, houses the Land Commission which removed the land of Ireland from the hands of the Ascendancy which Castlereagh epitomised.

1766   **Royal Hibernian Military School** (Phoenix Park). Now St Mary's Hospital. The chapel (Cooley) will be added in 1771.

1768   **Poolbeg Lighthouse** (Smyth) terminates the building of the South Wall.

1769   **City Hall** (Cooley) built as the Royal Exchange on Cork Hill. This replaces

Cork House, home of the Boyle family. The scientist who established Boyle's Law belonged to this family whose ornate tomb can be seen in St Patrick's.

Dame Street widened by Wide Streets Commission.

St Catherine's Church (Smyth) built on Thomas Street.

1770   **Lucan House**: Palladian villa built for Agmondisham Vesey, M P on the site of Sarsfield's castle.

Northland House (possibly by Ensor) built on Dawson Street. In 1785, the Royal Irish Academy will be founded here.

1771   **Powerscourt House** (Mack) built as town house in South William Street. Renovated as a shopping/dining complex in 1981.

New roof completed at St Patrick's Cathedral.

Sir Boyle Roche becomes a member of the Irish Parliament. Immortalized for his lateral thinking, many of his sayings are to be found in dictionaries of quotations. For example:

> 'Why should we take all this pain to provide for posterity, Mr Speaker? What has posterity ever done for us?'

> 'No man can be in two places at once, barring he's a bird.'

> 'It would surely be better, Mr Speaker, to give up not only a *part* but even the *whole* of our constitution to preserve the remainder.'

> 'If French principles take root in Ireland we should come down to breakfast one morning to find our bleeding heads upon the table staring us in the face.'

Between 1771 and 1782 many of the Penal Laws against Catholics will be abolished, but the elective franchise will not be granted till 1793.

1772   **House of Industry** opens in N. Brunswick Street. Eventually it will become the St Laurence Hospital complex (see Appendix on Hospitals). Poverty has increased amidst the grandeur and the number of beggars in Dublin has grown out of all proportion. The **Morning Star Hostel** will take over some of the premises of the House of Industry.

Gloucester Street (now Sean MacDermott Street) built. The Gloucester Diamond – still extant – was never fully developed.

1773   **King's Hospital** (Ivory) built on Blackhall Place. Now the home of the Incorporated Law Society (see 1670).

Green Street Prison (Cooley). Known as New Newgate, its hanging apparatus is placed (as in most Irish prisons) above the main door. Demolished 1839.

Jesuits suppressed by the Pope. The Order will be restored in 1814.

1774 **Dublin Paving Board** established for 'paving, cleaning, lighting, draining and improving' the streets of the city – except Sackville and Marlborough streets which have their own arrangements.

1775 **Chief Secretary's Lodge**, now U.S. Ambassador's Residence, is built in Phoenix Park by Sir John Blacquiere at public expense. Later, he will sell it to the State for £7,000.

Ely House (on Ely Place), now the headquarters of the Knights of St Columbanus, built as the Dublin home of Lord Ely, an eccentric nobleman who lived in Rathfarnham Castle and built a folly over 350 feet long in the Dublin mountains.

1776 While America is declaring its Independence, Arthur Young begins his famous **Tour in Ireland**, a description of which he will publish in 1780.

1777 **Trinity College**: building of the Theatre (Chambers) begins. Completed, 1786.

1778 Round Tower of St Mac Táil's (Ship Street) demolished: it was the only one in the city.

Clonmell House (17 Harcourt Street) built for 'Copper-faced Jack' Scott, the Chief Justice whose gardens across the road became the Coburg Gardens and are now the Iveagh Gardens. Lord Clonmell is the judge who rules in favour of the 'Sham Squire' (Francis Higgins proprietor of *The Freeman's Journal*) in his libel action against John Magee (Proprietor of the *Dublin Evening Post*). When Magee is released from jail he decides to take revenge on Lord Clonmell. In his newspaper he advertises a 'Grand Olympic Pig Hunt', to take place at Temple Hill, Blackrock. The venue, incidentally, is a field adjoining the judge's country seat, Neptune House, much admired for its splendid herbaceous borders and manicured lawns. On the appointed day countless thousands of Dubliners show up, described by Lord Cloncurry as 'the entire disposable mob of Dublin of both sexes'. Magee provides unlimited whiskey for one and all and goes off to prepare the pigs. When their tails are well soaped, he releases 'the cart-full of porkers' and announces that anyone can take home a pig if he catches it by the 'lubricated member'. The hogs head for, and through, the hedges surrounding Neptune House pursued by the lubricated populace. Clonmell rushes off to Dublin Castle where he informs the Viceroy that South County Dublin is in a state of insurrection, that the Privy Council must be summoned at once and the *Habeas Corpus* suspended!

1779 Despite the fun and games, it is reported that over 19,000 Dublin weavers are unemployed.

Trinity College: work on the Chapel (Chambers) begins. Completed, 1793.

Thomas Moore, author and melodist, born at his father's grocer's shop, 12 Aungier Street.

The offices of 'The Freeman's Journal' (see 1763).

Patio, 86 St Stephen's Green (see 1765 & 1854).

Looking up Lord Edward Street: left, Newcomen's Bank; centre, Christ Church Cathedral; right, 'Evening Mail' offices (see 1781, 1028, 1823);

Chimney urn by Vierpyl at Casino, Marino; Ceiling plasterwork at the Casino.

The Casino at Marino, 1758 with details.

The Chief Secretary's Lodge, Phoenix Park with interior.

Bedroom at the Ambassador's residence, formerly the Chief Secretary's Lodge (see 1775).

1780 **John Beresford**, who will commission the new Custom House in the following year, becomes Chief Commissioner of Revenue.

1781 New **Custom House** (Gandon) with sculptures by Smyth. Begun despite fierce protests from (a) the merchants, whose warehouses stand further upstream by the old Custom House; (b) the dockers, who live within easy walking distance of the old port; (c) the north side gentry who fear that their fashionable residential area of Lower Gardiner Street, Buckingham Street, etc. will be contaminated by the proximity of commerce – a fear which proves justified as Montgomery Street (now Foley Street) becomes the heart of the infamous night-spot known as 'Monto'. The Custom House will take ten years to complete.

Newcomen's Bank (Ivory) opened by Sir Thomas Newcomen, Snr. outside Dublin Castle. Now the Rates Office. The Newcomen family lived at Killester House. Sir Thomas Newcomen, Jnr. inherited the title, his mother's peerage and the Bank. Lord Newcomen committed suicide in 1825, unmarried, aged 48. No claimant appeared for the title, which became extinct – as did the bank.

1782 **Grattan's Parliament**: parliamentary independence is granted to Ireland by the British Government: 'Spirit of Swift! Spirit of Molyneux! Your genius has prevailed,' cries Grattan at the opening of the new parliament.

Birth of **John Field**, Dublin composer. Commemorated by a plaque on the wall of St Werburgh's.

Dunsink Observatory opens. The first three astronomers to work here are Rev Henry Ussher, John Brinkley and William Rowan Hamilton (see 1843).

Charles Maturin, dramatist, born at 37 York Street.

1783 **The Volunteers**: Convention held in the Rotunda, under the chairmanship of Lord Charlemont, demands that Parliament become more representative of the people. Still all Protestants, two-thirds of the members of the Irish House of Commons are either 'placemen' or 'pensioners': i.e. they hold positions which give them undemocratic access to seats in Parliament.

Dublin **Chamber of Commerce** is established, superseding the Ouzel Galley Society which had been founded in 1705. The *Ouzel Galley* was a ship that left Dublin fully laden in 1695, was presumed to have been captured by pirates, but returned to Dublin safely (after insurance had been paid) in 1700.

Bank of Ireland founded at 12 Mary's Abbey, off Capel Street.

Lady Morgan, novelist, born in Dublin. She will make her name with *The Wild Irish Girl* in 1806.

1784 **Sackville Street** (Lower O'Connell Street), Westmoreland Street and D'Olier Street laid out by Wide Streets Commission. Lord George Sackville, Duke of Dorset, is Viceroy; Jeremiah D'Olier is a Huguenot trustee of Mountjoy Square; for Westmoreland, see 1792 and for Upper O'Connell Street, see 1748.

Opposite: The Custom House from the top of a tram on O'Connell Bridge (see 1781).

Westmoreland Street (see 1784).

Sackville (later O'Connell) Street (see 1784), taken during the 1932 Congress.

New Assembly Rooms (R Johnston) built to supplement the Rotunda. Now the Gate Theatre.

Royal College of Surgeons founded. It had functioned in Mercer's Hospital and in Carmichael House on Aungier Street before moving to St Stephen's Green in 1810.

1785   **The Four Courts** (Gandon). Completed in 1801, it originally held the courts of Exchequer, Common Pleas, King's Bench and Chancery.

Parliament House: East Portico and House of Lords (Gandon). Now part of the Bank of Ireland, College Green.

Belvedere House (Stapleton). Built at a cost of £24,000, it will be sold to the Jesuits for £1,800 in 1841.

Royal Irish Academy founded. Originally in Grafton Street, it will move to Northland House (built 1770) in Dawson Street in 1852.

An air-balloon, the first in Ireland, ascends from Ranelagh Gardens.

1786   **Dublin Port and Docks Board** succeeds the Ballast Board. The Ballast Office on Westmoreland Street had a 'time-ball' on its roof which was controlled from Dunsink Observatory. It fell every day at 1.00 p.m. True Dublin Time. (The Dunsink clock itself was regulated from Greenwich: a gold watch in a chamois leather pouch was sent every day from London to Dublin with the right time. Two couriers and the captain of the Mail Boat co-operated.)

North Strand Church and School founded. An advertisement in one of the first issues of *Saunder's Newsletter* reads:

> Wanted for this Charity, a Person properly qualified to teach Children to read, and who is a Protestant, and capable of singing Psalms and of acting as Clerk to the chapel belonging to the above School which is to be opened for Divine Service on Sunday next, the 20th August.

1787   **Parliament House**: West Portico and House of Commons extensions (Gandon, Parke, Hayes).

1788   **Kilmainham Jail** (Trail). Enlarged 1848. With its cliff-like walls overlooking the River Camac, it will become infamous as the jail of Irish patriots and will be the site of execution of the leaders of the 1916 Rising. Now restored and open to the public on Sundays.

1789   **Royal Canal** reaches Dublin. Terminating at Broadstone Harbour, it passes under Blacquiere Bridge at Phibsborough Library (see 1775) and crosses Constitution Hill via the Foster Aqueduct. The connection with the Liffey will be added the following year, the bridge at Drumcondra Road being named after 'Long John' Binns, one of the founder members of the Royal Canal Company.

Carlisle (later O'Connell) Bridge (see 1794).

Belvedere House (see 1785).

Daly's Club (R Johnston) opens on Dame Street. Described by an English visitor as 'the most superb gambling-house in the world'.

Grand Canal is connected to the mouth of the Liffey.

Parliament House: West Wing (Parke): Note the walled-up doorway which gave the Members access to Daly's Club – of which they were the prime patrons.

Obelisk built at St James's Gate. Funerals circled this monument three times on their way to the grave-yard.

Botanic Gardens created at Glasnevin by (Royal) Dublin Society. (There had been a Botanic Garden at Mecklenburgh Street – now Railway Street – since 1735. At the same time, Trinity College had its own Botanic Garden where Jury's Hotel now stands in Ballsbridge).

1790   Sick and Indigent Roomkeepers' Society established. Its premises still stand in Palace Row, beside the City Hall.

1791   In this year **James Malton** executes his twenty-five drawings of views of Dublin. Reproduced in etching and aquatint, these will be published in one volume in 1799. As a contemporary reviewer put it: 'Dublin never before appeared as respectable!'.

Fitzwilliam Square is laid out on the south side.

Mountjoy Square goes one better for the north side: it is the first **square** square in Dublin – all the others are rectangles.

Establishment of **Apothecaries' Hall** and **Dublin Literary Society**.

Rutland Fountain (Francis Sandys) constructed on Merrion Square opposite the National Gallery. Named after the Viceroy who died in office in 1787, it was out of action for many years but is now spouting again.

Two distilleries open: **Power's** in Thomas Street and **Jameson's** in Bow Street.

United Irishmen founded: Wolfe Tone comes to prominence; Hon Simon Butler is chairman of the organization in Dublin and James Napper Tandy is its secretary.

1792   **Catholic Convention** meets in the Rotunda, under chairmanship of the business man, John Keogh, to demand the abolition of Penal Laws.

The Viceroy, Lord Westmoreland writes to Pitt: 'It is very extraordinary, but I believe the two sects of Irish hate and fear each other as much as they did one hundred years ago.'

Green Street Courthouse (Whitmore Davis). Most of the well-known republican prisoners (Tone, Emmet, et al.) will be tried here.

Marino Crescent built by Mr Ffolliott of Aungier Street who had a dispute with Lord Charlemont and built this terrace to obstruct the view of Dublin Bay from the Casino at Marino. To prevent the building, the Earl increases the transit charges along the North Strand – which he owns. Not to be outdone, Ffoliott ships the building materials by barge. The Crescent later achieves fame as the birthplace of Bram Stoker, author of *Dracula*, in 1847.

Back Lane Parliament meets in Tailors' Hall (see 1627).

1793 **Clarendon Street Church** (Papworth) built for the Discalced Carmelites.

Catholics allowed to vote in parliamentary elections for the first time since the 1630s. They are also admitted to Trinity College.

1794 **Carlisle Bridge** (Gandon). Later (1880) widened to become O'Connell Bridge. The original carved heads (by Smyth) can now be seen on the Tropical Fruit Company's premises on Sir John Rogerson's Quay. The building of this bridge completely changes the axis of Dublin to a north-south one: hitherto it had run east-west along the line of High Street/Castle Street/Dame Street. (Lord Edward Street is relatively recent: it was opened in 1896).

Sarah Bridge (at Islandbridge) named after Viceroy Westmoreland's wife.

George's Hill Convent is opened by Presentation Sisters who were founded in Cork by Nano Nagle in 1775.

1795 Fitzwilliam becomes Lord Lieutenant in January; sacked in February for pro-Catholic leanings at the instigation of John Beresford, the powerful Commissioner of the Revenue.

Design drawn for **King's Inns** (Gandon). Gandon's work on this building will be completed by Baker and extended in 1817 by F. Johnston.

The dignitaries of Dublin attend the opening of **Maynooth College**, originally named the Royal College of St Patrick.

1796 **Jervis Street Hospital** (see 1718) built on site of former house of Lord Charlemont. Subsequently rebuilt (1877).

Commercial Buildings (Parke) built on Dame Street. Recently demolished.

Aldborough House built on Portland Row. Last of the large Dublin residences, it will become The Feinaglian Institute (a boarding school run by a school-master from Luxembourg), a barracks, and eventually a store for the Department of Posts and Telegraphs. Outside this building, where Amiens Street meets the North Strand, **The Five Lamps** monument stands in memory of General Henry Hall of the Indian Army.

Royal Circus is designed by Luke Gardiner for a site between the present Mater Hospital and Mountjoy Jail. (The 'Circus' is actually shown on old maps of Dublin although it was never built.)

1797 **Samuel Lover**, novelist, born at 60 Grafton Street.

1798   'Who fears to speak of Ninety Eight?' asked the poet, John Kells Ingram, when a student at Trinity College. For years his ballad will be recited and sung all over Ireland in memory of the United Irishmen – much to the disgust of the poet who had become a staunch Unionist.

In Dublin, the Rebellion of '98 is nipped in the bud with the arrest, at 152 Thomas Street, of Lord Edward FitzGerald, brother of the Duke of Leinster. A plaque marks the spot, now the premises of the Irish Agricultural Wholesale Society. Lord Edward – after whom a new street will be named in 1896 – dies of injuries received during his arrest.

No fighting takes place in Dublin itself. Martial Law is proclaimed and a 9.00 p.m. to 5.00 a.m. curfew imposed. The bodies of rebels killed in County Dublin are carried into the city on carts and heaped up in the Castle Yard. Convicted rebels are hanged on Carlisle (O'Connell) Bridge.

Prisoners, including Hamilton Rowan, William Jackson, the Sheares brothers, Oliver Bond and Napper Tandy are defended by John Philpot Curran in Green Street Court and jailed in Newgate Prison nearby. (This notoriously horrific prison – which replaced the original jail that was part of the New Gate at Cornmarket – will eventually be razed to the ground. It is now a children's playground. A statue to the inmates stands in the centre.)

Matthew Tone and other executed rebels are buried in **Croppies Acre**,

Jones's Road, with entrance to Redd House in the distance (see 1799).

the railed-in plot in front of Collins Barracks. A new monument (1985) marks the spot.

The ring-leader, Theobald Wolfe Tone (who was born in Stafford Street, now Wolfe Tone Street), is arrested while trying to land with a French invading force in Lough Swilly. Brought as a prisoner to Dublin, he escapes execution by committing suicide.

During the rebellion, over 11,000 rebels fall in the field and 2,000 are hanged or deported. On the other side, Lord Mountjoy, grandson of Luke Gardiner (see 1730) is killed by the rebels at New Ross. (His Dublin house was in Henrietta Street, his 'country residence' in the Phoenix Park). 1,600 other soldiers are killed in action. Outside of Dublin – especially in Wexford – many Protestant civilians are slaughtered.

1799   **Dublin Stock Exchange** (Anglesea Street) is established by Act of Parliament. Present building dates from 1878.

Free Church (Robins) built on Great Charles Street as a Methodist church. It will be taken over and re-consecrated by the Church of Ireland in 1828.

Jones's Road built by Frederick (known as 'The Buck') Jones as a convenient route from his home at the Redd House to his new theatre in Crow Street (see 1758). The Redd House was built by Tristran Fortick; Clonliffe Road used to be called Fortick Road. After Jones died in 1834, the house became an adjunct to the Feinaglian Institute (see 1796); from 1845 to 1847 it became a barracks for the Revenue Police; later it was purchased by the RC Archdiocese of Dublin as the site for Clonliffe College.

ELSEWHERE: Catherine the Great becomes Czarina (1762). Rousseau's *Social Contract* (1762). Red Indian rising led by Pontiac near Detroit (1763). James Hargreaves invents the spinning jenny (1764) and Richard Arkwright the spinning frame (1769). Jesuits suppressed by the Pope (1773-1814). 'Boston Tea Party' (1773). Discovery of nitrogen by Daniel Rutherford (1722) and of oxygen by Joseph Priestley (1744). James Watt's steam engine (1775). American Declaration of Independence (1776). Adam Smith's *Wealth of Nations* (1776). The Derby first run at Epsom (1779). Kant's *Critique of Pure Reason* (1781). Treaty of Versailles: American independence recognised (1783). First steamboat (1783). English Channel crossed by hot-air balloon (1785). Edmund Cartwright invents the power loom (1785). George Washington becomes first U.S. President (1789). French Revolution begins (1789). Paine's *The Rights of Man* (1791). Louis XVI and Marie Antoinette executed (1793). Fall of Robespierre (1794). Napoleon Bonaparte disperses Paris mob with 'Whiff of Grape-shot' (1795), leads victorious campaign in Italy (1796), compels Austria to make peace at Campo Formio (1797), leads Egyptian campaign (1798) and becomes First Consul of France (1799). Irish Rebellion stamped out: Wexford rebels defeated by Gen. Lake at Vinegar Hill; Henry Joy McCracken hanged in Belfast; French force under Gen. Humbert – after initial success at Castlebar – yields to Gen. Cornwallis at Ballinamuck (1798).

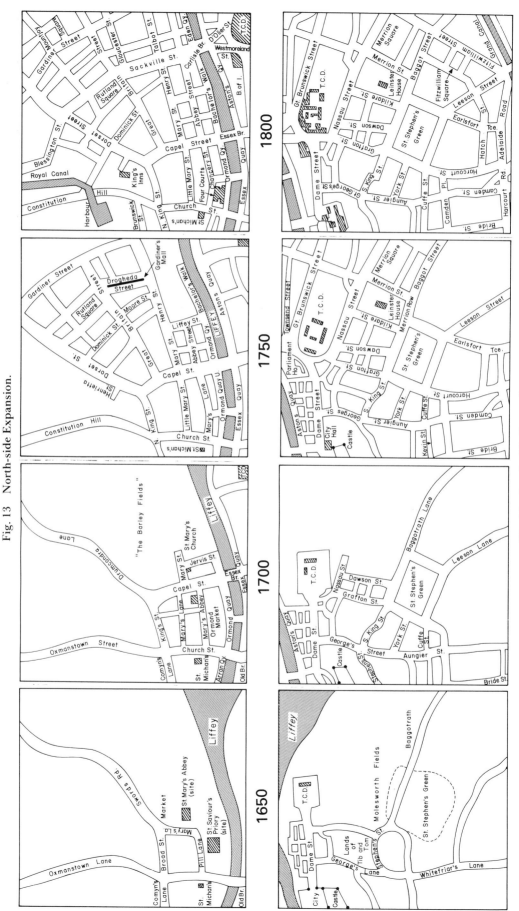

Fig. 13   North-side Expansion.

Fig. 14   South-side Expansion.

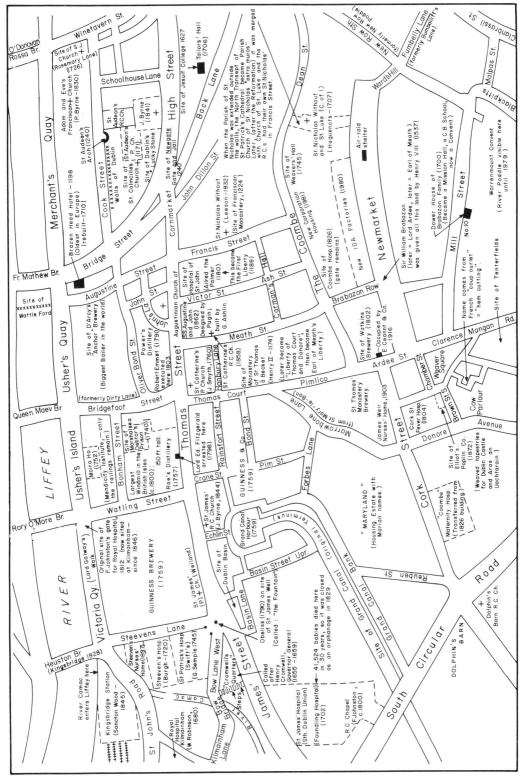

Fig. 15   Thomas Street and environs: The Liberties.

Sentry at the Bank of Ireland (see 1803).

AFTER THE UNION

In response to the Rebellion of 1798, it was decided to work towards the abolition of the Irish Parliament, towards Direct Rule from Westminster. This marked the beginning of a long decline for Dublin. When the Lords and members of the Lower House left their fine residences, professional people moved in. These soon abandoned the north side of the city. Henrietta Street, Mountjoy Square, Gardiner Street, Summerhill, etc. gradually became tenements and Dublin's slums became the worst in Europe 'with the exception of Naples, where at least they had the sun'. The key occurrence in the north side's decline was the sale of the Gardiner Estate, beginning in 1844.

1800   **Act of Union**: Irish Parliament, through the bribery of Castlereagh and FitzGibbon, abolished as of following January 1st.

Captain William Bligh, of *Mutiny on the Bounty* fame, draws an important map of Dublin harbour: it will be published in London in 1803.

1801   Vice-Regal Lodge, Phoenix Park enlarged by F Johnston (see 1751).

1802   **St George's Church** (F. Johnston) built on Hardwicke Street. Johnston lives nearby at 64 Eccles Street where he drives the neighbours mad by keeping a chime of bells in the back garden. Eventually he will donate them to St George's, which many believe to be Dublin's most beautiful church. Its spire resembles that of St Martin-in-the-Fields, London. It has the distinction of being the only church in Dublin with a greater width than length.

Ringsend Bridge swept away by the River Dodder.

1803   **Rebellion of Robert Emmet**. Murder of Lord Kilwarden in Victor Street leads to the execution of Emmet on Thomas Street, outside St Catherine's church. Kilwarden's home in County Dublin will become the club-house of Newlands Golf Club, only to be demolished in recent times.

James Clarence Mangan is born at 3 Fishamble Street.

Bank of Ireland takes over Parliament House on College Green. Shortly afterwards, Francis Johnston is employed to convert the building into one suitable for banking. He makes the Cash Office seventy feet long by fifty-two feet wide and converts the House of Commons into the Accountant-General's Office, the Board Room and the Governor's Room. The House of Lords is left untouched. It can still be viewed during normal banking hours.

1804   Between this year and 1806, twenty-one **Martello Towers** are constructed to protect Dublin from a threatened Napoleonic invasion. Built at Balbriggan, Skerries, Shenick's Island, Loughshinny, Rush, Portrane (two), Robertswall, Carrick Hill, Ireland's Eye, Howth, Sandymount, Williamstown, Seapoint, Dún Laoghaire, Sandycove, Bullock Harbour, Dalkey Island, Killiney, Shanganagh and Bray. Cost £1,800 each.

     Cow-pock Institution opens in North Cope Street: vaccinations against smallpox given in Dublin for the first time.

     Cork Street Fever Hospital opens.

1805   **Portobello Hotel** (Colbourne) built at Canal Harbour. Later it will become a nursing home; now it is a commercial premises with its cupola restored.

     Tholsel (on Christ Church Place) demolished (see 1325). The exterior statues of Charles II and James II (by William de Keyser) are preserved in the crypt of Christ Church Cathedral.

     Sir William Rowan Hamilton, mathematician and astronomer, born at 36 Dominick Street. Will become third chief-astronomer at Dunsink (see 1782).

1806   **Royal College of Surgeons** (Parke) erected on St Stephen's Green (see 1784). Completed in four years, the building will be extended by Murray in 1827.

     Ormonde Bridge swept away by a flood (see 1683 and 1813).

     Charles Lever, the writer, born at 35 Amiens Street.

1807   **Chapel Royal** (F. Johnston) is added to Dublin Castle. Now the Church of the Holy Trinity, the exterior has countless sculptured heads by Smyth.

     The building of **Howth Harbour** (Rennie) begins. Size: 52 acres. Unfortunately, it faces the wrong way and silts up quickly. Howth becomes the Mail Station for Dublin in 1818, but this service is transferred to Kingstown in 1834.

     Great storm. Hundreds of soldiers drown when the troopships *Rochdale* and *Prince of Wales* are driven ashore at Merrion Strand.

1808   **Sir Patrick Dun's Hospital** (Sir Richard Morrison). See Appendix on Hospitals, under 1788.

     Nelson Pillar (Wilkins and F. Johnston) is erected in Sackville (O'Connell) Street, with statue by Kirk. Blown up in 1966, Nelson's head can still be viewed in the Civic Museum. 134 feet tall, the pillar had 168 spiral steps.

M. W. Balfe (composer) born at 10 Pitt Street, off Grafton Street. (The name of this street was changed in honour of Balfe and a plaque marked his house until it was demolished recently.)

Daniel O'Connell begins his rise to fame as Catholicism's 'Liberator'.

Burgh Quay is named after Margaret Amelia Burgh, wife of John Foster, former Speaker of the Irish House of Commons.

1809   Formal re-establishment of the **Catholic Committee** at the Assembly Rooms in South William Street (see 1760).

1810   **Shaw's Bank** established in Foster Place, in the former premises of the United Service Club. (Foster, after whom the Aqueduct and the Avenue are also named, had been Speaker of the House of Commons.) This will become the Head-office of the Royal Bank in 1836. Now it is a branch of AIB.

1811   **Kildare Place Society** founded. Entrusted by parliament with the education of poor children. Often accused of proselytising.

   SS. Michael's and John's Church built on Exchange Street ('The Blind Quay'), on the site of Smock Alley Theatre.

   Richmond Hospital (F. Johnston).

   St Michan's (RC) Church (O'Brien and Gorman) built on Halston Street.

   A light-ship is permanently anchored on the Kish Bank in Dublin Bay.

1812   **Kilmainham Gate** (F. Johnston). This entrance to the Royal Hospital previously stood across the quays at Watling Street.

1813   **Richmond Bridge** built near the site of the old Ormonde Bridge (see 1683). It is now named O'Donovan Rossa Bridge after the Fenian leader.

   Petition of the Corporation of Dublin against further concessions to Roman Catholics presented by the Lord Mayor at London's House of Commons.

1814   **GPO** (F. Johnston). Will be opened for business in 1818 on the site where Catholics had hoped to build their cathedral.

   Dublin Society purchases Leinster House and moves there from Hawkins Street. It will become the **Royal** Dublin Society in 1820.

   Joseph Sheridan Le Fanu, novelist, born at 45 Lower Dominick Street.

   The present **Bailey Lighthouse** constructed at Howth Head. Beacons had been lit here since medieval times. A coal-burning lighthouse is marked on Collins' chart of 1686.

1815   **Molyneux Asylum** replaces Ashley's Amphitheatre (whose equestrian displays used to delight the citizenry) on Peter Street.

Dun Leary Harbour (see 1817).

Chapel Royal, Dublin Castle (see 1807).

Sisters of Charity founded by Mary Aikenhead: first convent at North William Street.

Pro-cathedral (Sweetman) on Marlborough Street. It was to have been on Sackville (O'Connell) Street, where the GPO stands now but Catholics were not yet emancipated. Sweetman, an amateur, based his design on the church of St Philippe-du-Roule in Paris. His work will be altered and the building completed in 1825 by Sir Richard Morrison. The portico will not be completed till after 1840. During the building, the Archbishop of Dublin, Dr Troy, resides at 3 Cavendish Row and staunchly maintains that Dublin will, one day, have a Catholic cathedral again.

Corn Exchange (Halpin) is built on Burgh Quay.

A Dubliner – born at 24 Merrion Street – defeats Napoleon at Waterloo. (Wellington, incidentally, wasn't too proud of being a Dubliner: 'Just because you were born in a stable,' he said, 'it doesn't mean you're a horse!')

Nine people killed at Royal Exchange (City Hall) in a crush to see a public whipping.

1816　**Wellington Bridge**. The only foot-bridge across the Liffey, it is familiarly known as the **Half-penny Bridge** from the original toll exacted. One of the earliest cast-iron bridges in the world, it is designed by John Windsor and cast at the Coalbrookdale Works in Shropshire.

Grangegorman: Mental Hospital and Richmond Jail (F. Johnston). The hospital was originally known as the Richmond Lunatic Asylum.

First steam-ship leaves Howth Harbour.

1817　**Wellington Testimonial** (Smirke) is begun in Phoenix Park. Completed in 1861, it was to have had an equestrian statue of the Iron Duke alongside but funds ran out. Nevertheless, it remains the largest obelisk in Europe and the second largest in the world – after the one in Washington.

Whitworth Hospital (F. Johnston) added to the Richmond (see 1811).

The building of **Dun Leary Harbour** (Rennie) begins. Its 251 acres make it the largest artificial harbour in the world at this time. The Mail Station will be transferred to here from Howth in 1834, with the opening of Ireland's first railway. (For the name 'Kingstown', see 1821).

First flight across the Irish Sea made by Mr Windham Sadler from Dublin to Anglesea . . . by balloon.

1818　**Whitworth Bridge** replaces the Old Bridge of 1428. (It is now named the 'Father Mathew Bridge' in honour of the temperance crusader).

Archduke Maximilian of Austria and Grand Duke Michael of Russia visit Dublin.

Views of Dublin drawn by **Henry Brocas**: twelve will be published between 1818 and 1829.

1819   **Much Cabra House**, home of the Arthur family and once the seat of James Seagrave (see 1537), is acquired by Dominican Sisters. (The house was called Much Cabra to distinguish it from Little Cabra House which stood near the Deaf and Dumb Institute).

Home's Royal Arcade, a two-storey shopping mall, built to link College Green with Suffolk Street. Burnt down in 1837.

1820   **William Howard Russell** born at Jobstown, Co. Dublin. He will become a famous war-correspondent, reporting from the Crimea, known as 'Russell of *The Times*'.

Bull Wall completed. It extends from Clontarf to within a hundred feet of the Poolbeg lighthouse. North Bull island, the city's most famous bird sanctuary, quickly builds up.

1821   **Theatre Royal** opens in Hawkins Street (see 1880).

George IV visits Dublin. 'Round Room' (Semple) added to the Mansion House for the occasion. Dun Leary is renamed 'Kingstown' at the King's departure. (It will become Dún Laoghaire in 1921).

1822   Frances Ball founds **Loreto Abbey** (A. W. Pugin) in Rathfarnham, the first Loreto Convent in Dublin.

The Wellington Testimonial, 1817, with the statue of Lord Lieutenant (1855-64) Carlisle, G. W. Frederick Howard.

Cook's Royal Map of Dublin gives twenty-five superb views of the city.

Dion Boucicault, dramatist, born at 47 Gardiner Street.

1823   First issue of *The Evening Mail* (see 1960 and 1962).

Catholic Association founded by Daniel O'Connell.

Royal Hibernian Academy of Arts founded. On the south side of Lower Abbey Street, its premises (F. Johnston) will be detroyed by fire during the 1916 Rising. Never restored.

1824   **Shelbourne Hotel** opens on site of Kerry House (which had been built in the 1770s by Thomas Fitzmaurice, first Earl of Kerry, and passed on to his son, the first Earl of Shelbourne).

St Stephen's Church (Bowden), familiarly known as the 'Pepper Pot', built in Mount Street.

Dublin Oil Gas Station (Cooke) built in Brunswick (Pearse) Street. This will become the Antient (*sic*) Concert Rooms. Now the Academy Theatre.

Provincial Bank of Ireland founded in London for the benefit of towns over 50 miles from Dublin. (In 1830 it will be allowed to open a Dublin office: 60 South William Street).

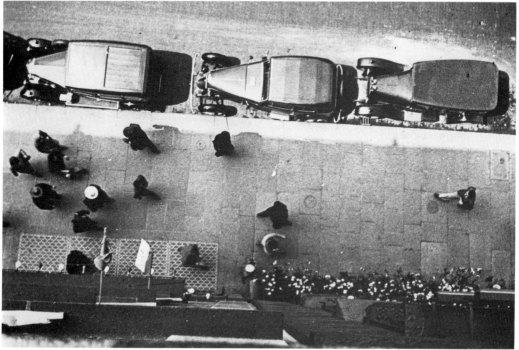

Looking down from the Shelbourne Hotel roof.

1825   **Hibernian Bank** founded. It opens at 81 Marlborough Street but in 1831 moves to the premises of Newcomen's Bank (see 1781), now the Rates Office.

Gas-light introduced to city streets for first time.

1826   **Sandford Church** built on Sandford Road and named after its benefactor. The present frontage (Lanyon and Lynn) is part of an extension added in 1859.

Mendicity Institute moves to Moira House from Copper Alley (see 1753).

1827   **St Paul's Church** rebuilt (see 1697).

1828   **Kingsbridge** (Papworth) built (i.e. the bridge, not the station). Now named Heuston Bridge, it carries little traffic since the building of a new bridge just beside it in 1982.

Catholic Model Schools. Foundation-stone laid by Daniel O'Connell. Now known as O'Connell's Schools.

1829   **Catholic Emancipation**. 'Relief Bill' passed by parliament.

Adelphi Theatre opens on Brunswick (Pearse) Street. Later it will become the Queen's Theatre. It will house the Abbey Theatre Company from 1951 to 1966. Then it will be demolished.

Gasworks (see 1825).

1830 **Adam & Eve's Church** (Byrne) built for the Franciscans on Merchant's Quay. Named after the tavern where Mass was celebrated during the Penal Days (see 1615), its official dedication is to the Immaculate Conception.

First **Dublin Horse Show** is held by the Royal Dublin Society at Leinster House. From 1880 onward, the annual Spring and Horse Shows will be held at Ballsbridge.

The Black Church (Semple) built off Mountjoy Street. Officially St Mary's Chapel-of-ease, it is now closed – but the devil is still supposed to appear if one runs around the church three times!

1831 **Primary Education** system instituted.

Dublin Zoo opens. One of the most picturesque anywhere in the world, this zoo is particularly successful for breeding lions in captivity. Despite the prevalent myth, however, the Metro-Goldwyn-Mayer lion is not a Dublin one.

Parliament authorises construction of Dublin-Kingstown Railway by William Dargan (see 1834). There is much opposition to the railway from landowners along the proposed route.

Nathaniel Hone, the Younger, painter, born in Dublin.

Music Festival held in Dublin. The great Paganini performs.

Sisters of Mercy founded by Catherine McAuley. Originally located in Baggot Street, they will receive Papal approval in 1835.

1832 **St Nicholas of Myra (RC) Church** (Leeson) built on Francis Street.

United Service Club founded. Originally in Foster Place, it will move to its present location on St Stephen's Green in 1848.

St Francis Xavier's Church (Esmonde and Keane), Gardiner Street. The former Jesuit church on Hardwicke Street becomes St Francis Xavier's College. In 1841 the school will move to Belvedere House (see 1785): it is now better known as Belvedere College, where James Joyce went to school.

Prospect Cemetery (Glasnevin) opens.

1833 **Loreto College** is founded on St Stephen's Green.

St Andrew's (RC) Church (Bolger) built on Westland Row.

Garnet Joseph, who will eventually become **General Wolseley**, commander-in-chief of the British army, born at Golden Bridge House, Dublin.

An English visitor is appalled at the state of St Stephen's Green: 'The hedge is ragged and gapped, the ditch full of dock-weed and dead cats, and all the trees have gone except for a few at the corner near Leeson Street where there is a rookery.' Some things *have* improved.

The Dublin to Kingstown railway at Serpentine Avenue.

ELSEWHERE: *Populations, 1800:* Great Britain 10.4 million; Ireland 5.2 million; USA 5.3 million; London 864,000; Dublin 172,084; New York 60,515. Peace of Amiens between Britain and France (1802). Thomas Wedgwood takes first photograph (1802). USA purchases Louisiana from France (1803). Napoleon becomes Emperor (1804). Anglo-Spanish War begins (1804). Nelson wins Battle of Trafalgar (1805). Napoleon defeats Russo-Austrian forces at Austerlitz (1805) and Prussians at Jena (1806). Beethoven's Fifth Symphony (1808). Peninsular War begins (1808). Sir John Moore dies at Coronna (1809). Argentina is first S. American country to become independent (1810). Napoleon's retreat from Moscow (1812). Grimm's *Fairy Tales* (1812). Wellington wins at Vitoria (1813), Toulouse (1814), Waterloo (1815). Napoleon banished to St Helena (1815). Congress of Vienna (1815). First steamship, *Savannah*, crosses the Atlantic (1818). 'Peterloo' massacre in Manchester when soldiers disperse Parliamentary Reform meeting (1819). Deaths of Keats (1821) and Shelley (1822). Schubert's 'Unfinished' Symphony (1822). 'Monroe Doctrine' expounded by U.S. President (1823). First railway runs from Stockton to Darlington (1825). George Stephenson's 'Rocket' (1829). Michael Faraday's electric transformer (1831). Deaths of Walter Scott, Jeremy Bentham and J. W. Goethe (1832). Samuel Morse invents telegraph (1832). 'Oxford Movement' begins (1833).

THE RAILWAY AGE

1834 **First Railway** in Ireland is built – from Dublin to Kingstown. Constructed by William Dargan (see 1853). The trains will run from Westland Row station to a terminus at the West Pier in Kingstown: the residents will not permit the 'puffing billies' to pollute their environment. The new railway serves the Mail Boat which is transferred from Howth to Kingstown this year.

Agricultural & Commercial Bank founded. Head-office at 63 Fleet Street.

St Vincent's Hospital established by Irish Sisters of Charity at St Stephen's Green, the first U.K. hospital to be run by women.

National Bank founded. As O'Connell is Chairman, it becomes known as 'The Liberator's Bank'. First Dublin branch will open at 53 Dame Street in 1836.

1835 **St Paul's Church** (Byrne), Arran Quay.

Clontarf Castle renovated by William Vitruvius Morrison (son of Sir Richard) who adds a peculiar Round Tower to the front gatehouse (see 1179).

The British Association meets in Dublin.

Jury's Hotel founded by William Jury on Anglesea Street/College Green.

1836 **Irish Constabulary** founded. This will become the RIC in 1867 and will be replaced by the Garda Síochána in 1923.

Royal Bank of Ireland founded; takes over Shaw's Bank (see 1810).

North Strand Church (see 1786) moves to its present site.

Mount Jerome Cemetery opens in Harold's Cross.

1837 **Dublin Metropolitan Police** established. Amalgamated with Garda Síochána in 1925.

Railway Commissioners publish maps of proposed lines, showing a Northern Terminus opposite the GPO and a line connecting Westland Row to Kingsbridge (cutting across Westmoreland Street and running down the quays). Fortunately, these plans will be scrapped.

Guinness & Mahon Bank founded at 26 South Frederick Street. (It will move to 17 College Green in 1854).

Mariners' Church, Kingstown, is opened. Now the Maritime Museum, Dún Laoghaire.

1838 **William Lecky**, historian, born at Cullenswood House, Ranelagh.

Trinity Church (Darley) built at Lower Gardiner Street. Later it will become a hotel; it is now an Employment Exchange.

Albert College (Agricultural Model School) opens in Glasnevin.

Lead mines, which also yield silver for a while, open at Ballycorus Hill (overlooking Cabinteely) in County Dublin. The prominent 'chimney' will be erected in 1862.

1839   **The Year of the Big Wind**. Great destruction is caused to life and property by storm on the night of 6 January. The Liffey overflows the quay walls in several places.

1840   **Scotch Church**, Adelaide Road, founded.

Royal Agricultural Society for Ireland founded.

1841   Daniel O'Connell becomes Lord Mayor of Dublin. An empty plinth bearing his name stands outside the City Hall: the statue which stood there has been taken inside to save it from the weather.

Belvedere College moves to Belvedere House (see 1785).

St Audoen's (RC) Church (Byrne) built on High Street.

1842   Views of Dublin drawn by **William Henry Bartlett**.

The Nation newspaper founded by the Young Irelanders, Charles Gavan Duffy, Thomas Davis and John Blake Dillon.

Richard Turner builds glass-houses at Botanic Gardens (see 1789). (His Hammersmith Works at Ballsbridge produced the Palm Houses of Kew and Belfast as well as the roof of Lime Street Station, Liverpool.)

All Hallows' College founded by Vincentians at Drumcondra House on land once owned by All Hallows' Priory (see 1162, 1537). Drumcondra House (Pearce) was built for Marmaduke Coghill in 1732.

1843   **Monster Meetings** are held by O'Connell for repeal of the Act of Union. The Clontarf meeting is called off to avoid violence.

Centenary Church (Farrell) built for Methodists on St Stephen's Green. It will be destroyed by fire in 1969 and has now been converted into offices.

Conciliation Hall (where O'Connell will hold his meetings) built on Burgh Quay. Later it became the Tivoli Music-Hall; now part of the *Irish Press* offices.

Incorporated Law Society founded. It will take over the old King's Hospital building Blackhall Place in 1979.

Dublin scientist, Sir William Hamilton Rowan discovers a mathematical formula for quaternions – and immediately carves it with a pen-knife on the Royal Canal bridge at Ballyboggan, near Cabra.

Adjusting the mailbag.

Dublin railway scenes. 'Locomotive'.

Looking in.

A Question.

1844   **Amiens Street Station** (W. Deane Butler) – now Connolly Station – built as terminus of the Dublin and Drogheda Railway, later to become the Great Northern.

St James's (RC) Church (Byrne) built on James's Street. The other, now spireless, (Protestant) St James's Church (Welland) across the street is presently a commercial premises.

Atmospheric Railway built from Kingstown to Dalkey. (There was no engine on these trains. The engine was on the top of Dalkey Hill and it used suction to haul the trains up from Kingstown; the force of gravity sufficed for the return journey. There was a problem, however. The front coach of the trains was joined to a piston which ran in a tube lying between the tracks. The piston-rod had to run through a groove along the top of this tube which had a leather flange to prevent air escaping. To keep the leather from stiffening, it had to be greased daily with tallow. Rats began to eat the tallow, leather and all, so the railway had to be abandoned after ten years.)

Daniel O'Connell serves four months of a twelve month sentence in Richmond Jail for disturbing the peace.

1845   **Kingsbridge Station** (Sancton Wood) built as terminus for the Great Southern and Western Railway.

Arbour Hill. Building begins on Military Prison and chapels for both Protestants and Catholics.

Museum of Irish Industry opens on east side of St Stephen's Green. With the help of the RDS, this will eventually develop into the Royal College of Science (see 1867).

Wesley College founded at St Stephen's Green. It will move to Dundrum in 1969.

1846   **Alfred Perceval Graves**, poet, born in Dublin.

Bewley's Café opens in Sycamore Alley, off Dame Street (see 1926).

1847   **The Great Famine** at its height. Soup-kitchens are set up around Dublin. The largest, with a 300-gallon cauldron, is sited in the field below the Royal (Collins') Barracks.

Funeral of Daniel O'Connell, who dies in Genoa, to Glasnevin Cemetery.

Rathmines becomes Dublin's first independent township, with its own Town Hall (see 1863).

1848   **Rebellion (Young Irelanders)**: William Smith O'Brien (whose statue once stood at the junction of Westmoreland Street and D'Olier Street and now stands in O'Connell Street) is sentenced to death but deported to Tasmania instead. John Mitchel is deported to Bermuda. Kilmainham Jail is enlarged to accommodate the rebels: Thomas Francis Meagher, T. B. McManus, Patrick

O'Donoghue, Kevin O'Doherty, John Martin, etc. Public disturbances in Dublin lead to the proclamation of the Crime & Outrage Act and the suspension of the *Habeas Corpus*.

Royal Irish Academy of Music (Westland Row) founded; it now examines over 18,000 students annually. The building has some magnificent plasterwork by Michael Stapleton; it was built in 1778 as a town house for Lord Conyngham.

Augustus St Gaudens (the sculptor of the Parnell Monument in O'Connell Street) born at 35 Charlemont Street (see 1911).

Sarah Purser, painter, designer and stained-glass artist, born in County Dublin (see 1903).

1849   **Queen Victoria** visits Dublin for the first time. It is not true that she commits the barbaric act of autographing the Book of Kells: she signs her name on a sheet of parchment which is afterwards bound into one of its volumes.

St Columba's College moves to Rathfarnham (from County Meath, where it was founded in 1842).

Royal Society of Antiquaries of Ireland is founded as the Kilkenny Archaeological Society. It will move to Dublin in 1868.

1850   **Broadstone Railway Station** (Skipton Mulvany) built as terminus for the Midland Great Western Railway.

Mountjoy Jail (Owen) completed.

Our Lady of Refuge Church (Byrne) built on Rathmines Road with one of the largest domes in Ireland.

World-famous **Rhododendron Garden** planted at Howth Castle, with additions being made until 1909. There are over two thousand different varieties now on view.

University Club opens in 17 St Stephen's Green (originally Milltown House, built by John Leeson).

Shaw's **Pictorial Directory of Dublin** published. Unfortunately, it does not get re-issued. A most unusual production, it contains drawings, not just of the streets, but of the houses along each street.

1851   **Benjamin Lee Guinness** gives a banquet of unprecedented splendour in the Mansion House on becoming Lord Mayor.

Star of the Sea Church (McCarthy) built at Sandymount.

Royal Irish Yacht Club (Mulvany) founded at Kingstown.

1852   **Electric Telegraph** laid between Dublin and Holyhead.

St Catherine (RC) Church (McCarthy) built on Meath Street.

Rathmines (see 1847).

Portraits, Áras an Uachtaráin: "The Fenians" (see 1858) and "Conradh na Gaeilge" (on right).

1853   **International Exhibition** on Leinster Lawn. Organized by William Dargan (of Kingstown Railway fame). The works of art on show will become the nucleus of the National Gallery nearby. That is why Dargan's statue (Farrell) stands outside. These pictures included Old Masters (predominantly Italian and French) and 'modern' paintings (by Bentley, Callow et al.) which had been borrowed from Irish collections.

    Queen Victoria attends Exhibition. Visits Dargan at his home, Mountainville (now Mount Anville Convent), and offers him a knighthood – which he refuses.

    Church of St Laurence O'Toole (Keane) built at Seville Place.

1854   **Catholic University** founded, St Stephen's Green. Cardinal Newman the first Rector.

    University Church (John Hungerford Pollen) built next door. Called 'Newman's church' because he had a hand in its Byzantine design.

    Oscar Fingall O'Flahertie Wills Wilde born at 21 Westland Row.

1855   **Trinity College**: Museum Building (Deane and Woodward). Stone carvings of monkeys, parrots and owls executed by the O'Shea brothers. The University authorities do not appreciate their work, so the brothers are dismissed before the building is completed.

    Donnybrook Fair abolished, having been in existence since 1204. The road out to Donnybrook is being developed at this time, including the area known as 'The Roads': Waterloo Road, Wellington Road, Elgin Road, Raglan Road, etc.

    Anthony Trollope lives for five years at Seaview Terrace, Donnybrook, where he writes *Barchester Towers*.

1856   **Mount Argus** (McCarthy) formally opened by Passionist Fathers on 15th August.

    George Bernard Shaw born at 33 Synge Street.

    Natural History Museum (Fowke) built on Merrion Square. Inaugural lecture delivered (1857) by Dr David Livingstone.

1857   Jewish house added to Fairview Cemetery (see 1718).

    Statue to the memory of Thomas Moore, melodist, erected at College Street. Designed by Foley, it is placed above a public convenience (henceforth known as 'The Meeting of the Waters').

1858   **Fenian movement** founded simultaneously in Dublin and New York by James Stephens, John O'Mahony, Charles Kickham, John O'Leary, Thomas Clarke Luby and Michael Doheny. Soon joined by Jeremiah O'Donovan Rossa. These men believe that the only route to independence is by physical force.

St Saviour's Church (McCarthy), built for the Dominicans on Dominick Street, retains the name of their old priory by the Liffey.

Trinity College: new roof for Library (Deane and Woodward). A semi-circular tunnel-vault of timber is supported by matching tunnel-vaults over the aisles (see 1710).

Queen Victoria Bridge replaces Barrack Bridge (see 1674). Now named Rory O'More Bridge.

1859   **Harcourt Street Railway Station** (Wilkinson) is built as the terminus for the Dublin and South Eastern Railway which runs via Dundrum and Bray to Wexford.

Kildare Street Club (Deane and Woodward) is rebuilt in Venetian style. (Now the Alliance Française.) The decorative stone carvings are by the O'Shea brothers. This club for conservative gentlemen was founded in 1782. Cricketer, W G Grace once broke a window of this building hitting a 'six' from College Park.

National Gallery (Fowke and Lanyon). Formally opened by the Earl of Carlisle in 1862. It will gradually acquire an internationally famous collection of paintings (see 1853).

First issue of *The Irish Times*.

Walter Osborne, artist, born in Rathmines.

ELSEWHERE: 'Tolpuddle Martyrs': workers deported from Dorset for joining trade union (1834). Texas becomes independent of Mexico (1836) and a US state (1845). Anglo-Chinese 'Opium War' begins (1839). Penny postage instituted in Britain (1840). Hong Kong acquired by British (1841). Liszt's *Preludes* (1845). Rebellions in Sicily, France, Austria, Venice, Prussia, Italy, Poland, Ireland (Tipperary), Bohemia and Hungary (1848). Communist *Manifesto* by Marx and Engels (1848). Insurrection in Rome: Pius IX flees to Gaeta (1848) but can return to Rome when French crush Garibaldi (1849). Gold rush to California (1849) and to Australia (1851). Isaac Singer's sewing machine (1851). Verdi's *Rigoletto* (1851). Thoreau's *Walden* (1854). Crimean War: Alma, Sevastopol, Balaklava, Inkerman, 'Charge of Light Brigade' (1854-55). Livingstone discovers Victoria Falls (1855). Berlioz' *Te Deum* (1855). Flaubert's *Madame Bovary* (1856). Indian Mutiny: Relief of Lucknow (1857). Ottawa becomes capital of Canada (1858). Darwin's *The Origin of the Species* (1859). Gounod's *Faust* (1859). Dickens' *A Tale of Two Cities* (1859).

THE FENIAN ERA

1860   Archbishop (later Cardinal) Cullen lays the foundation stone of the Catholic diocesan seminary, **Clonliffe College** of the Holy Cross.

John's Lane Church (E W Pugin and Ashlin) built for the Augustinians on Thomas Street. Dedicated to St John and St Augustine, it is called 'the Fenian Church' because many of its builders are members of that movement.

Blackrock College founded by Holy Ghost Fathers. Originally known as 'The French College' because of the nationality of its priests.

Mount Temple (later to become Mountjoy Schools) built by the magistrate, J. C. Stronge. This property belonged to Alexander Richey, agent of Lord Charlemont. Mountjoy Schools will take possession of the property in the 1940s. In the 1960s they will be joined by the Hibernian Marine and Bertrand and Rutland schools. Now the Mount Temple Comprehensive.

Terenure College founded by Carmelite Fathers.

1861   **Mater Hospital** (Bourke) built for the Sisters of Mercy.

Horse-drawn trams. Six passengers drown in Portobello lock when a tram plunges into the canal. (The lock-keeper thought he could 'float' the tram to safety but the consequences of his opening the sluices were disastrous).

Queen Victoria pays a third visit to Dublin.

St James's (P) Church (Welland) built on James's Street.

1862   **Dublin Fire Brigade** established. Before this, insurance companies had run their own fire-brigades for the buildings they had covered. Dublin's first Fire Brigade Station is at Whitehorse Yard, off Winetavern Street. Another will be opened in 1863 in what is now the Civic Museum, South William Street.

Crampton Memorial. Strange monument erected on site of Viking 'steine'. Cosgrave's *Illustrated Dictionary of Dublin* has this to say:

> The Crampton Memorial at the junction of College-street with Gt Brunswick-street, was erected from the design of J. Kirk R H A. A paper of 1862 states: 'The sculptor hopes it will be a monument to himself as well as to Sir P. Crampton'. It is generally called 'The Water Babe' but less flattering names have been applied. It consists of a stone base with three drinking fountains; above rises a tall pyramid of bronze built up of water lilies and other aquatic plants; swans and a bust of Crampton nestle in its foliage. It is a curious production. The following inscription was composed by Lord Carlisle:

This fountain has been placed here,
A type of health and usefulness,
by the friends and admirers
Of Sir Philip Crampton, Bart.,
Surgeon-General to His Majesty's Forces.
It but feebly represents
The sparkle of his genial fancy,
The depth of his calm sagacity,
The clearness of his spotless honour,
The flow of his boundless benevolence.

The Crampton Memorial

1863   First issue of **The Irish People**, Fenian newspaper edited by John O'Mahony and published by Jeremiah O'Donovan Rossa.

Iveagh House (Young) built for Lord Iveagh on St Stephen's Green. Now the Department of Foreign Affairs.

Unitarian Church (St Stephen's Green).

Pembroke (including Donnybrook, Ballsbridge, etc.) becomes Dublin's second independent township (after Rathmines, see 1847). Its Town Hall, at the junction of Merrion and Anglesea roads, is now the administrative offices of the Dublin City Vocational Education Committee. Stephen Gwynn writes:

> Bills embodying Pembroke and Rathmines into the city were rejected by the House of Lords. Officially, for purposes of enumeration, these are separate towns, comprising a population of over 100,000. Their inhabitants contribute nothing to city rating, and the upkeep of the most important parts of the town falls heavily on the shopkeeping community and on the poor.

1864   James Stephens declares that 1865 will be the year of the Fenian insurrection (see 1867).

Abbey Church, Parnell Square (Heaton) – called 'Findlater's Church' after the Presbyterian grocer who funded it. Besides his large shop in Sackville Street, Alexander Findlater had branches throughout the city and suburbs.

Restoration of **St Patrick's Cathedral** begins. Financed by Sir Benjamin Lee Guinness, the brewer. His sons, Lord Ardilaun and Lord Ivedagh, will finance further restoration work (by Sir Thomas Drew) in the early 1900s.

Goldsmith's Statue unveiled. The sculptor, John Foley, was born in Montgomery (now Foley) Street in 1818. (For other Foley statues, see 1868, 1876 and 1882).

The present Capuchin **Church of St Mary of the Angels** erected on Church Street. Earlier Capuchin foundations had been erected here in 1720 and 1796.

Synge Street School founded by Christian Brothers.

1865   **The Irish People**: Fenian newspaper offices in Parliament Street raided by the police. James Stephens arrested, but escapes from Richmond Jail. Many others arrested – but are not so lucky.

William Butler Yeats born at Georgeville, Sandymount Avenue. Son of John Butler Yeats and brother of Jack B. Yeats, painters.

Dublin International Exhibition opens at the Winter Garden at Earlsfort Terrace. The Great Hall will become part of University College and is now the National Concert Hall.

1866   **Alexandra College** (Parry) founded on Earlsfort Terrace. It will move to Milltown in 1972.

Masonic Hall (Holmes) built on Molesworth Street. Note the brass fittings on its entrance-steps – these held the carpet-rods of the red carpet so often laid down for the Prince of Wales.

Archbishop Cullen of Dublin becomes first Irish Cardinal.

1867   **Fenian Rebellion**. Skirmish at Tallaght. Becuase most of the leaders are betrayed and imprisoned, the revolt, like the Young Ireland one of 1848, is no more than a gesture.

Catholic University School founded by Marist Fathers, Leeson Street.

George Russell ('AE') born in Lurgan. He will come to Dublin at the age of eleven and spend the rest of his life here.

St Bartholomew's Church (Wyatt) built on Clyde Road.

Royal College of Science founded as an off-shoot of the Royal Dublin Society. It will move to its magnificent new premises on Merrion Street in 1911.

ELSEWHERE: Garibaldi, with help of Cavour, makes Victor Emmanuel of Sardinia King of Italy (1860). Abraham Lincoln becomes President of USA: Civil War begins (1861). Steel-making processes invented by William Siemens in UK and by Pierre Martin in France (1861). Hugo's *Les Miserables* (1862). Bismarck rises to power in Prussia (1862). Battle of Gettysburg (1863). Louis Pasteur invents 'pasteurisation' (1864). Maximilian of Austria becomes President of Mexico (1864); executed (1867). Lee surrenders to Grant: end of US Civil War (1865). Lincoln assassinated (1865). Joseph Lister founds antiseptic surgery (1865). Transatlantic cable completed (1865). Pierre Lallement builds 'bone-shaker' bicycle (1865). Lewis Carroll's *Alice in Wonderland* (1865). Alfred Nobel invents dynamite (1866). Dostoievsky's *Crime and Punishment* (1866). Strauss' *Blue Danube* Waltz (1867). Russia sells Alaska to USA for $7,200,000 (1867). Ibsen's *Peer Gynt*, Turgeniev's *Smoke* and Zola's *Thérèse Raquin* (1867).

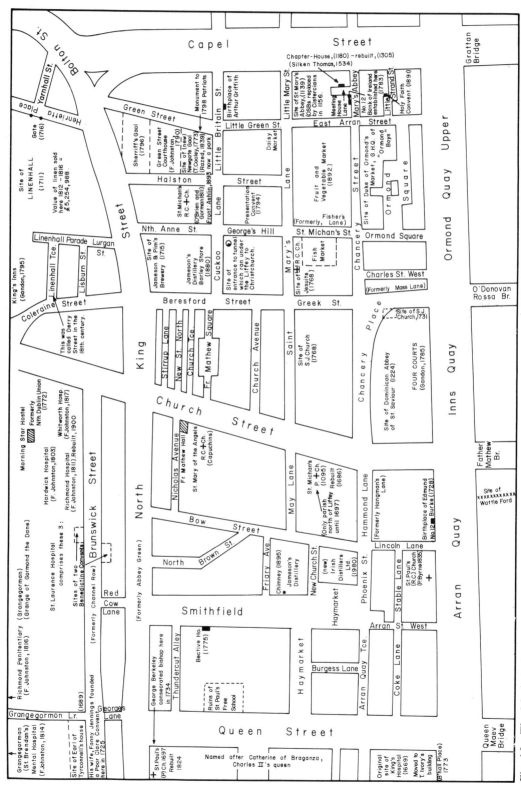

Fig. 16 The Markets Area.

THE HOME RULE ERA

1868 **Vartry Water** comes to Dublin – from the River Vartry in Wicklow. Sir John Gray, chairman of the Waterworks Committee, will be commemorated with a statue in Sackville Street, by Farrell, in 1879.

 Statue of Edmund Burke by Foley unveiled outside Trinity College.

 St Ann's Church (Sr T N Deane), Dawson Street. St Ann's was originally built in 1720 to the design of Isaac Wills.

 Katherine Tynan, writer, born at Whitehall House, Clondalkin.

1869 **Disestablishment of Church of Ireland**.

 William Carleton dies at Woodville, Sandford Road.

1870 **Home Rule Movement** launched by Isaac Butt at the Rotunda.

 The High School founded at Harcourt Street. Here W. B. Yeats went to school. The establishment will move to Rathgar in 1971.

1871 Restoration of **Christ Church Cathedral** (George Edmund Street) begins. Financed by Henry Roe, the distiller, Street's work will take seven years to complete and will result in the addition of a new Chapter House – where the old Church of St Michael had stood – and its linking bridge across the top of Winetavern Street.

 Gaiety Theatre opens.

 John Millington Synge born at 2 Newtown Villas, Rathfarnham.

1872 **Dublin Tramway Company** founded. The numbers of the trams, from 1 to 31, all operating from Nelson Pillar, will form the basis of the present bus-numbers. They radiated around the city, beginning at the south. Number 1 went to Poolbeg, 2 and 3 to Sandymount, 4 to Ballsbridge, 5 to 8 to Blackrock/Dalkey 9 and 10 to Donnybrook, 11 to Clonskeagh, 12 to Palmerstown Park etc., up to number 31 (Howth).

 Dublin Exhibition of Arts, Industries and Manufactures is held at Earlsfort Terrace. Designed to promote Irish goods, the exhibition is sponsored by the Guinness family and comprises a Manufacturers Department, a Loan Museum and a National Portrait Gallery. Open for 154 days, the Exhibition is attended by 420,000 people.

1873 **Trinity College** 'freed from religious restrictions': i.e. Roman Catholics are admitted to fellowship and College offices for the first time (see 1793).

Michael Healy, painter and stained-glass artist, born in Dublin. In time he will design beautiful windows all over Ireland (e.g. St Eunan's Cathedral, Letterkenny, Blackrock College, Dublin and Rochestown, Co. Cork). Dies 1941.

1874   **Essex Bridge** (better known as Capel Street Bridge), rebuilt (see 1676 and 1753).

1875   **St Patrick's Training College** opens on Drumcondra Road, in the house facing down Clonliffe Road which is now the Sacred Heart Home. In 1883, St Patrick's will move to its present location beyond Drumcondra Bridge. (For primary education, see 1831).

Charles Stewart Parnell begins his rise to fame, becoming MP for Meath.

Rugby Union: Ireland's first home international match (against England) played at the Leinster Cricket Ground, Rathmines. The Irish Champion Athletic Club's ground at Lansdowne Road is deemed to be 'quite inadequate for an international rugby match'. England win by a goal and a try to nil. (The first international to be played at Lansdowne Road will be on 16th December 1876.England will win by two goals and a try to nil.)

Essex Bridge re-named 'Grattan Bridge'.

1876   **'Star of Erin' Theatre** opens, popularly known as 'Dan Lowry's' after the owner. It will close in 1897 but re-open as the Empire Palace Theatre. Now the **Olympia Theatre**.

Grattan Monument, by Foley, erected in College Green.

Sir William Wilde, surgeon, antiquary, author, father of Oscar, dies at his home at 1 Merrion Square.

1877   **Parnell** elected president of the Home Rule Confederation – in place of Butt.

Jervis Street Hospital rebuilt (see 1796).

North Wall Railway Station opens, the only Dublin passenger terminus owned by an English company (the London and North Western Railway). It has a Railway Hotel next door (now the British Rail offices).

Over six hundred hacked Viking skulls are found near the Donnybrook end of Ailesbury Road.

Teacher Training College opens in Baggot Street. It will move to its present location at Carysfort, Blackrock, in 1884.

National Library of Ireland is the new name given to the Royal Dublin Society's library which is taken over by the State in this year. It will move (from Leinster House) into its present premises, designed by Sir T M Deane, in 1883 and officially open in 1890.

1878   **Intermediate Education Act.**

Church of Ireland Training College founded. Originally in Kildare Place, it is now in Rathmines.

Oliver St John Gogarty born at 5 Parnell Square. Surgeon and writer, he will also achieve fame as 'Buck Mulligan' in James Joyce's *Ulysses*.

South City Markets (Lockwood and Mawson) built as a Victorian extravaganza off South Great George's Street. Partly reconstructed after a fire in 1892.

Sir William Orpen, painter, born in County Dublin.

1879 **Butt Bridge**, the last bridge built for vehicular traffic till 1978.

Drumcondra becomes the north side's first township.

Irish National Land League founded by Michael Davitt. Parnell agrees to become its president.

1880 **O'Connell Bridge** (called Carlisle Bridge till 1882 when the statue of 'the Liberator' will be unveiled) replaces Gandon's bridge of 1794.

St Joseph's Church (Ashlin and Coleman), Berkeley Road.

Theatre Royal burnt down. Re-opened in 1897, it will be demolished in 1962 to make way for 'Hawkins House' office-block.

St Stephen's Green opened to the public, thanks to Lord Ardilaun who is commemorated there by a statue (Farrell).

Tom Kettle, writer and patriot, born in Artane.

Irish Rugby Football Union holds its inaugural meeting at 63 Grafton Street. Formed from amalgamation of Irish Football Union and Northern Football Union of Ireland.

1881 **Electric light** comes to Dublin streets; electricity will soon (1896) power the hitherto horse-drawn trams.

Land League agitation. Davitt jailed in Portland. Parnell and other leaders jailed in Kilmainham. Major riots in Dublin.

Royal University established as examining and degree-conferring institution.

1882 **Phoenix Park Murders**. Lord Frederick Cavendish (Chief Secretary) and T. H. Burke (Under-secretary) assassinated by 'the Invincibles' Brady and Kelly. A cross in the grass opposite Áras an Uachtaráin marks the spot.

O'Connell Monument, by Foley, completed on Sackville (now O'Connell Street). The foundation-stone had been laid in 1864.

James Stephens, writer, born at 5 Thomas Court.

National League founded, replacing the Land League and dominated by Parnell's parliamentary party at Westminster.

Dominican College founded on Eccles Street.

James Joyce (who will make Eccles Street world-famous) born at 41 Brighton Square.

1883   **National Library** (Sir T M Deane) Kildare Street (see 1877).

The administration of **University College** is given to the Jesuit Order. It will become part of the new National University in 1908.

1884   Foundation of the **National Museum** (Sir T M Deane) in Kildare Street. Its collections originally belonged to the Royal Dublin Society and the Royal Irish Academy. The building will be opened to the public in 1890.

Sean O'Casey born at 85 Upper Dorset Street.

Dublin Public Libraries are started with the branches in Capel Street and Thomas Street.

1885   **Munster & Leinster Bank** founded. It replaces the Munster Bank which had taken over the La Touche Bank in Castle Street (see 1735).

Golf: Dublin's first golf-club founded: Royal Dublin on Bull Island.

Salvation Army established in Ireland.

1886   **First Home Rule Bill** of Gladstone defeated by Commons at Westminster.

Samuel Ferguson, poet, dies at his home, 20 North Great George's Street.

1887   **St Joseph's School** founded by the Christian Brothers at Fairview.

Joseph Mary Plunkett born at Larkfield, Kimmage Road.

Bohernabreena reservoirs (originally for Rathmines Township) completed at Glen-na-Smól on the River Dodder. The upper reservoir holds 360 million gallons of water, the lower one 156 million.

Kevin Street Technical School opens. Now the College of Technology.

Dublin illuminated and all public offices closed in honour of Queen Victoria's Golden Jubilee.

1888   **Barry Fitzgerald**, Abbey and Hollywood actor, born in Dublin.

1889   **John Boyd Dunlop** opens world's first pneumatic tyre factory at Upper Stephen's Street. (The inventor lived at 46 Ailesbury Road.)

Fall of Parnell. Captain O'Shea files petition for divorce from his wife, Kitty, citing Parnell as co-respondent.

Elizabeth Bowen born at 15 Herbert Place.

Death of Father **Gerard Manley Hopkins**, SJ, poet. Professor of Greek at University College, he is buried in Glasnevin Cemetery.

Statue of Father Theobald Mathew, apostle of temperance, erected in Sackville Street. Designed by Mary Redmond.

Pneumatic tyres (see 1889).

A new era (see 1903).

Parnell Monument (see 1911).

City market (see 1892).

1890   **Fairview Presbyterian Church** built: the congregation had previously occupied the little Doric-style temple which still stands in Seán Mac Dermott Street.

       College of Physicians granted new charter by Queen Victoria; it thus becomes the Royal College of Physicians of Ireland (see 1667 and 1692).

       St Mary's College founded by Holy Ghost Fathers in Rathmines.

       Catholic Archbishop's House built by Dr Walsh in Drumcondra.

1891   **Death of Parnell**. John Redmond becomes new leader of the Irish Party.

       First issue of *Evening Herald*.

       City of Dublin Junction Railway: familiarly known as the Loop Line, its hideous Butt Bridge obliterates the view of the Custom House from O'Connell Bridge to the regret of generations of Dubliners.

1892   **Belfast Bank** opens its first Dublin branch at 69-70 Dame Street.

       North City Markets open on Mary's Lane, topped with Arms of Dublin by Harrison's of Pearse Street.

1893   **Second Home Rule Bill** of Gladstone is defeated by Lords at Westminster.

       Belfast City Hall erected by the Dublin contractors, H. and J. Martin. Completed in 1906.

1894   **Gaelic League** (Conradh na Gaeilge) founded by Douglas Hyde and Eoin Mac Neill to keep the Irish language alive.

       Evie Hone, stained-glass artist, born in Dublin.

       St Andrew's College founded at St Stephen's Green. It will move to Donnybrook in 1938 and to Booterstown in 1973.

1895   First issue of **Irish Homestead**, weekly publication of the Irish Agricultural Wholesale Society, Thomas Street.

1896   **Austin Clarke**, poet, born in Manor Street.

       Lady Wilde, 'Speranza', authoress and mother of Oscar, dies at her home, 1 Merrion Square.

       Lord Edward Street laid out and named after the FitzGerald patriot (see 1798).

1897   **Mainie Jellett**, painter, born in Dublin.

       Dublin illuminated and all public offices closed in honour of Queen Victoria's Diamond Jubilee.

1898　**Dublin City Council** is established when a Local Government Act reforms the old Corporation.

Workers' Republic newspaper founded by James Connolly.

Pioneer Total Abstinence Association founded at St Francis Xavier's, Gardiner Street, by Fr James Cullen SJ.

1899　**United Irishman** newspaper founded by Arthur Griffith.

Marlborough Barracks (now McKee Barracks) built for the cavalry at Black Horse Lane. An 'old chestnut' has it that this should have been built in India, and the Indian one in Dublin, but the architect's plans were mailed to the wrong address.

Irish Literary Theatre, later to become 'The Abbey', founded by W. B. Yeats, Lady Gregory, et al.

1900　**Queen Victoria** visits Dublin for the fourth and last time. A statue of the queen (to be erected outside Leinster House in 1908) will not be removed till 1948.

Cumann na nGaedhael political party founded by Arthur Griffith.

1901　**George Moore**, writer, settles in Ely Place.

Pan-Celtic Congress held in Dublin.

Soccer: first match played in **Dalymount Park**. Bohemians (founded 1890) play Shelbourne. ('Bohs' win by two goals to nil.)

1902　**Irish National Theatre Society** develops from Literary Theatre of 1899.

German fleet, under the command of Prince Henry of Prussia, visits Kingstown.

1903　**Edward VII** visits Dublin. Athur Griffith's **National Council** opposes visit.

Flourishing of Dublin crafts: **Dún Emer Guild** founded by Evelyn Gleeson, Elizabeth and Lily Yeats (who will later establish the Cuala Press); **An Túr Gloine** founded by Sarah Purser.

Trinity College: women students admitted to degrees for first time.

Gordon Bennett Motor Race heralds the era of the motor car. Famous as world's first race to be held on a closed circuit, the cars are weighed-in at the Royal Irish Automobile Club (Dawson Street). The event is reported for the French media by James Joyce.

1904　**Abbey Theatre** opens – on site of the City Morgue! (see 1899).

Edward VII visits Dublin again with Queen Alexandra.

Strangway's Map of Dublin attempts to identify the streets shown on Phillipps' map of 1685.

St Mary's College of Education founded in Marino. In 1975 it will become associated with Trinity College.

Memorial Arch begun at Grafton Street corner of Stephen's Green to honour the Dublin soldiers who fell in the Boer War. Completed in 1907, it is known to Nationalist Dubliners as 'Traitors' Gate'.

June 16th is **Bloomsday** of James Joyce's *Ulysses*.

1905　**Sinn Féin League** founded at meeting of National Council in the Rotunda. Arthur Griffith the main mover.

Dublin's wettest day on record: nearly four inches of rain on 25th August. Eighty-one years later, to the day, history will repeat itself.

First issue of *The Irish Independent*, and *The Sunday Independent*. The former is a continuation of *The Irish Daily Independent*, first published in 1891.

1906　**Samuel Beckett** born in Foxrock, Co. Dublin.

1907　**Edward VII** visits Dublin Exhibition in Herbert Park. Ireland's Crown Jewels stolen from Dublin Castle to mark the occasion. (They have never been recovered.)

Disturbances at Abbey Theatre during first performance of John Synge's **The Playboy of the Western World** (see 1926).

Iveagh Markets opened.

1908　**Irish Universities Act** institutes National University of Ireland: three constituent colleges – at Dublin, Cork and Galway – and one recognised college – St Patrick's, Maynooth.

Royal University (1881) abolished.

Municipal Gallery of modern art opens in Clonmell House, Harcourt Street. Later, it will move to Parnell Square (see 1933).

1909　**ITGWU** founded. James Larkin becomes secretary of this Irish Transport and General Workers' Union.

1910　James Larkin sentenced to a year in jail; he will found *The Irish Worker* in 1911.

1911　**St Peter's Church** (Ashlin) is built for the Vincentians at Phibsborough. This replaces an earlier church by Patrick Byrne.

Royal College of Science (Webb) and Government Offices built on Merrion Street.

Parnell Monument, by Augustus St Gaudens, erected at top of Sackville (O'Connell) Street. Parnell Street was formerly named Great Britain Street.

George V becomes the last British monarch to visit Dublin. Scenes of great enthusiasm.

'Our Country calls' (see 1914).

Violence in Sackville Street (see 1913).

Bolton Street Technical School opens. Now the College of Technology.

Seven people killed when a tenement house collapses in Church Street: Commission set up to inquire into the housing of the working classes.

1912 **Third Home Rule Bill** is passed by Commons at Westminster: rejoicing in Dublin.

Edward Carson, the Dublin lawyer, organizes 'Solemn League and Covenant' in Ulster in opposition to Home Rule.

First issue of *Studies, An Irish Review*.

1913 **UVF** (Ulster Volunteer Force) established by Edward Carson. By way of response, Eoin Mac Neill advocates the formation of a national volunteer force; his article, 'The North Began' is published in *An Claidheamh Soluis*.

Irish Volunteers set up by Eoin Mac Neill, Pádraig Pearse, Bulmer Hobson, The O'Rahilly and others.

Gaelic Games: City & Suburban Grounds on Jones's Road purchased by the Gaelic Athletic Association and named Croke Memorial Park.

Third Home Rule Bill defeated by House of Lords: dejection in Dublin.

Rathfarnham Castle purchased by the Jesuits (see 1585 and 1986).

The most important event of 1913 is **The Great Strike**. Organized workers (under James Larkin of the ITGWU) 'take on' organized employers (under William Martin Murphy, owner of *The Irish Independent* and head of the Dublin United Tramway company). Englishman, Arnold Wright's 337-page history of the strike, called *Disturbed Dublin* (1914), begins as follows:

> In the latter half of 1913 Dublin was convulsed by an industrial struggle of a very remarkable kind. For several months the industries of the city, with few exceptions, were completely paralysed. The wharves, usually hives of industry, were for the most part silent and deserted. Very little trade came into the port and as little left it. Thousands of idle men swarmed the streets, from which much of the heavy vehicular traffic customarily seen in them had disappeared. The ordinary current of life was at several points entirely interrupted by ominous gatherings of strikers who, under the stimulus of inflammatory oratory, broke out into riotous disturbances, accompanied in one instance by pillage. It was a time more anxious for all involved, whether of the governing class or the governed, than any in the recent history of the Irish capital. Nor was it mere concern for the public peace that agitated men's minds. There were features in the struggle which differentiated it in a marked and alarming way from any previous industrial uprising in Irish history, or indeed in the history of the United Kingdom. The striker, by a vicious process of reasoning, became a revolutionary invested with the revolutionary's powers of mischief. Not only was trade arbitrarily interrupted and the ordinary

relations of life made difficult, but the whole fabric of civilisation was menaced by the promulgation and attempted enforcement of strange new doctrines which cut at the very roots of social order. The sinister character of the movement aroused the Dublin commercial world to a special effort to defeat it. There was a long and bitter conflict, but slowly common sense and determination carried the day. In the end Dublin was emancipated from a domination which, if it had been made effective, must almost inevitably have ruined the trade of the city for a generation.

The Irish Worker gives a more factual account of the disturbances, detailing the brutality of the police during riots at Ringsend, Beresford Place, the North Strand, Kilmainham, Inchicore and Talbot Street. Thousands gather in Sackville Street to hear Mr Larkin speak from a first-floor window of the Imperial Hotel (now Clery's department-store). Hundreds are injured when mounted police baton-charge the crowd. Two men die of fractured skulls.

Arnold Wright also points out that most Dubliners now call Sackville Street O'Connell Street. In fact, the name will not be finally changed until 1924. In 1885, the Vice-Chancellor of Ireland H E Chatterton obtained an injunction restraining the Corporation from changing the name. In retaliation, the Corporation refused to repaint the street signs for 39 years!

1914   **Third Home Rule Bill** is passed by Commons at Westminster for the third (and decisive) time. Bill receives Royal Assent but implementation is suspended due to the outbreak of World War I. Thousands of Dubliners join the British Army.

William Lawrence, Sackville Street photographer (1841-1932) is at his prime. His 40,000 glass negatives will be purchased by the State for £300 in 1942. His main photographer was Robert French.

ELSEWHERE: Suez Canal opens (1869). Franco-Prussian War (1870-1). Napoleon III capitulates at Sedan; Commune of Paris declared and crushed (1871). Whistler's *Mother* (1871). Remington typewriter (1873). Bell invents telephone (1876). Custer's 'Last Stand' (1876). Brahms' First Symphony (1876). Edison and Swan produce electric light (1880). Tchaikovsky's '1812 Overture' (1880). Revolt of the Mahdi in Sudan (1881). Stephenson's *Treasure Island* (1883). Twain's *Huckleberry Finn* (1884). Gilbert & Sullivan's *The Mikado* (1885). Gordon slain at Khartoum (1885). Daimler builds frst motor-car (1886). Eastman's 'Kodak' camera (1888). Tragic death of Prince Rudolf at Mayerling (1889). Second Socialist International (1889). Dvořák's 'New World' Symphony (1893). Wilde's *The Importance of Being Earnest* (1895). Lumière brothers invent cinematograph (1895). Marconi invents radio (1895). Röntgen discovers X-rays (1895). The Curies discover radium (1898). Boer War (1899-1902). Gold-rush to Klondyke (1899). Boxer Rising in China (1900). First flight of Wright brothers (1903). San Francisco earthquake (1906). Peary reaches N. Pole (1909). Blériot flies English Channel (1909). Ford's 'Model T' cars (1909). Amundsen reaches Pole (1911). Scott's expedition perishes in Antarctic (1912). *Titanic* sinks (1912). Assassination of Archduke Franz Ferdinand at Sarajevo leads to outbreak of First World War (1914).

THE STRUGGLE FOR INDEPENDENCE

The length of this chapter is no measure of its importance. So much has been written on the 1916 Rising, the War of Independence and the Irish Civil War that entries here have been kept to a minimum. As Dublin became the capital of the Irish Free State, much of the city centre was destroyed by fire and bomb. An appendix lists the main sites occupied during the Rising of 1916.

1914 **Howth Gun-running**: Erskine Childers brings arms to Howth for the Irish Volunteers on board the *Asgard*, a yacht now on view at Kilmainham Jail.

Bachelor's Walk Massacre. Four civilians killed and thirty-eight wounded by the King's Own Scottish Borderers in riot following the gun-running.

University College Dublin (Butler): The National University builds its Dublin college on Earlsfort Terrace. The building will take four years to complete. The Great Hall of the university building, which is now the auditorium of the National Concert Hall, is a legacy from the Dublin Exhibition of 1872.

Publication of James Joyce's *Dubliners*.

1915 **Pádraig Pearse** makes his famous grave-side speech in Glasnevin cemetery at the funeral of O'Donovan Rossa.

Sir Hugh Lane drowns in the **Lusitania** (see 1908 and 1933).

Oisín Kelly, sculptor, born in Dublin.

1916 **Easter Rising**. Proclamation of the Irish Republic is signed by Pearse, Clarke, Mac Diarmada, Ceannt, Plunkett, Mac Donagh and Connolly. Irish Volunteers and Citizen Army seize the GPO and other public buildings. Looting breaks out. Martial Law proclaimed. The most dreadful conflagration ever seen in Dublin causes £3,000,000 damage in the city centre. The number of casualties of the Rising: Military and Constabulary: 124 killed, 397 wounded; Civilian: 186 killed, 616 wounded. Execution of rebel leaders at Kilmainham Jail transforms Dublin's disapproval of the Rising into support for the Cause: 'A terrible beauty is born'. For further details, see Appendix.

Publication of James Joyce's *A Portrait of the Artist as a Young Man*.

1917 **Sinn Féin** movement gains popular support. Éamon de Valera elected member of Parliament.

The mailboat 'Leinster' (see 1918).

The 1916 Proclamation in the President's study at Áras an Uachtaráin.

Jewish Synagogue opens in Walworth Road (see 1985).

Irish Convention meets in Trinity College under the chairmanship of Horace Plunkett. Convoked by Lloyd George, this is to be 'a Convention of Irishmen of all parties for the purpose of producing a scheme of Irish self-government'. Sinn Féin party abstains.

1918   The mail-boat *Leinster*, en route from Kingstown to Holyhead, is sunk by a German submarine on 10th October with loss of 501 lives.

End of World War I.

General Election: Sinn Féin party wins landslide victory in Ireland: 73 seats as against 26 for the Unionists and 6 for the Irish Parliamentary Party.

1919   **First Dáil Éireann** meets in the Round Room of the Mansion House: a 'private' meeting of Sinn Féin adopts a provisional constitution and declaration of independence. Éamon de Valera is elected President of Dáil Éireann.

Anglo-Irish War begins (and will last till 1921). The 'Irish Volunteers' – now known as the Old IRA, take on the British Army, its Auxiliaries and 'Black and Tans'. A major 'Black and Tan' reprisal was the sack of Balbriggan, Co. Dublin (in 1920), burning business premises, factories and houses.

Despite the violence, philanthropic work continues. For example, Canon David Hall builds 176 houses for poor people in the North Strand area. Far ahead of their time in design, these will become the model for the first Dublin Corporation housing schemes at Marino, Donnycarney and Crumlin.

Attempted assassination of the Lord Lieutenant, Viscount French, at Ashtown Railway Station by Sean Tracy, Dan Breen, Martin Savage and others (*not* Michael Collins).

1920   **Government of Ireland Act** provides for separate Parliaments for Northern Ireland and Southern Ireland.

Bloody Sunday: twelve spectators massacred by British forces during a football match at Croke Park in retaliation for fourteen IRA killings.

Kevin Barry, medical student, hanged in Mountjoy Jail for murder of soldier: first of twenty-four executions.

IRA-man **Sean Treacy** and British Intelligence Officer Price kill one another in a shoot-out at Talbot Street. A Dublin newsagent, Mr Corringham, is killed by a stray bullet from one of their guns.

1921   **Custom House** burnt down by IRA.

Second Dáil meets in the Oak Room of the Mansion House. It is an illegal body until the **Anglo-Irish Treaty** is signed on 6th December. 26 of the 32 counties of Ireland become the Irish Free State.

Kingstown is renamed Dún Laoghaire, the Irish version of its original name (see 1821).

1922   **Dáil Éireann** approves the Treaty by a majority of seven after protracted discussion. Provisional Government of the Irish Free State constituted, with Arthur Griffith elected President of Dáil Éireann. British forces and officials leave Dublin: formal 'Changing of the Guard' at Dublin Castle.

Liam O'Flaherty, writer, in protest at the plight of the poor and unemployed, with a handful of unemployed dockers, seizes the Rotunda in January and raises a red flag. The Rotunda – a maternity hospital (see 1750) – was chosen because 'it was unlikely that the Free Staters would bombard it!' This token 'Irish Soviet Republic' fell in three days without a shot being fired. An old Dublin woman was heard to describe O'Flaherty as 'the man that tried to sell Dublin to the Bolsheviks'. O'Flaherty's Dublin thrillers will include *The Assassin*, based on the assassination of Kevin O'Higgins (see 1927).

Death of Arthur Griffith.

First meeting of newly-elected Dáil in Leinster House: William T. Cosgrave becomes **first Taoiseach**. Michael Collins comes to prominence as a minister.

Timothy Healy appointed first Governor-General of Irish Free State.

Civil War begins (to last till 1923) between the supporters and the opponents of the Treaty.

Four Courts bombarded and mined: Ireland's official Public Records go up in smoke.

Publication (in Paris) of James Joyce's Dublin saga, *Ulysses*.

ELSEWHERE: Panama Canal opens (1914). Battles of the Marne and Ypres (1914). Gas used in war on Western Front (1915). Einstein's General Theory of Relativity (1915). Picasso's *Harlequin* (1915). Battles of the Somme and Verdun (1916). Bolshevist Revolution in Russia (1917). Czar Nicholas II murdererd at Ekatherinburg with his wife and children (1918). Russo-German armistice signed at Brest-Litovsk (March, 1918). General armistice ends First World War (11.00 am, 11.11.1918). Votes for women in Britain (1918). Hopkins' *Poems* published posthumously (1918). Paris Peace Conference (1919-20). First transatlantic fight by Alcock and Brown (1919). German fleet scuttled at Skapa Flow, Orkney (1919). First meeting of League of Nations (1920). 'Prohibition' in USA (1920). Charlie Chaplin in *The Kid* (1921). Mussolini's 'March on Rome' (1922). Discovery of Tutankhamun's tomb in Egypt (1922). First insulin injection (1922). Vaughan Williams' 'Pastoral' Symphony (1922).

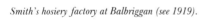

Smith's hosiery factory at Balbriggan (see 1919).

Garda Síochána (see 1923).

MODERN DUBLIN

Since Dublin became the capital of the Irish Free State in 1922 and of the Irish Republic in 1949, its size and character has changed almost beyond recognition. In the 1950s, the Corporation demolished many inner-city tenements and built vast new housing estates at Crumlin, Drimnagh, Cabra West and Ballyfermot. In the 1960s, further new estates were added at Walkinstown, Finglas etc. and many people were moved from their delapidated dwellings 'down town' to high-rise flats at Ballymun. In the 1970s, more successful re-housing schemes were completed at Irishtown, The Coombe, City Quay, etc. By the mid 1980s there were over one million inhabitants of Dublin if one includes its new satellite towns of Blanchardstown, Clondalkin and Tallaght. Comprehensive and community schools were opened in the new suburbs where American-style shopping-centres radically changed consumer spending patterns. Despite these changes, the city centre remains a lively place. There are lavish plans for dockland redevelopment at Custom House Quay and incentives for the restoration of the upper quays and other derelict areas such as Henrietta Street and Gardiner Street.

1923   **Civil War** ends.

Cumann na nGaedhael political party founded by William Cosgrave who supports Anglo-Irish Treaty of 1921 and forms a government which will remain in office until 1932. (Arthur Griffith's Cumann na nGaedhael party – see 1900 – had come to an end with the foundation of Sinn Féin in 1905).

Cenotaph in honour of Arthur Griffith and Michael Collins is unveiled outside Leinster House.

Garda Síochána established (see 1925 below).

Irish Free State joins **League of Nations**.

W B Yeats wins Nobel Prize for Literature.

Members of the **Legion of Mary** begin rehabilitation work among Dublin's prostitutes. (The Legion – originally named the Association of Our Lady of Mercy – had been founded by Frank Duff, a Dubliner, in 1921).

173

Brendan Behan born at 14 Russell Street.

1924   Ceremonial inauguration of the first Chief Justice of the Irish Free State in Dublin Castle. The Irish language is used in court for the first time in centuries.

The release of 15,000 Civil War prisoners in Dublin and throughout the country is unique insofar as this happens so soon after the cessation of hostilities.

1925   **George Bernard Shaw** is awarded the Nobel Prize for Literature.

Royal Dublin Society moves from Leinster House to Ballsbridge.

Dublin Metropolitan Police amalgamated with the Garda Síochána.

1926   **Radio Station 2RN** begins broadcasting. The predecessor of Radio Éireann, it has its first studio in Little Denmark Street and its one-kilowatt transmitter in McKee Barracks.

Fianna Fáil party formed by Éamon de Valera from old Sinn Féin: it refuses to take the 'Treaty Oath' or to sit in Dáil Éireann.

Bewley's Café opens in Grafton Street. Joshua Bewley, an Englishman, opened his first café in Sycamore Alley in 1846. He soon moved to South Great George's Street. In 1916, a second branch was opened in Westmoreland Street. In 1972, Victor Bewley will transfer control of the company to 'the Bewley community' (employees of at least three years' service). The Taoiseach, Garret FitzGerald, will intervene directly to save this Dublin 'institution' from financial disaster in 1986: it will be taken over by Campbell's later that year.

'Disturbances' at The Abbey Theatre during Sean O'Casey's play, *The Plough and the Stars*. W B Yeats tells the audience: 'You have disgraced yourselves again!' (see 1907).

1927   **Fianna Fáil** deputies decide to take 'Treaty Oath' and enter Dáil Éireann.

Kevin O'Higgins, Minister for Justice, is assassinated.

James MacNeill appointed Governor-General on retirement of Timothy Healy.

1928   Irish Free State issues its **first coins** and currency-notes.

Irish Manuscripts Commission is appointed, with Eoin MacNeill as chairman.

Lord Longford opens **Gate Theatre**. Hilton Edwards and Mícheál MacLiammóir find a stage. The **Peacock Theatre** is also founded – for modern drama.

W B Yeats writes to Sean O'Casey on behalf of Abbey Theatre rejecting *The Silver Tassie*. O'Casey, like many another Dublin writer will remain in London in voluntary exile.

Listening to the wireless (see 1926).

1929   **GPO** re-opens for first time since 1916.

      Civic Week Pageant is held outside the Mansion House. Written and designed by Mícheál MacLiammóir, it is produced by Hilton Edwards.

      Centenary of Catholic Emancipation: 400,000 people attend Mass in Phoenix Park.

      William Smith O'Brien's statue is moved to O'Connell Street (from D'Olier Street); statue of William of Orange removed from College Green – by nationalists' gun-powder! (This equestrian statue had been the target of numerous attacks since its unveiling in 1701).

1930   Borough of Dún Laoghaire established.

      Censorship Board appointed: in due course, it will ban most modern classics in the English language.

      Dublin's urban area extended to include Pembroke and Rathmines (see 1863).

      H V Morton, the English travel-writer, visits the Dublin Zoo and is fascinated by a preserved elephant's foot bearing the inscription; 'Sita, who killed her keeper and was shot, 11th June, 1903.'

1931   River Dodder bursts its banks and causes damage estimated at £40,000.

      First issue of *The Irish Press*.

      Death of **Harry Clarke**, stained-glass designer.

A pageant at the Mansion House – for the Irish Hospitals Sweepstakes (see 1938).

Irish Academy of Letters founded by Yeats and Shaw in Dublin. Its first members are: Austin Clarke, Padraic Colum, St John Ervine, Oliver Gogarty, Frederick Robert Higgins, Brinsley MacNamara, George Moore, T C Murray, Frank O'Connor, Peadar O'Donnell, Sean O'Faolain, Liam O'Flaherty, Seumas O'Sullivan, Forrest Reid, Lennox Robinson, George W Russell (AE), G B Shaw, Miss E OE Somerville, James Stephens, Francis Stuart and W B Yeats. Sean O'Casey refuses (violently) to join; James Joyce also refuses.

Bi-centenary celebrations of Royal Dublin Society.

1932 **Eucharistic Congress**: massive crowds celebrate in Phoenix Park and on O'Connell Bridge. Cardinal Lauri attends as Papal Delegate.

Army Comrades Association founded (see 1933).

General Election: Fianna Fáil win. Éamon de Valera becomes Taoiseach (for next sixteen years). **Domhnall Ó Buachalla** sworn in as Governor-General – with instructions to make a nonsense of the Office.

1933 **General Eóin O'Duffy** is elected leader of Army Comrades Association, now known as the National Guard (The Blueshirts). The Association is soon banned. Under a new name, the Young Ireland Association, it will be banned again the following year. Fascist-type demonstrations are held at the Mansion House and around the country. O'Duffy will lead 700 volunteers to fight for Franco in the Spanish Civil War in 1936.

Municipal Gallery opens in remodelled Charlemont House (see 1762) on

No parking! (see 1925).

O'Connell Street thronged for Benediction, and (below) Mass in the Phoenix Park – G K Chesterton and Count John McCormack in left foreground (see 1932).

Parnell Square, with a room left empty for Hugh Lane's donation of paintings which have been (controversially) kept by the National Gallery in London. Up to this time, the gallery was in Clonmell House, Harcourt Street (see 1908).

United Irish Party (later to be called Fine Gael) is launched under presidency of Eóin O'Duffy.

1934   Statue of Cú Chulainn (Sheppard) unveiled in GPO.

Eóin O'Duffy resigns from the Fine Gael party.

No Dublin newspapers from July to October due to a trade dispute.

1935   Transport strike in Dublin lasts from March to May.

Sale or importation of contraceptives forbidden.

Death of the writer and painter, George Russell (AE).

1936   **Aer Lingus**: inaugural flight from Dublin to Bristol under the name of Irish Sea Airways. Dublin Airport (see 1940) has yet to be built, so the flight leaves from Baldonnel airfield.

Ireland's first seismograph built at Rathfarnham Castle: it will earn an international reputation for its accuracy in measuring earthquakes. Now in Maynooth College Museum.

Liffey Reservoir Act empowers ESB to carry out hydro-electric scheme at Poulaphuca.

1937   **New Constitution**. Irish Free State becomes 'Éire'.

General Election: Fianna Fáil win again.

The altar in the Phoenix Park. Eucharistic Congress.   *First seismograph, 1936.*

World War II, 1939.

'Business as Usual', 1939.

1938 **Anglo-Irish Agreement** signed in London. 'Treaty Ports' returned by Great Britain. *The Irish Times* comments:

> No British Government would survive for twenty-four hours if it should attempt to bring undue pressure to bear on Belfast . . . Only by the promotion of more intimate relations between Dublin and London can the suspicions of Northern Ireland be allayed; but the process will take time.

Hospitals Trust formed as statutory body. First sweepstake had been held in 1930. Will close in 1987 on the arrival of the National Lottery.

Douglas Hyde, a Protestant, is elected first President of Éire. Vice-regal Lodge becomes Áras an Uachtaráin, the presidential residence.

First meeting of new Irish Senate, **Seanad Éireann**. (It was in the old Senate – 1922 – of the Irish Free State that Edward MacLysaght, Gogarty and W B Yeats were members; this was abolished in 1936).

Another **General Election** won by Fianna Fáil.

Éamon de Valera is elected president of assembly of **League of Nations**.

1939 **World War II** starts. Ireland neutral. Petrol rationed.

W B Yeats dies at Rocquebrune, France.

Magazine Fort (Phoenix Park) raided by the IRA at Christmas: over a million rounds of ammunition stolen.

Publication (in Paris) of James Joyce's *Finnegans Wake*.

1940 First issue of *The Bell* magazine, edited by Sean O'Faolain. It will last until 1954.

Institute for Advanced Studies founded.

Dublin Airport (D FitzGerald) opens (see 1936).

John Charles McQuaid becomes Catholic Archbishop of Dublin, a post he will hold until his retirement in 1972.

Poulaphuca Reservoir built. By 1987, it will supply 24,000,000 gallons of water to Dublin every day. For Poulaphuca Power Station, see 1943.

Corpus Christi Church (J. Robinson) opens in Whitehall.

1941 Dublin Fire Brigade rushes to Belfast to help in aftermath of bombing. The *Daily Telegraph* reports:

> A wave of gratitude for Éire's errand of mercy has swept the city (of Belfast) overnight, establishing a bond of sympathy between North and South Ireland which no British or Irish statesman has been able to establish in a generation.

Call to arms (see 1939).

Turf banks in the Phoenix Park (see 1942).

German bombs fall in Terenure and Harold's Cross in January: no casualties. In May, however, the North Strand is bombed with 37 people killed and 90 injured. After the War, West Germany will pay over £327,000 compensation.

Molyneux Asylum closes (see 1815).

Dublin Grand Opera Society founded. It succeeds the Dublin Operatic Society which had been founded in 1928 by Signor Viani. First production: *Il Trovatore*, at the Gaiety Theatre.

James Joyce dies in Zurich.

1942   Food rationing intensified.

Petrol shortage keeps Dublin cars off the streets till end of War. Due to fuel shortage, Dublin trams have to stop running at 9.30 pm.

Federated Union of Employers is certified as a trade union.

Howth Urban District is absorbed into County Dublin.

Central Bank established as currency authority.

1943   **Electricity**: the Liffey scheme begins to come on stream for the ESB with four megawatts coming from Golden Falls. In the following year, Poulaphuca will generate 15mw and in 1947 a further 15mw. The scheme will be completed in 1949 with the 4mw power-station at Leixlip.

General Election: Fianna Fáil retain power.

1944   **General Election**: Fianna Fáil retain power again.

Córas Iompair Éireann established. It takes over the Great Southern Railways Company and the Dublin United Tramway Company and is 'to generally control and reorganize transport'.

1945   **World War II** ends. Dublin Government attacked by Churchill in victory speech. Éamon de Valera responds in a memorable statement which may be read in full in *The Irish Press*, 17th May, 1945.

John McCormack, the operatic and concerto singer, dies and is buried at Deansgrange.

Seán T O'Kelly elected President.

1946   Thousands of Dubliners volunteer to save the precarious harvest.

Clann na Poblachta, left-wing party, founded by Seán MacBride.

Teachers' strike leaves 40,000 pupils out of primary school from 20th March to 31st October.

Dublin Airport, 1940.

Construction of Poulaphuca dam, 1940.

City bakery (see 1947).

Funeral of Dr Paschal Robinson (see 1948).

1947   Éamon de Valera signs Marshall Aid-to-Europe plan on behalf of Éire.

Bread rationed in Dublin.

Celtic Congress meets in Dublin with overseas delegations from Brittany, Cornwall, the Isle of Man, Scotland and Wales.

1948   **General Election**: John A Costello takes over from Éamon de Valera as Taoiseach. Coalition Government.

Foundation of **An Taisce**, the National Trust for Ireland. Headquarters now at Tailors' Hall (see 1627).

Statue of Queen Victoria is removed from the fore-court of Leinster House.

Death of Dr Paschal Robinson, Éire's first Papal Nuncio.

1949   **Republic of Ireland** established.

College of Industrial Relations holds its first classes in 35 Lower Leeson Street under the name of the Catholic Worker's College. It will move to its present location in Ranelagh in 1951.

The **last Dublin tram** runs from Nelson Pillar to Dalkey on 10th July.

First issue of *The Sunday Press*.

1950   **George Bernard Shaw**, Dublin playwright, dies in England.

Gonzaga College founded by Jesuit Order in former home of the Bewley family, Ranelagh.

Industrial Development Authority established.

Banks closed from December 6th (for 2 months) owing to a strike of their officials.

1951   Archbishop of Dublin, John Charles McQuaid, and other Catholic bishops object to government's Mother and Child Scheme by which free medical care would be given to mothers and their children up to sixteen years of age. The Minister for Health, Dr Noel Browne (who had organised the fight against tuberculosis since 1948), resigns. Government falls.

General Election won by Fianna Fáil: Éamon de Valera returns as Taoiseach.

Professor E T S Walton of Trinity College Dublin shares Nobel Prize for Physics. (He had worked on the transmutation of atomic nuclei).

Abbey Theatre burnt down. It will reopen in 1966. (For interim, see 1829.

1952   No Dublin newspapers for six weeks due to dispute in printing trade.

Inaugural meeting of **Irish Management Institute**.

Bord Fáilte established to promote tourism.

1953   **Chester Beatty Library** opens. Priceless collection of oriental art treasures donated to the State by the American oil magnate, Sir Alfred Chester Beatty, Ireland's first honorary citizen.

Busáras (Michael Scott) opens. Dublin's first modern office-block and Central Bus Station is derided as 'The Glass House'.

An Tóstal: Community Festival. The flower-bed on O'Connell Bridge with its Bowl of Light is nick-named 'The Tomb of the Unknown Gurrier'.

1954   **General Election**: John A Costello again becomes Taoiseach of Coalition Government.

Evening Press launched.

Tolka Bridge collapses due to flood: the fallen bridge acts as a dam and causes even more flooding. Local residents have to be rescued by rowing-boat. Until a Bailey bridge is erected, the Belfast trains have their terminus at the tiny Clontarf station.

1955   Ireland joins the **United Nations**.

First performance (in London) of Samuel Beckett's *Waiting for Godot*.

1956   Death of **Alfie Byrne** who was ten times Lord Mayor between 1930 and 1955.

Dubliner Ronnie Delany wins 1500 metres at Melbourne Olympics.

1957   Fianna Fáil returns to office at **General Election**, with Éamon de Valera back as Taoiseach.

Samuel Beckett's *Fin de partie* is performed for first time (again in London).

First Dublin **Theatre Festival**.

Alan Simpson, director of the Pike Theatre, is arrested for producing *The Rose Tattoo*, by Tennessee Williams.

Gough Monument (Phoenix Park) blown up. The equestrian statue (by Foley) of the hero of the Peninsular War had been erected in 1880.

1958   Inauguration of Aer Lingus flights to North America.

An Foras Talúntais (Agricultural Research Institute) established.

British Association for the Advancement of Science meets in Dublin.

First public performance of Brendan Behan's *The Hostage* at the Halla Damer, St Stephen's Green.

1959   **Éamon de Valera** resigns as Taoiseach to become President of Ireland.

Seán Lemass becomes Taoiseach until 1966.

Harcourt Street railway station (and the line to Bray) is closed.

Inaugural conference in Dublin of Irish Congress of Trade Unions.

1960 Dáil decides to transfer UCD from Earlsfort Terrace to Belfield.

George Morrison's film, *Mise Éire*, produced by Gael-Linn, with music by Seán Ó Riada.

Irish UN Troops leave Dublin for peace-keeping work in Congo: ten of them will be killed there.

Dubliner, Frederick Boland, elected President of UN General Assembly.

1961 Ireland joins UNESCO.

Patrician Year. Celebrations in Dublin mark the fifteen hundredth anniversary of the death of St Patrick.

Television transmissions begin with inauguration of Radio Telefís Éireann. Big crowd turns out to celebrate this event outside the Gresham Hotel, O'Connell Street, on New Year's Eve.

Samuel Beckett's *Happy Days* is performed for the first time (at Cherry Lane Theatre, New York).

1962 **Theatre Royal** demolished to make way for an office-block (see 1821).

The Dubliners ballad group hits the top.

First transmission of RTE television's **Late Late Show**. Its host, Gay Byrne, will become an influential figure in Irish society, with his show still running after twenty-five years.

Final issue of *Evening Mail* (see 1823). It had been taken over by *The Irish Times* in 1960.

1963 US **President Kennedy** visits Dublin five months before his assassination.

First meeting of **National Industrial Economic Council**.

1964 **US Embassy** (Johansen and Scott) completed in Ballsbridge.

Deaths of Sean O'Casey and Brendan Behan.

Irish troops leave Dublin for UN peace-keeping duty in Cyprus.

Liberty Hall (Rea O'Kelly) rebuilt, its disproportionate height causing untold distress to architectural purists. It will be formally opened on May Day in 1965.

Roger Casement's remains returned to Dublin for burial in Glasnevin.

An Foras Forbartha (National Institute for Physical Planning and Construction Research) incorporated.

1965 Death of **W T Cosgrave** (President, exec. council, Irish Free State, 1922-32).

Historic visit of the Taoiseach, Seán Lemass, to Stormont where he is greeted by Northern Ireland premier, Terence O'Neill.

Bank of Ireland Group formed from Bank of Ireland, National and Hibernian Banks.

General Election won by Fianna Fáil.

Death of Dublin's best-loved comedian, **Jimmy O'Dea**.

1966 **Nelson Pillar** is blown up by nationalists (to mark Golden Jubilee of 1916 Rising) in the early hours of the morning. Little further damage done. The army, however, break hundreds of windows in O'Connell Street when removing the stump of the pillar by 'controlled' explosion.

Garden of Remembrance (Hanly) laid out in Parnell Square to mark the same Jubilee. The sculpture of the Children of Lir is by Oisín Kelly.

Abbey Threatre (Scott) rebuilt, fire having destroyed the original one in 1951.

Myles na Gopaleen (Brian O'Nolan) dies in Dublin (see Literary Appendix).

New Taoiseach: Jack Lynch takes over from Seán Lemass.

Death of **Seán T O'Kelly** (President 1945-59).

Allied Irish Banks formed from Munster & Leinster, Provincial and Royal Banks.

A barge comes from Athy (see 1967).

1967 **AnCO**, the Industrial Training Authority, established.

Cargo aircraft crashes at Dublin Airport: two of its crew killed.

New Library (Koralek) opens at Trinity College.

ROSC, an international art exhibition, is held for the first time at the RDS (see 1984).

The new postal **Sorting Office** at Sheriff Street can handle one million items a day.

Peacock Theatre re-opens as an off-shoot of the Abbey.

Memorial to **Wolfe Tone** (Delaney) erected at St Stephen's Green. On account of its monolithic design, it is promptly nick-named 'Tonehenge'.

Jammet's, the gourmet Dublin restaurant, closes its doors. At another restaurant, The Bailey in Duke Street, an extra door is added as a show-piece: originally it was at 7 Eccles Street, the home of Joyce's Leopold Bloom.

Patrick Kavanagh, the writer, dies in Dublin. A canal-bank seat stands in his honour at Baggot Street Bridge. Why? Because he wrote:

> O commemorate me where there is water,
> Canal water preferably, so stilly
> Greeny at the heart of summer. Brother
> Commemorate me thus beautifully
> Where by a lock Niagariously roars
> The falls for those who sit in the tremendous silence
> Of mid-July. No one will speak in prose
> Who finds his way to these Parnassian islands.
> A swan goes by head low with many apologies,
> Fantastic light looks through the eyes of bridges –
> And look! a barge comes bringing from Athy
> And other far-flung towns mythologies.
> O commemorate me with no hero-courageous
> Tomb – just a canal-bank seat for the passer-by.

1968 Ireland's Eye and 220 acres of land at Howth are presented to the nation by Christopher Gaisford-St Lawrence.

Death of **Sir Alfred Chester Beatty** (see 1953) in Monte Carlo. State funeral in Dublin.

Statue of **Robert Emmet** (Connor) unveiled in St Stephen's Green, near his birthplace.

Traffic wardens appear on the streets of Dublin for the first time.

Higher Education Authority established.

New **College of Technology** opens in Kevin Street.

New wing is added to the **National Gallery**.

1969   Dublin City Council is dissolved for failing to strike a sufficient rate.

Dublin show-jumper, **Iris Kellett**, wins Queen Elizabeth Cup at Wembley.

Dublin Festival of 20th Century Music is held for the first time.

Secondary schools are closed for a month because of teachers' strike.

People's Democracy rally at GPO is attended by 4,000 people.

Publication of *Strumpet City* by **James Plunkett**.

Samuel Beckett wins Nobel Prize for Literature.

Hume Street: crowds protest at demolition of two eighteenth-century houses.

The International Society for the Rehabilitation of Disabled holds its world congress at the RDS.

1970   **Dublin Arms Trial**: ex Government Ministers Blaney and Haughey acquitted of charge of conspiracy to illegally import arms and ammunition into the State.

6,000 people protest on Lansdowne Road against 'apartheid' when Ireland plays rugby with South Africa.

Parking meters come to Dublin.

St Vincent's Hospital moves to Elm Park after 136 years on St Stephen's Green.

Irish School of Ecumenics inaugurated at Milltown Park by Rev Eugene Carson Blake, General Secretary of the World Council of Churches.

St Enda's School, Rathfarnham is presented to the nation. It will become the Pádraig Pearse Museum.

The Soviet news agency, TASS, opens its Dublin office.

Two Dublin printers, Derry Lindsay and Jackie Smith win the Eurovision Song Contest in Amsterdam. Their song, *All Kinds of Everything*, is sung by Dana.

1971   Death of Seán Lemass (Taoiseach 1959-66).

Dublin's first **bus lane** is introduced on an experimental basis.

Members of the Irish Women's Liberation Movement bring contraceptives by train from Belfast to Dublin in protest against the ban on their importation.

Decimal currency introduced.

Dublin telephone subscribers can now dial London and Belfast directly.

National College of Art and Design established. The original establishment dates back to Robert West's 18th century academy which was taken over by RDS in 1749. Renamed 'Dublin Metropolitan School of Art' in 1877, it became the 'National College of Art' in 1936. It has done an imaginative conversion job on its new premises in Thomas Street, formerly Power's distillery.

Demolition of Oliver St John Gogarty's house in Ely Place.

1972   One-man show: **Jack McGowran** brings Samuel Beckett's works to the Gaiety Theatre. The actor will die in New York the following year.

Protests against the demolition of Frascati House, Blackrock; formerly the home of Lord Edward FitzGerald.

Closure of **The Capitol** in Prince's Street. The theatre/cinema had been opened in 1920 as the La Scala Opera House.

British Embassy burnt down in reprisal for Bloody Sunday massacre in Derry. Thousands of Dubliners join in protest.

Dr Dermot Ryan attends a service in Christ Church Cathedral – the first RC Archbishop to do so since the Reformation.

Two **car-bombs** in central Dublin kill two and injure 127 people: Ulster extremists blamed.

New **Irish Farm Centre** (housing eighteen farming organizations) opens at Bluebell, Clondalkin.

Death of the poet, **Pádraic Colum**.

Dmitri Shostakovich, the Russian composer, receives an honorary doctorate in music at Trinity College.

Republic of Ireland joins **EEC** at midnight on 31st December.

1973   **General Election** brings Coalition Government to power: Liam Cosgrave becomes Taoiseach.

Dockrell's, the builders' providers establishment on South Great George's Street, is burnt to the ground.

John O'Conor, the Dublin pianist, wins the Beethoven Competition in Vienna.

Car-bomb explodes in Sackville Place, killing one and injuring thirteen: Ulster extremists blamed again.

Dublin City Council restored (see 1969).

Erskine Childers becomes President, Éamon de Valera retiring from public life. A Protestant, he is the son of the Howth gun-runner of 1914.

The Supreme Court decides that the ban on the importation of contraceptives is unconstitutional.

Bank of Ireland Group Head-office (Scott Tallon Walker) opens on Baggot Street: to make way for it, Georgian houses were demolished.

Thirteen letter-bombs, posted in Northern Ireland and Britain, are safely defused in Dublin.

Edward Heath visits Dublin: first UK Prime Minister to do so since foundation of the State.

First appearance of the new popular tabloid, *The Sunday World*.

1974　Irish University Press (publishers of a 1,000 volume series of British parliamentary papers – cited in *The Guinness Book of Records*) closes down.

Publishing revival leads to foundation of new Dublin companies including Wolfhound Press and The O'Brien Press.

More **car bombs**: 25 people killed when three cars explode during the evening rush-hour in the city centre. Although UDA and UVF deny responsibility, two of the three cars had been hijacked earlier in so-called 'Loyalist' areas of Belfast.

7,000 students march in protest against low education grants.

Cearbhall Ó Dálaigh becomes President on death of Erskine Childers.

The first official strike in its 215-year history takes plact at Guinness's Brewery.

Seán MacBride wins Nobel Peace Prize.

Dublin **bus strike** lasts for nine weeks.

RC Archbishop Ryan hands over Merrion Square to the people of Dublin as a public park.

Gaelic football: Dublin wins the All-Ireland championship (and will do so again in 1976, 1977, and 1983). Asked what he thought about this resurgence of 'The Dubs', an old man in the Liberties replies: 'Dubs how-are-yeh! Sure they're a crowd o' culchies from Fairview and Marino!'

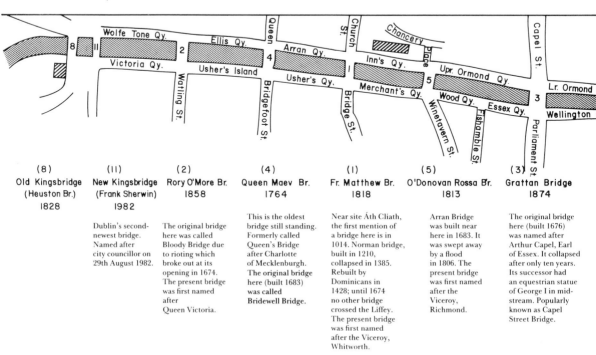

(8) Old Kingsbridge (Heuston Br.) 1828	(11) New Kingsbridge (Frank Sherwin) 1982	(2) Rory O'More Br. 1858	(4) Queen Maev Br. 1764	(1) Fr. Matthew Br. 1818	(5) O'Donovan Rossa Br. 1813	(3) Grattan Bridge 1874
Dublin's second-newest bridge. Named after city councillor on 29th August 1982.	The original bridge here was called Bloody Bridge due to rioting which broke out at its opening in 1674. The present bridge was first named after Queen Victoria.	This is the oldest bridge still standing. Formerly called Queen's Bridge after Charlotte of Mecklenburgh. **The original bridge here (built 1683) was called Bridewell Bridge.**	Near site Áth Cliath, the first mention of a bridge here is in 1014. Norman bridge, built in 1210, collapsed in 1385. Rebuilt by Dominicans in 1428; until 1674 no other bridge crossed the Liffey. The present bridge was first named after the Viceroy, Whitworth.	Arran Bridge was built near here in 1683. It was swept away by a flood in 1806. The present bridge was first named after the Viceroy, Richmond.	The original bridge here (built 1676) was named after Arthur Capel, Earl of Essex. It collapsed after only ten years. Its successor had an equestrian statue of George I in mid-stream. Popularly known as Capel Street Bridge.

1975 Ireland's first full-time community law centre opens in Coolock.

Wood Quay saga begins. Archaeologists claim that mechanical diggers are destroying the remains of medieval timber structures.

Project Arts Centre is opened by President Ó Dálaigh.

Bomb explodes at Dublin Airport, killing one and injuring five: UDA claims responsibility.

Guinness Fountain, the well-known landmark of the Liberties, is wrecked by a reversing lorry.

Three members of Dublin's Miami Show Band are killed at the Border by UVF extremists.

Eight gardaí and 150 fans injured during disturbances at pop concert in Star Cinema, Crumlin.

Death of Éamon de Valera, aged ninety-two. 70,000 people pay their respects at his lying-in-state at Dublin Castle. He is buried in Glasnevin on a day of national mourning.

1976 **Patrick Hillery** becomes President in place of Cearbhall Ó Dálaigh who resigns 'to protect the dignity of the Office' when called 'a thundering disgrace' by Defence Minister Donegan.

Seventy architectural students stage a sit-in at Bord na Móna headquarters, Pembroke Street, in an attempt to prevent demolition of Georgian buildings.

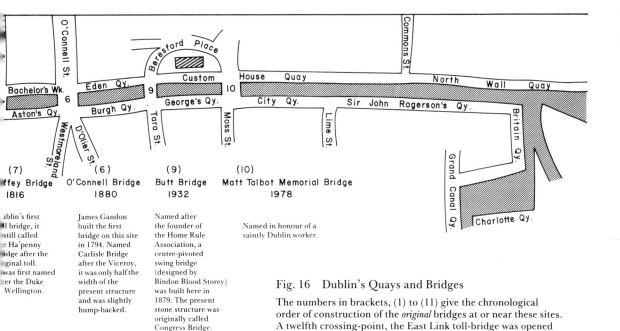

(7)	(6)	(9)	(10)
ffey Bridge	O'Connell Bridge	Butt Bridge	Matt Talbot Memorial Bridge
1816	1880	1932	1978

blin's first ll bridge, it still called e Ha'penny dge after the ginal toll. was first named er the Duke Wellington.

James Gandon built the first bridge on this site in 1794. Named Carlisle Bridge after the Viceroy, it was only half the width of the present structure and was slightly hump-backed.

Named after the founder of the Home Rule Association, a centre-pivoted swing bridge (designed by Bindon Blood Storey) was built here in 1879. The present stone structure was originally called Congress Bridge.

Named in honour of a saintly Dublin worker.

Fig. 16 Dublin's Quays and Bridges

The numbers in brackets, (1) to (11) give the chronological order of construction of the *original* bridges at or near these sites. A twelfth crossing-point, the East Link toll-bridge was opened further downstream in 1985.

Assassination of British Ambassador, Christopher Ewart-Biggs, outside his home at Sandyford by the Provisional IRA. Civil servant, Judith Cooke, also dies in blast.

In Dublin magazine launched.

10,000 people attend Easter Rising jubilee rally outside the GPO convened by Provisional IRA despite government ban.

Bank-strike lasts from 28th June to 6th September.

'Undignified' scenes at Forty-Foot bathing-place, Sandycove: women occupy the 'Gentlemen Only' bastion.

1977 **General Election** won by Fianna Fáil. Jack Lynch back as Taoiseach.

Multi-fountained memorial to **Thomas Davis** (Delaney) erected on College Green. Promptly nick-named 'Urination Once Again'.

Death of artist Seán Keating.

1978 **Central Bank** (Stephenson) completed in Dame Street, causing a storm of controversy because of its lack of proportion to adjacent buildings.

Wood Quay saga continues. Vain attempts to save Viking Dublin. (see 1979 and 1983). The High Court declares a portion of the Wood Quay site to be a national monument.

Irish Life Centre (Devane) opens in Abbey Street: wits refer to the statue outside as 'The Mad Milkman of Abbey Street'.

Dublin Institute of Technology founded.

Matt Talbot Memorial Bridge opened: it commemorates a saintly Dublin worker who died in 1925 and was declared 'venerable' by the Pope in 1975.

Wettest December since records began in 1829.

1979 Taoiseach retires: Jack Lynch replaced by **Charles Haughey**.

To halt destruction of national monument at **Wood Quay** for the building of civic offices, the site is occupied peacefully by a group of distinguished citizens.

Dublin business disrupted by strikes of busmen, barmen, binmen and postmen. The postal dispute, the first national one in over fifty years, lasts from 19th February to 25th June.

200,000 PAYE tax-payers march through Dublin demanding tax reform.

Papal Visit of Pope John Paul II. Over a million people congregate in Phoenix Park, the biggest crowd to assemble in Ireland since 1932.

Statue of **James Larkin** (Oisín Kelly) unveiled in O'Connell Street (see 1913).

£500,000 stolen from Trinity Bank Ltd.

Summit Meeting of EEC premiers held in Dublin Castle.

Dublin's first **women bus-conductors** introduced.

Thirty-three people injured in a train crash at Dalkey.

1980   **Derrynaflan Hoard** of ninth century silver-work found in Co Tipperary on view at National Museum, Dublin. In 1986, the High Court will decide that it should be returned to its finders. (Appeal to Supreme Court pending.)

National Institute for Higher Education founded on site of old Albert College in Glasnevin.

700,000 PAYE workers take part in the biggest nation-wide protest ever mounted.

Allied Irish Banks opens new Group Headquarters (Devane) in Ballsbridge. Most expensive building to date (but Dublin Corporation is still at work on Wood Quay!).

Boomtown Rats give rock concert at Leixlip: 14,000 fans of the Dublin group attend.

Johnny Logan wins Eurovision Song Contest with Shay Healy's song, *What's Another Year?*

1981   **General Election**: Garret Fitzgerald becomes Taoiseach of Coalition Government.

Death of **Thomas Dudley**, the famous Dublin character known as 'Bang! Bang!' because of his habit of 'shooting' people with an imaginary gun.

H-Block demonstration in Dublin leads to riot. Damage estimated at over a million pounds.

Dublin City Marathon: the first run around the streets since 1753.

Dubliner **Éamonn Coghlan** sets a new world record for the indoor mile (in San Diego).

National Concert Hall opens in Earlsfort Terrace (see 1865).

New airline, Avair, links Dublin with Derry.

Powerscourt House, South William Street, renovated and opened as a shopping complex (see 1771).

Death of the sculptor, Oisín Kelly.

Royal Dublin Society celebrates its 250th anniversary.

Over 50,000 farmers paralyse traffic in the centre of Dublin in protest at falling farm incomes.

The Stardust Disco Fire. Forty-eight young people die in worst Dublin tragedy since 1596.

1982   January snowstorm cripples Dublin for a week.

20,000 fans attend Simon & Garfunkel concert at RDS.

New bridge is opened across the Liffey near Kingsbridge: officially named 'Frank Sherwin Memorial Bridge' after a hard-working Dublin City Councillor.

Grafton Street is zoned for pedestrians only.

New Dublin Gas piped from Kinsale, Co Cork.

Celebrations mark the centenary of James Joyce's birthday. *Ulysses* is enacted on the streets, with real Dublin extras. The complete text of *Ulysses* is broadcast (without interruption) on RTE. It begins at 6.30 am on Bloomsday (16th June) and ends at 12.45 pm the following day.

Two **General Elections**: Charles Haughey forms minority Fianna Fáil Government in February with the support of Independent TD Tony Gregory who is promised £91m for the development of Dublin's inner city. Garret FitzGerald becomes Taoiseach of new Coalition Government in December.

Royal Hibernian Hotel, one of Dublin's oldest, closes on Dawson Street.

Attorney General, Patrick Connolly resigns after a man is arrested at his flat on a charge of murder. Charles Haughey describes the incident as 'grotesque, unprecedented, bizarre, unique': thus the word 'GUBU' is added to Dublin vocabulary.

1983   **Howth Harbour** renovated at far over the estimated cost.

Dublin Chamber of Commerce celebrates its bicentenary.

DART: Howth to Bray railway electrified. Named after BART, Bay Area Rapid Transit, in California. With the help of feeder buses, it is capable of carrying 80,000 passengers daily.

Mercer's Hospital is closed (see 1734).

Dublin Corporation Offices, Wood Quay, built on site of Viking Dublin. The substantial remains of tenth century houses, streets and quay walls are seen for the last time.

3,000 people take part in anti-nuclear demonstration outside US and Soviet embassies.

Book of Kells (kept at Trinity College) is valued by Sotheby's at £15,000,000.

Éamonn Coghlan becomes the world 5,000 metres champion (in Helsinki).

Christ Church Cathedral gets another face-lift (see 1871).

Brooking's Map of Dublin (see 1728) re-issued by the Irish Architectural Archive.

Referendum: Proposed amendment to Constitution reads: '. . . the State acknowledges the right to life of the unborn, and with due regard to the equal right to life of the mother, guarantees in its laws to respect, and as far as practicable, by its laws to defend and vindicate that right.' The amendment is carried by 841,233 votes to 416,136, but support for it was only half as strong in Dublin as in the rest of the Republic.

First issue of *The Sunday Tribune*. (An earlier, short-lived *Sunday Tribune* had been published in 1980).

1984 Report of **New Ireland Forum** published. Apart from putting forward constructive proposals for the political future of Ireland, it states that the Republic has spent two billion pounds on security – as against the UK's five billion – since 1976. (The Forum, which held its public sessions in Dublin Castle, was a joint effort on the part of major political parties in Ireland, North and South, with the exception of the Unionists – who refused to attend).

Death of **Luke Kelly**, one of 'The Dubliners' (see 1962). Ballybough Bridge will be renamed after him.

Visit of US President **Ronald Reagan**.

The Hop Store at Guinness's Brewery is remodelled as an exhibition centre (Scott) and hosts a ROSC exhibition. Begun in 1967, ROSC exhibitions had been held in 1971, 1977 and 1980.

St Audoen's Park, on old city walls, wins European award for civic improvement. Full marks to Dublin Corporation.

The centenary of the birth of John McCormack: wreath-laying ceremony is held at the tenor's grave in Deansgrange.

Nine people – including prominent Dublin journalists and restauranteurs – are killed in plane crash *en route* from Dublin to Paris to take part in the annual Beaujolais wine race.

An Taisce takes over Tailors' Hall (see 1627).

Casino, Marino, renovated and opened to the public (see 1758).

Irish UN soldiers killed in Lebanon: military funerals bring grief to Dublin.

Dining Hall of Trinity College (see 1734) destroyed by fire. The East Chapel is destroyed in another fire.

East Link Bridge opens: the first toll-bridge since 1816.

1985 **Royal Hospital Kilmainham** renovated and opened to the public. In 1986 it will win the Europa Nostra Medal for architectural conservation. Its first public exhibiton is of the Chinese Emperor's Warriors.

'Steine' (Clíona Cussen) erected on old Viking site, College Street (see 841).

20,000 teachers attend rally in Croke Park to demand that their pay award be granted by the government. School strikes follow.

European Special Olympics for the mentally handicapped held in Dublin.

President Hillery re-elected for another term in Office.

Death of **Hector Grey**, successful businessman and Dublin's best-known trader for nearly fifty years.

Dubliner **Bob Geldof** organizes international *Live Aid* television spectacular to raise funds for famine relief in Africa. Ireland contributes generously.

Jewish Museum is opened by President Herzog of Israel on Walworth Road – around the corner from his childhood home (see 1917).

Hillsborough Agreement signed between Irish and British Governments. Ulster extremists threaten to bomb Dublin.

Drugs dealer, Larry Dunne, is sentenced to fourteen years imprisonment.

Death of **Noel Purcell**, actor and Dubliner.

Concert of Dublin pop-group, **U2**, fills Croke Park stadium (see 1987).

1986　Excavations at **Dublin Castle** begun. Foundations of the Powder Tower uncovered. Part of the original moat comes to light (see 1204). The excavations are providing much new information on the construction of the original castle.

New political party, The Progressive Democrats, holds its first public meeting in Dublin.

Dining Hall of Trinity College (burnt in 1984) beautifully restored (Blacan & Meagher).

Six Loreto nuns die in fire at their convent, St Stephen's Green.

Gonzaga College (see 1950).

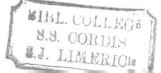

Rathfarnham Castle declared a National Monument (see 1585 and 1987).

Small riot breaks out when the army moves in to clear away rubbish mounting up during bin-men's strike.

Mrs Jennifer Guinness is abducted from her home in Howth; released, unharmed, after eight days in captivity.

On the eightieth birthday of **Samuel Beckett**, the Taoiseach presents a gold torc to the author's niece, on her self-exiled uncle's behalf, at a ceremony in Dublin. The torc is the highest honour that can be conferred by Irish artists on one of their fellows: it symbolizes the position of *saoí* (see chapter on The Celts).

Divorce Referendum: Dublin still differs from the rest of Ireland:

	For	Against
Dublin	49.9	49.7
Rest of Leinster	34.2	65.0
Munster	29.5	63.1
Connacht	27.9	71.3
Ulster	27.8	71.8

Newbridge House is opened to the public (see 1737).

Self Aid: Bob Geldof helps RTE to organize a televised concert at RDS with a view to easing the unemployment crisis.

Sir Patrick Dun's Hospital closes (see 1808).

August 25th: **Hurricane Charlie** causes devastation. 3.1 inches of rain fall in Dublin in 24 hours, the heaviest rainfall since 1905. All the rivers except the Liffey burst their banks: Anna Livia has been tamed.

Ultra-modern **Dublin Public Library** opens in the ILAC Centre, Henry Street.

The **Bolshoi Ballet** performs at the RDS.

1987   **Gas explosion** in Ballsbridge wrecks block of flats, killing three people.

Rathfarnham Castle purchased by the State (see 1986).

General Election: Charles Haughey becomes Taoiseach of another minority Fianna Fáil government.

Johnny Logan wins Eurovision Song Contest for a record second time (see 1980) with his own song, *Hold Me Now*.

New National Lottery is launched in Dublin by An Post. There had been a State Lottery in the eighteenth century: the Lottery Office at Capel Street Bridge is shown on a Malton water-colour of 1800.

The Dubliners ballad-group makes the UK charts again (see 1962).

Dublin cyclist, **Stephen Roche**, wins the Giro d'Italia, the Tour de France and the World Championship in Austria.

On 24th May in Christ Church Cathedral, five hundred years to the day since the event took place, Professor F X Martin gives a public lecture on the crowning of Lambert Simnel as King Edward VI (see 1487).

Dublin rock singers **U2** make the front cover of *Time* magazine during their tour of the United States. Their Dublin concerts in Croke Park stadium on 27th and 28th June are attended by over 100,00 fans.

Health cuts: Protest marches and doctors' strike in reaction to budgetary economies. Dr Steevens Hospital (see 1720) is to be closed.

One of the New Assembly Rooms (see 1784) is beautifully restored at the Rotunda.

Re-appearance of the humorous magazine, *Dublin Opinion*. First issued in March, 1922, it had stopped publication in 1970.

Referendum on **Single European Act**: 65.7% of Dubliners who vote favour the Act; in the rest of the country, the majority is 69.9%.

Beaumont Hospital due to open as we go to press.

1988   **Millennium** celebrations in Dublin (see preamble to chapter on Hiberno-Norse Dublin, page 47.

1988   Centenary year of *The Irish Catholic* newspaper.

Centenary of *Sacred Heart Messenger*, Ireland's largest religious periodical with a circulation of over 200,000 copies monthly. Always based in Dublin, the original Messenger Office in Great Denmark Street was burnt down in 1948.

View from the roof of the old 'Messenger Office' (see 1988) including Findlater's Church spire (renovated in 1986).

The main hall at Rathfarnham Castle (see 1987).

ELSEWHERE: Hitler's *Mein Kampf* (1925). Baird invents television (1926). Fleming discovers penicillin (1928). Wall Street Crash (1929). Hitler becomes German Chancellor (1933) and Führer (1934). Watson-Watt devises radar (1935). Spanish Civil War (1936-39). Whittle invents jet engine (1937). Germany annexes Austria (1938). Müller invents DDT (1939). German invasion of Poland starts Second World War (1939). Dunkirk; Fall of France; Battle of Britain (1940). Japanese attack Pearl Harbour (1941). Montgomery defeats Rommel at El Alamein (1942). Fermi splits atom (1942). Fall of Mussolini (1943). Russians advance on Germany's Eastern Front (1943). Normandy Landings: D-Day (1944). Jewish 'Holocaust' (1944-45). Atomic bombs dropped by USA on Hiroshima and Nagasaki (1945). World War II ends (1945). Mahatma Gandhi assassinated (1948). Korean War (1950-53). Hillary and Tensing climb Everest (1953). Bannister's 'Four Minute Mile' (1954). Hungarian Revolution (1956). Treaty of Rome sets up EEC (1957). Russia launches *Sputnik I* (1957). Berlin Wall built (1961). First space-man: Yuri Gargarin (1961). President Kennedy assassinated (1963). Vietnamese War (1965-73). First heart transplant (1967). Martin Luther King and Robert Kennedy assassinated (1968). First test-tube baby (1969). Man lands on moon (1969). 'Bloody Sunday' in Derry (1972). Watergate break-in (1972) leads to resignation of President Nixon (1974). Earthquake in Tangshan, China, kills 655,237 people (1976). Falklands crisis (1982). 'Apartheid' riots in Soweto, S. Africa (1985). Lebanese civil war ends (1986). Car-ferry sinks at Zeebrugge with loss of 188 lives (1987).

CONCLUSION

In the year 1915, Stephen Gwynn wrote:

> Dublin has been called 'a faded capital', and the description is true; in the eighteenth century she was the capital of a resident aristocracy, and in the nineteenth century she faded. A new life, a new growth, a new flowering and fruitage may be before her as the metropolis of an Irish nation at last finally and fully developed; she may rise out of the squalor that hangs about her, like a draggled skirt on a beautiful woman; she may breed clean and strong generations for the uses of the world. Yet whatever happens to her, if she retain her nature, she will not despise the days of her adversity; she will keep her remembering heart, and have a tenderness for the old bad times and for those who in discouraging hours kept alive the faith of nationality.
>
> *The Famous Cities of Ireland*, p.267

Little did the author realise that less than a year later tremendous events would rock the city to its foundations. If we link Stephen Gwynn's prophecy with that of St Patrick (see the year 450), we do not need a particularly vivid imagination to see Dublin as a city of destiny.

In these pages we have seen that the modern capital of Ireland replaced the British seat of government which the Anglo-Normans took over from the Hiberno-Norse who inherited the site of Viking Dublin. Before the Vikings there was a Christian settlement; before Christ Church Cathedral there was Cill Céle Crist. Recent anthropological studies would lead us to suppose that there was a pagan shrine in existence before the Christian church, a shrine whose location would have been determined by druids. Using a science now lost to man, the druids were able to respond – like diviners – to fields of energy and electricity. They fixed on a point where physical and spiritual forces combined to produce equilibrium. As Dr Lyall Watson puts it, they were able to respond to 'a set of stimuli that give certain places, and only those places, a necessary, special and magical quality'.

Appendix I
ROLL OF THE HONORARY FREEDOM OF THE CITY OF DUBLIN

Among the muniments of Dublin Corporation in the City Hall, dating back to the twelfth century there are rolls of "free citizens" who received a key to the city gates. The list below gives the names of those who were granted the freedom of the city since the British parliament passed an Act (1876) enabling the City Council "to elect and admit persons to be honorary burgesses".

Isaac Butt, QC, 4 Sept 1876
Rt Hon William Edward Gladstone, PC, MP,
 1 Nov 1877
Ulysses S Grant, ex-President USA, 30 Dec 1878
Edward E Potter, Captain of the Relief Ship
 Constellation US Navy, 26 April 1880
Charles S Parnell, MP, 3 Jan 1882
John Dillon, MP, 3 Jan 1882
Kevin Izod O'Doherty, 10 Aug 1885
Hon Patrick A Collins, Senator USA, 22 July 1887
William O'Brien, MP, 22 July 1887
Timothy Daniel Sullivan, MP, 10; Dec 1887
Thomas Sexton, MP, 28 Dec 1887
Rt Hon The Marquis of Ripon, PC, 16 Jan 1888
Rt Hon John Morley, PC, MP, 16 Jan 1888
His Eminence Cardinal Moran, 1 Oct 1888
Lady Sandhurst, 19 Sept 1889
Rt Hon James Stansfield, PC, MP, 19 Sept 1890
The Rev George Salmon, DD, Provost, TCD,
 14 March 1892
Rt Hon Stuart Knill, Lord Mayor of London,
 23 Dec 1892
Patrick A McHugh, MP, 30 Oct 1901
John E Redmond, BL, MP, 18 Dec 1901
(An Craobhín Aoibhinn), President Douglas Hyde,
 LL D, 29 June 1906
Richard Croker, 1 July 1907
Spencer Harty, CE, Borough Surveyor of Dublin,
 2 Sept 1907
Hugh P Lane, 10 Feb 1908
E O'Meagher Condon, 28 Sept 1909
Sir Chas A. Cameron, CB, Executive Sanitary
 Officer, 30 Sept 1910
Dr Kuno Meyer, 18 July 1911
An Canonach Peadar Ua Laoghaire, 18 July 1911
Most Rev Daniel Mannix, DD, Archbishop of
 Melbourne, 5 Aug 1920
John Count McCormack, 3 Sept 1923
Ehrenfried Gunther, Baron von Hunefeld,
 30 June 1928
Captain Hermann Koehl, 30 June 1928
Major James Fitzmaurice, 30 June 1928
The Hon Frank B Kellogg, LL D, Secretary of
 State USA, 25 Aug 1928

His Eminence Lorenzo Cardinal Lauri, Papal
 Legate to the 31st International Eucharistic
 Congress, 27 June 1932
Sir John Lavery, RA, RHA, 17 Sept 1935
Sir John Purser Griffith, MAI, MInst CE,
 8 June 1936
George Bernard Shaw, 28 Aug 1946
Most Rev Richard J Cushing, DD, Archbishop
 of Boston, 16 Sept 1949
The Hon Paul Dever, Governor of Massachusetts,
 USA, 16 Sept 1949
His Excellency Sean T Ó Ceallaigh, Uachtarán
 na hÉireann, 2 June 1953
His Eminence John Cardinal Dalton, DD,
 Archbishop of Armagh and Primate of
 All Ireland, 2 June 1953
His Excellency Gerald P O'Hara, DD, Archbishop
 of Savannah, Georgia, USA and Papal Nuncio
 to Ireland, 27 July 1954
Sir Alfred Chester Beatty, FSA, LL D, DSc,
 26 July 1956
Most Rev John Francis Norton, BA, DD, LL D,
 Bishop of Bathurst, New South Wales,
 28 Oct 1958
His Eminence Gregory Peter Cardinal Agagianian,
 Papal Legate to the Dublin Congress of the
 Patrician Year 1961, 22 June 1961
His Eminence Michael Cardinal Browne, OP,
 23 Aug 1962
John F Kennedy, President, USA, 28 June 1963
Hilton R H Edwards, 22 June 1973
Dr Micheál Mac Liammóir, 22 June 1973
Éamon de Valera, President of Ireland,
 7 March 1975
John A Costello, 7 March 1973
His Holiness Pope John Paul II, 29 Sept 1979
Noel Purcell, 28 June 1984
Maureen Potter, 28 June 1984
His Imperial Highness Akihito, Crown Prince
 of Japan, 4 March 1985
Her Imperial Highness Michiko, Crown Princess
 of Japan, 4 March 1985
Stephen Roche, 29 September 1987

Appendix II
SOME LITERARY CONNECTIONS
(Living writers excluded)

Addison, Joseph
b England, 1672; wrote many of his *Essays* in Dublin while secretary to the Lord Lieutenant, 1708-11 and 1714-15.

Ashe, Thomas
b Glasnevin, 1770; went to France with British Army; jailed for duelling; on return to Dublin wrote travel books, including *Memoirs and Confessions*; novels: *The Spirit of the Book, The Soldier of Fortune, The Liberal Critic*, etc; d 1835.

Barlow, Jane
b Clontarf, 1857; lived in Bray; poet and novelist; works include *The Land of Elfintown, Kerrigan's Quality, The Founding of Fortunes, Flaws, Doings and Dealings, Between Doubting and Daring*; d 1917.

Barrington, Jonah
b Abbeyleix, 1760; educated at TCD; became MP for Tuam, Clogher and Banagher; political works include *Historic Anecdotes and Secret Memoirs of the Legislative Union between Great Britain and Ireland* and *Personal Sketches of his Own Time*; d 1834.

Behan, Brendan
b 14 Russell Street (off North Circular Road) 1923; *Borstal Boy, The Quare Fellow, The Hostage*, etc; d Dublin 1964; last home: 5 Anglesea Road.

Berkeley, George
b Co. Kilkenny, 1685; educated at TCD; philosophical works include *Treatise concerning the Principles of Human Knowledge* and *Essay towards a New Theory of Vision* which he wrote as Fellow of TCD; became Bishop of Cloyne; d 1753.

Boucicault, Dion
b 47 Gardiner Street, 1822; drama: *The Colleen Bawn, Arrah-na-Pogue, The Shaughraun*, etc; d 1890.

Bowen, Elizabeth
b 15 Herbert Place, 1889; novels: *Death of the Heart, The Last September*, etc; d London, 1973.

Burke, Edmund
b 12 Arran Quay, 1729; studied at TCD; founded Debating Society; statesman and orator; essays: *Reflections on the Revolution in France*, etc; d 1797.

Byrne, Seamus
b Dublin, 1904; jailed for involvement with IRA, 1940; had two plays produced in Dublin: *Design for a Tombstone* and *Little City*; d 1968.

Carleton, William
b Trillick, Co Tyrone, 1794; moved to Dublin and wrote *The Black Prophet, The Black Spectre*, etc, at 3 Marino Terrace; later moved to Rathgar; last home: 2 Woodville, Sandford Road; d 1869.

Clarke, Austin
b Manor Street, 1896; school at Belvedere; lived in Mountjoy Street; went to UCD; *Collected Poems*; *Twice Round the Black Church* (novel) etc; d 1974.

Colum, Pádraic
b Longford, 1881; moved to Sandycove as a boy; school in Glasthule; taught in St Enda's; *Poems* (An Old Woman of the Roads), etc; before emigrating to USA lived at 11 Edenvale Road, Ranelagh; d 1972; buried in St Fintan's, Sutton.

Congreve, William
This English author (1670-1729) came to Ireland as an infant, spent his childhood here and wrote his first book, *Incognita*, while a student at TCD in 1687.

D'Alton, Louis
b Dublin, 1900; two early novels: *Death is so Fair* and *Rags and Sticks*; drama: *The Man in the Cloak, Lovers Meeting, The Money Doesn't Matter, This Other Eden*, etc; d 1951.

Davis, Thomas
b Mallow, 1814; moved to Dublin and went to TCD; lived at 67 Lower Baggot Street; co-founder of *The Nation*; wrote *Poems, Literary & Historical Essays*; etc; d 1845.

Devlin, Denis
b Greenock, 1908; educated at Belvedere and UCD; spent life in diplomatic service; several collections of poems: *Lough Derg and Other Poems, Selected Poems*, etc; d 1959.

Ferguson, Samuel
b Belfast, 1810; moved to Dublin and lived at 20 North Gt George's St; translator of Goethe; *Collected Poems, Deirdre*, etc; influenced William Butler Yeats; d 1886.

Figgis, Darrell
b Rathmines, 1882; lived in India as a child; bought arms for Howth gun-running, 1914; became MP for County Dublin; novels: *The Return of the Hero* (under pseudonym of Michael Ireland), *Children of Earth, The House of Success*, etc; d 1925.

Gogarty, O St John
b 5 Parnell Square, 1878 (opp Gate Theatre); attended O'Connell's Schools; lived in 25 Ely Place; surgeon; senator, 1922-36; *As I was going down Sackville Street*, etc; d 1957.

Goldsmith, Oliver
b 1728 in Co Longford; came to TCD in 1747; left after Black Dog Riot; poems: *The Deserted Village*, etc; plays: *She Stoops to Conquer*, etc; novels: *The Vicar of Wakefield*, etc; d London, 1774.

Graves, Alfred P
b Dublin, 1846; son of Bishop of Limerick; prolific writer of popular poems using Irish material, eg *Songs of Killarney, Father O'Flynn and other Irish Lyrics, An Irish Faery Book*; plus an anthology, *The Book of Irish Poetry*; d 1931.

Green, A Stopford
b Kells, Co Meath, 1847; studied history in London; returned to Dublin and lived at 90 St Stephen's Green; historical works include *The Making of Ireland and Its Undoing* and *The History of the Early Irish State to 1014*; d 1929.

Gwynn, Stephen
b Rathfarnham, 1864; educated at St Columba's College; wrote poems, novels, sketches, stories, essays, political works and biographies of Swift, Moore, Scott, Goldsmith, Stevenson *et al*; *The History of Ireland, Dublin Old and New, The Famous Cities of Ireland*, etc; d 1950.

Healy, Gerard
b Dublin, 1918; educated at CBS Synge St; joined Gate Theatre Company; plays: *Thy Dear Father* and *The Black Stranger*; d 1963.

Holloway, Joseph
b Dublin 1861; attended School of Art, Kildare St; became famous Dublin 'character'; wrote *Joseph Holloway's Abbey Theatre* and a 3-vol history of the Irish theatre; d 1944.

Hopkins, Gerard Manley
The English Jesuit poet (1844-1889) spent the last five years of his life at 86 St Stephen's Green while Professor of Greek at University College; *The Wreck of the Deutschland, The Windhover, Pied Beauty*, etc; buried in Glasnevin Cemetery.

Hyde, Douglas
b French Park, Co Roscommon, 1860; went to TCD; Irish scholar; founded *Gaelic League*; *Legends of Saints and Sinners, A Literary History of Ireland*, etc; first President of Ireland (1938-1944); d 1949.

Ingram, John Kells
b 1823 in Co Donegal; became Professor of English and eventually Vice-Provost at TCD; lived at 38 Upper Mount Street; wrote *The Memory of the Dead* (which opens with the famous lines: 'Who fears to speak of Ninety-Eight?'); d 1907.

Johnston, Denis
b Dublin, 1901; educated at St Andrew's; plays: *The Old Lady Says No, The Moon on the Yellow River, Storm Song, The Golden Cuckoo, The Scythe and the Sunset*, etc; biography: *In Search of Swift*; d 1984.

Joyce, James
b 41 Brighton Square, 1882; Belvedere College, Clongowes, Catholic University; lived at 14 Fitzgibbon Street, 17 North Richmond Street, etc; stayed (briefly) in Martello Tower, Sandycove (now Joyce Museum); *Dubliners, Portrait of the Artist as a Young Man, Ulysses, Finnegans Wake*, etc; d Zurich, 1941.

Kavanagh, Patrick
b Monaghan, 1904; moved to Dublin 1939; lived at 62 Pembroke Road, etc; fiction: *The Green Fool, Tarry Flynn*; poems: *The Great Hunger, A Soul for Sale, Come Dance with Kitty Stobling*, etc; editor of periodical *Kavanagh's Weekly*; d 1967. Canal Seat memorial at Baggot Street Bridge.

Kettle, Tom
b Artane, Co Dublin 1880; school at Clongowes; economist; wrote *Home Rule Finance*, etc; also *Poems & Parodies*; d (in World War I) 1916.

Lawless, Emily
b Dublin, 1845; daughter of Baron Cloncurry; novels, essays and short stories; *Grania, Maelcho, With the Wild Geese*, etc; d 1913.

Lecky, William
b Cullenswood House, Ranelagh, 1838; became Professor of History at TCD; wrote 8-volume *History of England in the Eighteenth Century*; d 1903.

Le Fanu, J Sheridan
b 45 Lower Dominick Street in 1814; grand-nephew of R B Sheridan; owned *The Evening Mail*; lived at 70 Merrion Square; novels include *The House by the Churchyard, The Cock and Anchor*, etc; d 1873.

Lever, Charles
b 35 Amiens Street (where the Station stands now) in 1806; lived in Templeogue House; his *Collected Works* run to 37 volumes; *Charles O'Malley*, etc; d Trieste, 1872.

Lover, Samuel
b 60 Grafton Street, 1797; novels include *Rory O'More, Handy Andy*, etc; lived at 9 D'Olier Street; d 1868.

MacDonagh, Donagh
b Dublin, 1912; son of Thomas MacDonagh (signatory of 1916 Proclamation); educated at Belvedere and UCD; plays include *Happy as Larry, God's Gentry, Step-in-the-Hollow, Lady Spider*; also wrote poetry and co-edited *Oxford Book of Irish Verse*; d 1968.

Mahaffy, J. Pentland
b Switzerland, 1839; educated at TCD where he became Provost for 55 years; Greek scholar; works include *A History of Classical Greek Literature, Greek Life and Thought*; co-edited *Georgian Society Records*; d 1919.

Mangan, James Clarence
b 3 Lord Edward Street, 1803; school at Courtney's Academy, Derby Square; lived at 6 York Street; worked in Ordnance Survey, 21 Great Charles Street; *Poems and Translations from Irish*; *My Dark Rosaleen*, etc; d 1849.

Maturin, Charles
b 37 York Street, 1782; studied at TCD; wrote horror novels, eg *Melmoth the Wanderer* and a play, *Bertram*; d 1824.

Moore, George
b Co Mayo, 1852; came to Dublin and lived at 4 Ely Place; wrote *A Drama in Muslin, Hail and Farewell, Esther Waters, The Lake*, etc; d 1933.

Moore, Thomas
b 12 Aungier Street, 1779; one of the first Roman Catholics to enter TCD; wrote 9 volumes of *Irish Melodies* and 6 volumes of *National Airs*; d 1852.

Morgan, Lady Sydney
b 1783 in Dublin; *née* Sydney Owenson; married Sir Thomas Morgan and lived for eighteen years at 39 Kildare Street; novels include *The Wild Irish Girl*; famous for her literary *salon*; d 1859.

Murray, T C
b Macroom, Co Cork, 1873; came to Dublin to attend St Patrick's Training College, Drumcondra; became Headmaster of Inchicore Model Schools in 1915; one of the Abbey Theatre's greatest playwrights; *Birthright, Maurice Harte, Autumn Fire*, etc; lived at 11 Sandymount Avenue; d 1959.

O'Casey, Sean
b 85 Upper Dorset Street, 1880; lived 35 Mountjoy Square, Abercorn Road, Hawthorn Terrace, Leo Street (off North Circular Road, now called 'Sean O'Casey House'); drama: *The Plough and the Stars, The Shadow of a Gunman, Juno and the Paycock, The Silver Tassie*, etc; d 1964.

O'Connor, Frank
b Cork, 1903; real name Michael O'Donovan; moved to Dublin and became municipal librarian at Ballsbridge; lived in Sandymount Green and Anglesea Road before moving to Court Flats, Wilton Place; one of the greatest Irish short-story writers; *Guests of the Nation*, etc; novel: *The Saint and Mary Kate*; d 1966.

O'Duffy, Eimar
b Dublin, 1893; educated at Stonyhurst and UCD; called 'modern Ireland's only prose satirist'; plays: *The Walls of Athens, The Phoenix on the Roof, Bricriu's Feast*, etc; major novel: *The Wasted Island*; d 1935.

Ó Faracháin, Roibeárd
b Robert Farren, Dublin, 1909; became director of Abbey Theatre 1940-73; worked for 21 years at Radio Éireann (where he became Controller of Programmes); plays: *Assembly at Druim Ceat, Lost Light*, etc; poems: *The First Exile, Thronging Feet, Time's Wall Asunder*, etc; d 1984.

O'Flaherty, Liam
b Aran Islands, 1897; spent early 1920s in Dublin where he wrote Dublin based thrillers: *The Informer, The Assassin, Mr Gilhooley, The Puritan*; a master of the short-story; returned to Dublin in 1950; d 1984.

O'Keeffe, John
b 6 Abbey Street, 1747; educated by the Jesuits at Saul's Court Academy, off Fishamble Street; moved to London, 1780; wrote numerous comic operas: *The Toy, Wild Oats, Doldrum*, etc; d Southampton, 1833.

O'Nolan, Brian
b Strabane, Co Tyrone, 1911; better known as Flann O'Brien or Myles na Gopaleen; lived at Belmont Avenue, Donnybrook; *At Swim-two-Birds, An Béal Bocht, The Dalkey Archive, The Third Policeman, Faustus Kelly*, etc; his column, *Cruiskeen Lawn*, ran for twenty years in *The Irish Times*; d 1966.

O'Riordan, Conal
b Dublin, 1874; educated at Clongowes; became managing director, Abbey Theatre, 1909; revived Synge's *Playboy* there; novels: *Adam of Dublin, Adam and Caroline*, etc; historical novels and series *Soldier Born, Soldier's End* etc; d 1948.

O'Sullivan, Seumas
b Dublin, 1879; as editor of *The Dublin Magazine* he published first works of Beckett, Kavanagh, Clarke *et al*; own works include *The Twilight People, The Rose and the Bottle, Requiem and Other Poems* etc; d 1958.

Parnell, Thomas
b Dublin, 1679; educated at TCD; befriended by Swift; wrote *Poems on Several Occasions, The Hermit*, etc; often collaborated with Pope and wrote introduction to his *Iliad*; d 1718.

Petrie, George
b Dublin, 1790; distinguished antiquarian; *On the History and Antiquities of Tara Hill, The Ecclesiastical Architecture of Ireland, The Petrie Collection of the Ancient Music of Ireland*, etc; d 1866.

Plunkett, Joseph M
b Larkfield, Kimmage Road, 1887; school at CUS, Belvedere and Stonyhurst; poet: *I see His Blood upon the Rose*, etc; editor of the *Irish Review*; executed 1916.

Robinson, Lennox
b Co Cork, 1886; associated with Abbey Theatre as writer, producer and director 1908-58; plays: *The Whiteheaded Boy, The Round Table, The White Blackbird, The Far-Off Hills, The Big House*, etc; d 1958.

Russell, George (AE)
b Lurgan, 1867; came to Dublin when 11 years old; lived at 33 Emorville Avenue (off South Circular Road); helped start Abbey Theatre; worked at 84 Merrion Sq; later addresses include 10 Grove Terrace, 66 Castlewood Avenue, 17 Rathgar Avenue and 28 Upper Mount Pleasant Avenue; *Homeward*; *Songs by the Way, The Divine Vision and Other Poems*, etc; d 1935.

Ryan, Cornelius
b 33 Heytesbury Street, 1920; became a journalist and emigrated to USA; novels: *The Longest Day, The Last Battle, A Bridge Too Far*; d 1974.

Sarr, Kenneth
b Dublin, 1895; educated at Belvedere, Clongowes and UCD; had two one-act plays produced at Abbey Theatre; Dublin novels: *Somewhere to the Sea, Another Shore, Young Man with a Dream*; d 1967.

Shaw, George Bernard
b 33 Synge Street, 1856; emigrated to England; Nobel Prize, 1925; *Pygmalion, Major Barbara, Man and Superman, Heartbreak House, Arms and the Man*, etc; d 1950.

Sheridan, John D
b Dublin, 1903; humorous essayist, poet and novelist; *I Laugh to Think, The Rest is Silence, Paradise Alley, Include Me Out*, etc; d 1980.

Sheridan, R Brinsley
b 12 Upper Dorset Street, 1751; left for Harrow, aged 11, never to return; *The School for Scandal, The Duenna, The Rivals, The Relapse* etc; d 1816.

Shorter, Dora Sigerson
b Dublin, 1866; poetical works include *Ballads and Poems, Through Wintry Terrors, As the Sparks Fly Upward, The Troubadour and Other Poems*; d 1918.

Sigerson, George
b Strabane, 1836; moved to Dublin and lived at 3 Clare Street; historical works include *Bards of the Gael and the Gall, Modern Ireland*, etc; d 1915.

Smithson, Annie M P
b Sandymount, 1883; convert to Catholicism and nationalism; novels: *The White Owl, Winter Heather, Katherine Devoy, The Light of Other Days, Tangled Threads* etc; d 1948.

Southerne, Thomas
b Co Dublin, 1660; educated at TCD; collaborated with Dryden; tragedies: *The Fatal Marriage, Oroonoko* etc; d 1746.

Steele, Sir Richard
b Dublin, 1672; founder of *The Tatler* and associated with Joseph Addison on *The Spectator*; later founded *The Guardian*; famous as an essayist; d 1729.

Stephens, James
b 5 Thomas Court, 1882; worked at 9 Eustace Street; later lived at 8 St Joseph's Road, 30 York Street, 2 Leinster Square, 17 Pearse Street and 42 Fitzwilliam Place; *The Crock of Gold, The Charwoman's Daughter, Irish Fairy Tales*, etc; d 1950.

Stoker, Bram
b 15 Marino Crescent, 1847; became best-selling Irish writer ever; lived at 16 Harcourt Street; wrote *Dracula*, and other horror stories; d 1912.

Swift, Jonathan
b Hoey's Court, off Werburgh Street, 1667; studied divinity at TCD; became Dean of St Patrick's, 1713; satires include *A Tale of a Tub, Gulliver's Travels, Drapier's Letters, A Modest Proposal*, etc; many poems and letters; *Journal to Stella*, etc; d 1745.

Synge, John M
2 Newtown Villas, Rathfarnham, 1871; lived 4 Orwell Park and 31 Crosthwaite Street, Dún Laoghaire; *Playboy of the Western World, Shadow of the Glen, Riders to the Sea, The Well of the Saints, Deirdre of the Sorrows*, etc; d 1909.

Todhunter, John
b Dublin, 1839; educated at TCD; taught at Alexandra College; plays: *Helena in Troas, The Black Cat, A Comedy of Sighs, A Sicilian Idyll, Alcestis* etc; d 1916.

Trollope, Anthony
The English novelist (1815-1822) lived for five years (1855-1860) at 6 Seaview Terrace, Donnybrook, where he wrote: *Barchester Towers and Castle Richmond*.

Tynan, Katherine
b Whitehall House, Clondalkin, 1868; published works run to 125 vols; *Ballads and Lyrics, The Holy War*, etc; d 1931.

Ussher, James
b Dublin 1581; lived in Cook St; educated at TCD; became (Protestant) Archbishop of Armagh, 1635; 17 vols of published works include the very popular *Biblical Chronology*; d 1656.

Wilde, Lady Jane
b Dublin, 1825; inspired by Thomas Davis, wrote many articles and poems for *The Nation* under the pen-name 'Speranza'; under her own name wrote *Driftwood from Scandinavia, Legends of Ireland* and *Social Studies*; wife of Sir William Wilde and mother of Oscar; her *salon* (1 Merrion Square) was the most famous in Dublin; d 1896.

Wilde, Oscar
b 21 Westland Row, 1854; lived at 1 Merrion Square; emigrated to England; novelist, poet and playwright, works include *The Picture of Dorian Gray, The Importance of Being Earnest, Lady Windermere's Fan, A Woman of No Importance, The Ballad of Reading Gaol, Salomé*, etc; d 1900.

Wilde, Sir William
b Co Roscommon, 1815; moved to Dublin, 1833, to become a doctor, Royal College of Surgeons; wrote text-book, *Aural Surgery*, which became a standard work; many papers on archaeology and antiquities; wrote *The Beauties of the Boyne and Blackwater, Lough Corrib*, etc; lived at 21 Westland Row (where his son, Oscar, was born); moved to 1 Merrion Square (where his wife, Lady Jane, held her *salon*); d 1876.

Wolseley, Viscount G J
b Golden Bridge House, Dublin, 1833; served all around the Empire in the British Army, eventually becoming General and Commander-in-chief; wrote *Story of a Soldier's Life, Narrative of the War with China in 1860, Soldier's Pocket Book, Field Manoeuvres, Marley Castle, Life of Marlborough* (2 vols), *The Decline and Fall of Napoleon*; d 1913.

Yeats, William Butler
b 'Georgeville', Sandymount Avenue, 1865; educated in The High School; lived at 10 Ashfield Terrace, Rathgar, and 82 Merrion Square; Nobel Prize, 1923; senator, 1923-28; plays: *Cathleen Ní Houlihan, Deirdre*, etc; poems: *The Tower, The Winding Stair, Michael Robartes and the Dancer, The Wild Swans at Coole* etc; founded the Irish Literary Society, 1892; helped found the Abbey Theatre, 1903; edited *The Oxford Book of Modern Verse*, 1936; d 1939.

Appendix III
JOYCE'S NAMES FOR DUBLIN IN FINNEGANS WAKE

the turn at the fourth of the hurdles
The Heart of Midleinster
athclete bally bathfeet
dear dutchy deeplins
ford of hurdlestown
Bauliaughacleeagh

the furt on the turn of the hurdles
town of the Fords in a huddle
Ballyaughacleeaghbally
Ceadurbar-atha-Cleath
Hungerford-on-Mudway
Tumblin-on-the-Leafy

devlins	Eblana	dabblin	doublin
Dobbelin	Dirtby	Ni-non	Dovlen
Dyfflin	Dubblann	Shuvlin	Dubloonik
Durlbin	Bully Acre	Delvan	Dumnlimn
Nilbud	Dumplan	diveline	d'lin
Dumbaling	Babbalong	Livienbad	Dyb!
Inbeen	Dalbania	Divlun	durdin
Urovivla	Ebblannah	dubble	wumblin
Dvlyn	wubblin	Eblinn	deevlin
Lionndub	Nublid	goblin	oldun
D. Blayncy	dulpen	Ibdullin	bludyn
delving	doubling	dyfflun	Libaud
bally clay	troublin	Diaeblen	Defblin
Babylon	Dobelan	cubblin	Linduff
Ebblawn	Diddlem	dompling	dobbling
Dubville	Elleb Inam	daulimbs	Athclee
dabnal	Libnius	dibblin	ballyheart
Nilfit	D'Oblong	Dungbin	doveling
duvlin	Blath	Deblinity	Livmouth
Dumpling	DVbLIn	doubthing	Dubbeldorf
doherlynt	dullard	darblun	Eblinia
Doubtlynn	Lynn-Duff	doubling	dumblynass
Dephilim	Publin	Dunlob	Niluna
Rivapool	Annapolis	Darby	Ebblawn
Puddlin	Dybblin	Tupling	stabling
Nublinia	Doolin	wabblin	Deblinity
Ballaclay	Budlim	dubilden	doubtling
dobblins	tippling	dabbling	Tumplan
Balkley	Dbln.	daulphin	Lublin
diublin	riverpool	Dolando	Deublan
tublin	Delvin	tumbling	hungerford
Djublian	Dybbling	bubblin	Dilluvia
durblin	Ebblin	Dupling	Nephilim
Dulby	Delville	oldbrawn	Ntamphlin
Drooplin	Deblance	Durblana	Luvillicit
Doublin	Doveland	Debbling	Aud Dub
Dyoublong	Evlyn	Dubs	Durban
Ublanium	Diablan	Dirt Dump	Deva
Dabblin	Liverpoor	duv	Delvin
Doublands	Doubloon	dapple inn	Londub
Devlin	Hublin	Analbe	d' of Linn
Poolblack	Dumbil	gambling	
Dublinos	Dubbeltye	dulvin	
Bullyclubber	Dullokbloon	Hurdlebury Fenn	Dablena Tertia
hundled furth	Athacleeath	Hurdlestown	baileycliaver
Poplinstown	Labbeycliath	double inns	Hurtleforth
Dellabelliney	Huddlesford	Fort Dunlip	Dyfflinsborg
Strathlyffe	Cleethabola	Hurtereford	elbiduubled
nill, Budd!	Eblanamagna	dub him Lynn	Arans Duhkha

Appendix IV
DUBLIN ARCHITECTS, 1680-1880

Burgh, Thomas
Royal Barracks (Collins'), 1701
St Mary's Church, 1702
Old Custom House, 1707
Infirmary of Royal Hospital, 1711
The Library, Trinity College, 1712
St Werburgh's Church, 1715
Dr Steeven's Hospital, 1720

Butler, William Deane
Amiens St (now Connolly) Railway Station, 1844

Byrne, Patrick
Adam & Eve's Church, Merchant's Quay, 1830
St Paul's Church, Arran Quay, 1835
St Audoen's R.C. Church, 1841
St James's R.C. Church, 1844
Our Lady of Refuge, Rathmines, 1850

Cassels, Richard
80 St Stephen's Green, 1730
9-10 Henrietta St, 1730
Powerscourt House, Co Wicklow, 1731
TCD: Printing House, 1734
Newbridge House, Donabate, (probably), 1737
Carton, Maynooth, 1739
Clanwilliam House (85 St Stephen's Green), 1739
Tyrone House, Marlborough Street, 1740
Music Hall, Fishamble Street, 1741
Leinster House, 1745
Rotunda Hospital, 1750

Chambers, William
Casino, Marino, 1758
Charlemont House (now Municiapl Gallery), 1762
TCD: Theatre, 1777
TCD: Chapel, 1779

Cooley, Thomas
City Hall (Royal Exchange), 1769
Hibernian Marine School, 1770
Chapel, St Mary's Hospital, (Phoenix Park).
   (Originally the Royal Hibernian
   Military School), 1771
Green Street Prison, 1773
Public Offices, Inns Quay, 1779. (These were
   incorporated into the Four Courts, with
   additions and subtractions, by James Gandon)

Deane & Woodward
TCD Museum Building, 1855
Dundrum Court House, 1855
Dundrum Schools, 1857
St Ann's Schools (Dawson Street), 1857
   (now demolished)
TCD Library Roof, 1858
St Stephen's Schools (Mount Street Bridge), 1859

Kildare Street Club, 1859
(Benjamin Woodward's partner, Sir Thomas
   Newenham Deane, was responsible for the new
   design of St Ann's Church on Dawson Street in
   1868.)

Deane, Sir Thomas Manley
National Library, 1883
National Museum, 1884

Ensor, John
Merrion Square Houses, 1762
Rotunda (now Ambassador Cinema), 1764
Gardiner's Row, 1765
Antrim House, 1778

Ensor, George
Rutland (now Parnell) Square Houses, 1750
St John's Church (now gone), 1766

Gandon, James
Custom House, 1781
Four Courts, 1785 (following Cooley)
Parliament Buildings (now Bank of Ireland): East
   Portico and House of Lords extensions, 1785
Army GHQ, 1786
Parliament Buildings (now Bank of Ireland): West
   Portico and House of Commons extensions, 1787
Carlisle Bridge, predecessor of
   O'Connell Bridge, 1791
Beresford Place Crescent, 1791
King's Inns, 1795

Ivory, Thomas
King's Hospital, 1773
Corporation Rates' Office (originally
   Newcomen's Bank), 1781

Jacobsen, Theodore
TCD: West Front, College Green, 1752 (despite
   statements to the contrary)

Johnston, Francis
St Andrew's Church (remodelling), 1793
Viceregal Lodge, Phoenix Park, 1801
St George's Church, 1802
Bank of Ireland Cash Office, 1803
Hardwicke Hospital, 1803
Chapel Royal, Dublin Castle, 1807
Nelson Pillar (with Wilkins), 1808
Richmond Hospital, 1811
Kilmainham Gate, (which originally straddled
   the quays at Watling Street), 1812
General Post Office, 1814
Grangegorman Mental Hospital (now
   St Brendan's), 1816
Whitworth Hospital, 1817

King's Inns (completed the work of Gandon), 1817

Johnston, Richard
Daly's Club, College Green, 1789
Gate Theatre (originally New Assembly Rooms), 1784

Keane, J. B.
Gardiner Street Church, 1832
Seville Place Church, 1844

McCarthy, J. J.
Chapel, All Hallows College, 1848. (Now replaced by Ashlin)
Star of the Sea Church, Sandymount, 1851
St Catherine's Church, Meath Street, 1852
Mount Argus, 1856
St Saviour's Church, Dominick St, 1858

Morrison, Sir Richard
Sir Patrick Dun's Hospital, 1808
Carton, Maynooth (after others), 1815
Pro-Cathedral (after Sweetman), 1816

Mulvany, John Skipton
Broadstone Railway Station, 1850
Royal Irish Yacht Club, 1851
Dún Laoghaire Railway Station, 1852

Papworth, George
Clarendon Street Church, 1793
Kingsbridge (bridge) 1808

Parke, Edward
Parliament Buildings, (Bank of Ireland) West Wing, 1790
Commercial Buildings, Dame Street, 1796
College of Surgeons, 1806

Pearce, Edward Lovett
Castletown House, Celbridge (with A. Galilei), 1722 (?)
Houses of Parliament (Bank of Ireland), 1729
9 Henrietta Street, 1730
State Apartments, Dublin Castle, 1730 (?) – his design used by Joseph Jarrat, 1746 (?)
Obelisk, Stillorgan, 1731
Drumcondra House (All Hallows), 1732
Aungier Street Theatre, 1733

Robinson, William
Royal Hospital, Kilmainham, 1680
Dublin Castle: part of Staqte Apartments, 1684
Marsh's Library, 1702
Hall of South Dublin Union, 1703 (?)

Semple, John
Round Room (The Mansion House), 1821
The Black Church, 1830
Protestant Churches at:
Whitechurch, 1825; Kilternan, 1826; Donnybrook, 1827; Tallaght, 1829; Monkstown, 1832; Rathmines, 1833.

Smyth, John
St Thomas's Church, Marlborough Street, 1758 (now demolished)
Poolbeg Lighthouse, 1768
St Catherine's Church, Thomas Street, 1769

Stapleton, Michael
Royal Irish Academy of Music, 1778
Dunsany Castle, 1780
Belvedere House (now College), 1785

Wood, Sancton
Kingsbridge (now Heuston) Railway Station, 1844

Appendix V — BRITISH MONARCHS

(Asterisks mark those who visited Ireland, with the dates of their visits given outside the brackets.)

*Henry II (1171-89) 1172
Richard I (Lionheart) (1189-99)
*John (1199-1216) 1185, 1210
Henry III (1216-72)
Edward I (1272-1307)
Edward II (1307-27)
Edward III (1327-77)
*Richard II (1377-99) 1394, 1399
Henry IV (1399-1413)
Henry V (1413-22)
Henry VI (1422-61)
Edward IV (1461-83)
Edward V (1483)
Richard III (1483-85)
Henry VII (1485-1509)
Henry VIII (1509-47)
Edward VI (1547-53)
Mary I (1553-58)
Elizabeth I (1558-1603)

James I (1603-25)
Charles I (1625-49)
(Cromwell)
Charles II (1660-85)
*James II (1685-88) 1689-90
*William III (1689-1702) 1690
Mary II (1689-94)
Anne (1702-14)
George I (1714-27)
George II (1727-60)
George III (1760-1820)
*George IV (1820-30) 1821
William IV (1830-37)
*Victoria (1837-1901) 1849, 1853, 1861, 1900
*Edward VII (1901-1910), 1903, 1904, 1907
*George V (1910-1936) 1911
Edward VIII (Jan-Dec 1936)
George VI (1936-1952)
(Éire left the Commonwealth in 1949)

Appendix VI — EASTER RISING, 1916

LIST OF THE DUBLIN BUILDINGS OCCUPIED BY THE IRISH VOLUNTEERS, IRISH CITIZEN ARMY, IRB, ETC.

Blanchardstown Mills, North King Street
Boland's Bakery, Grand Canal Street
Boland's Mills, Grand Canal Street
Bridewell Police Station, Chancery Street
Carrisbrooke House, Northumberland Road
Church of Ireland Synod Hall, Christ Church Place
City Hall
Clanwilliam House, Lr Mount Street
College of Surgeons, St Stephen's Green
Colmcille Hall, Blackhall Place
Davy's Pub, Portobello
Delahunt's Pub, Camden Street
Dublin Bread Company, O'Connell Street
Evening Mail Offices, Lord Edward Street
Father Mathew Hall, Church Street
Four Courts
Gas Works, Macken Street
GPO
Harcourt Street Railway Station
Henry & James Ltd, Parliament Street
Hopkins & Hopkins Ltd, O'Connell Street
Imperial Hotel, O'Connell Street
Jacob's Factory, Bishop Street
Kapp & Peterson Ltd, O'Connell Street

Liberty Hall
Little's Pub, Cuffe Street
Linenhall Barracks, Lisburn Street
Louth Dairy, North King Street
Marrowbone Lane Distillery
Mendicity Institute, Usher's Island
Metropole Hotel, Abbey Street
Monks's Bakery, North King Street
Moore Street, No 16
Northumberland Road, No 25
Parochial Schools, Mount Street Bridge
Railway Works, South Lotts Road
Reilly's Pub, North King Street
Reis & Co, O'Connell Street
Roe's Distillery, James's Street
St Stephen's Parochial Hall, Northumberland Road
Ship Tavern, Abbey Street
South Dublin Union, James's Street
Thom & Co, Cork Street
Turkish Baths, St Stephen's Green
Watkins' Brewery, Ardee Street
Westland Row Railway Station
Williams & Woods Ltd, Parnell Street

Appendix VII — IRISH PRESIDENTS

Douglas Hyde (1938-45)
Seán T. O'Kelly (1945-59)
Éamon de Valera (1959-73)

Erskine Childers (1973-74)
Cearbhall Ó Dálaigh (1974-76)
Patrick Hillery (1976-   )

Appendix VIII — POPULATION OF DUBLIN

Nobody really knows the population of Dublin in its earliest days. Even the first four figures given below are "educated guesses".

A glance at the other numbers on this page shows that there were two major declines in the city's population. Between 1300 and 1400, thousands died of the 'Black Death' and other plagues; between 1650 and 1660, the Cromwellian Wars took a severe toll.

The figures here *exclude* the coastal Borough of Dún Laoghaire. The so-called 'Greater Dublin Area' now (1987) has a population of over one million people.

Year	Population	Year	Population	Year	Population	Year	Population	Year	Population
1000	2,500	1500	12,000	1750	150,000	1920	360,000	1970	560,000
1100	8,000	1600	18,000	1800	172,000	1930	410,000	1980	600,000
1200	10,000	1650	24,000	1850	250,000	1940	450,000		
1300	12,000	1660	9,000	1900	280,000	1950	500,000		
1400	8,000	1700	40,000	1910	300,000	1960	510,000		

Appendix IX
LIST OF THE CHIEF GOVERNORS OF IRELAND — 1660-1922

The complete list of the chief governors from the time of the Norman Conquest to 1922 is given in several histories and directories. The following list, which makes no distinction between Lords Deputy and Lords Lieutenant, is given as an aid to dating Dublin buildings and street-names.

1660 George Monck, Duke of Albemarle
     (Never came over)
     John Robartes, Baron Robartes
     (Never came over)
1662 James Butler, Duke of Ormonde
1664 Thomas Butler, Earl of Ossory
1669 John Robartes, Baron Robartes
1670 John Berkeley, Lord Berkeley
1672 Arthur Capel, Earl of Essex
1677 James Butler, Duke of Ormonde
1682 Richard Butler, Earl of Arran
1685 Henry Hyde, Earl of Clarendon
     Richard Talbot, Earl of Tyrconnell
1689 King James II in person
1690 King William III in person
1692 Henry Sidney, Viscount Sidney
1695 Henry Capel, Earl of Essex
1702 Laurence Hyde, Earl of Rochester
1702 James Butler, Duke of Ormond
1707 Thomas Herbert, Earl of Pembroke
1709 Thomas Wharton, Earl of Wharton
1710 James Butler, Duke of Ormonde
1713 Charles Talbot, Duke of Shrewsbury
1714 Charles Spencer, Earl of Sunderland
     (Never came over)
1716 Charles Townshend, Viscount Townshend
     (Never came over)
1717 Charles Townshend, Duke of Bolton
1721 Charles Fitzroy, Duke of Grafton
1724 John Carteret, Lord Carteret
1731 Lionel Sackville, Duke of Dorset
1737 William Cavendish, Duke of Devonshire
1745 Philip Stanhope, Earl of Chesterfield
1747 William Stanhope, Earl of Harrington
1751 Lionel Sackville, Duke of Dorset
1755 William Cavendish, Marquis of Hartington
1757 John Russell, Duke of Bedford
1761 George Dunk, Earl of Halifax
1763 Hugh Percy, Earl of Northumberland
1765 Thomas Thynne, Viscount Weymouth
     (Never came over)
     Francis Seymour, Earl of Hertford
1766 George William Hervey, Earl of Bristol
     (Never came over)
1767 George Townshend, Viscount Townshend
1772 Simon Harcourt, Earl Harcourt
1777 John Hobart, Earl of Buckinghamshire
1780 Frederick Howard, Earl of Carlisle
1782 William Bentinck, Duke of Portland
     George Grenville, Earl Temple
1783 Robert Henley, Earl of Northington
1784 Charles Manners, Duke of Rutland

1787 George Grenville, later Marquis of
     Buckingham
1790 John Fane, Earl of Westmoreland
1794 William Wentworth, Earl Fitzwilliam
1795 John Pratt, Earl Camden
1798 Charles Cornwallis, Marquis Cornwallis
1801 Philip Yorke, Earl of Hardwicke
1805 Edward Powis, Earl Powis
     (Never came over)
1806 John Russell, Duke of Bedford
1807 Charles Lennox, Duke of Richmond
1813 Charles Whitworth, Viscount and
     Earl Whitworth
1818 Charles Chetwynd, Earl Talbot
1821 Richard Wellesley, Marquis Wellesley
1828 William Paget, Marquis of Anglesea
1829 Hugh Percy, Duke of Northumberland
1830 William Paget, Marquis of Anglesea
1833 Richard Wellesley, Marquis Wellesley
1834 Thomas Hamilton, Earl of Haddington
1835 Henry Constantine, Earl of Mulgrave
1839 Hugh Fortesque, Viscount Ebrington,
1841 Thomas Philip, Earl de Grey
1844 William A'Court, Baron Heytesbury
1846 John Ponsonby, Earl of Bessborough
1847 George Villiers, Earl of Clarendon
1852 Archibald Montgomerie, Earl of Eglinton
1853 Edward Granville Eliot, Earl of St Germans
1855 Frederick Howard, Earl of Carlisle
1858 Arthur William, Earl of Eglinton and
     Winton
1859 Frederick Howard, Earl of Carlisle
1864 John Wodehouse, Baron Wodehouse
1866 James Hamilton, Marquis of Abercorn
1868 John Poyntz, Earl Spencer
1874 James Hamilton, Duke of Abercorn
1876 John Churchill, Duke of Marlborough
1880 Francis de Grey, Earl Cowper
1882 John Poyntz, Earl Spencer
1885 Henry Molyneux, Earl of Carnarvon
1886 John Gordon, Earl of Aberdeen
     Charles Stewart, Marquis of Londonderry
     Laurence Dundas, Marquis of Zetland
1892 Robert Milnes, Lord Houghton, afterwards
     Earl of Crewe
1895 George Henry Cadogan, Earl Cadogan
1902 William Humble Ward, Earl of Dudley
1905 John Gordan, Earl of Aberdeen
1915 Ivor Guest, Baron Wimborne
1918 John French, Viscount French
1921 Edmund Talbot, Viscount FitzAlan

Appendix X
STREET-NAME CHANGES

It would be virtually impossible (and it would serve no particularly useful purpose) to give a complete list of all the Dublin streets whose names have been changed over the years. This list gives a sample of some changes that were made for different reasons: to commemorate patriots, to remove improprieties, etc.

Amiens Street was The Strand
Ardee Street was Crooked Staff
Aughrim Street was part of Blackhorse Lane
Back Lane was Rochel Street
Balfe Street was Pitt Street
Belmont Avenue was Coldblow Lane
Benburb Street was Barrack Street
Bishop Street was Great Boater Lane
Blackhall Place was The Gravel Walk
Bow Lane was Elbow Lane
Bow Street was Lough Buoy
Brabazon Street was Cuckold's Row
Bridgefoot Street was Dirty Lane
Brookfield Avenue was Watery Lane
Brookfield Road was Cutthroat Lane
Camden Street was St Kevin's Port
Cathal Brugha Street was Gregg Lane
Cathedral Lane was Cabbage Garden Lane
Chancery Place was Mass Lane
Christchurch Place was Skinners' Row
Clonliffe Road was Fortick Road
College Green was Hoggen Green
Constitution Hill was Glasmanogue
Dame Street was Tengmouth Street
Dean Street was Cross Poddle
Digges Lane was Goat Alley
Dorset Street was Drumcondra Lane
Engine Alley was Indian Alley
Essex Street West was Orange Street and,
  earlier, Smock Alley
Exchange Street Lower was The Blind Quay
Exchequer Street was Chequer Street
Foley Street was Montgomery Street and,
  earlier, World's End Lane
Glover's Alley was Rapparee Alley
Green Street was Abbey Green
Haddington Road was Cottage Terrace
Hammond Lane was Hangman's Lane
Harrington Street was Whitworth Street
High Street was Main Street
Hill Street was Lower Temple Street
Infirmary Road was Aberdeen Street
Island Street was Dunghill Lane
Lansdowne Road was Watery Lane
Lincoln Lane was Pudding Lane

Lincoln Place was Park Street and, earlier,
  St Patrick's Well Lane
Little Green Street was Bradogue Lane
Little Ship Street was Pole Mill Street
Lower Baggot Street was Gallows Road
Lower Gardiner Street was The Old Rope Walk
Mary's Lane was Broad Street
Mercer Street was French Street
Mespil Road was Gibbet Meadow
North Brunswick Street was Channel Row
North Lotts was Newfoundland
O'Connell Street was Sackville Street. Earlier,
  Upper O'Connell Street was Drogheda Street
Old Kilmainham was Murdering Lane
Oliver Bond Street was Mullinahack
Parnell Square was Rutland Square
Parnell Street was Great Britain Street
Pearse Street was Great Brunswick Street
Pimlico was Donour Street
Prussia Street was Cabragh Lane
Railway Street was Upper Tyrone Street and,
  earlier, a part of Mecklenburgh Street (see
  Waterford Street)
Sackville Place was Tucker's Row
Sean McDermott Street was Gloucester Street and,
  earlier, Great Martin's Lane
Shelbourne Road was Artichoke Road
St Andrew's Street was Hog Hill and, earlier,
  Hoggen Hill
St Michael's Lane was Macgillamocholmog's
  Street
St Stephen's Green North was Beaux Walk
St Stephen's Green South was Leeson's Walk
St Stephen's Green East was Monks's Walk
St Stephen's Green West was French Walk
Talbot Street was Cope Street North
Townsend Street was Lazy Hill and, earlier,
  Lazar's Hill
Usher's Lane was Dog & Duck Yard
Waterford Street was Lower Tyrone Street
  and, earlier, part of Mecklenburgh Street
  (see, Railway Street)
Wellington Street was Paradise Row
Wolfe Tone Street was Stafford Street

Appendix XI
DUBLIN'S OLDEST BUSINESS CONCERNS

The following list is intended only as a starting point and is not complete. It has been mainly compiled from a comparison of companies listed in *The Industries of Dublin* (published by Spencer Blackett in London, c. 1886) with the current *Thom's Directory*. The firms listed are, in some shape or form, at least one hundred years old (1988). Any omissions are regretted. The author will be glad if these are brought to his attention for inclusion in the next edition.

Arnott & Co, Drapers, Department Store
Barnardo & Co, Furriers
Bewley's Cafés
Brown Thomas & Co, Department Store
Browne & Nolan, Printers
Buswell's Hotel
G & T Crampton Ltd, Builders
Dockrell & Co, Builders Providers
Dollard Printinghouse
Dunns Ltd, Fish and Poultry Merchants
Eason & Son, Booksellers
Gaiety Theatre
Ganly & Co, Auctioneers
M H Gill & Son, Publishers
Goulding Ltd, Fertilizer Manufacturers
Guinness & Co, Brewers
Hafners Ltd, Pork Butchers
Hayes & Co, Chemists
Hely & Co, Stationers
The Irish Times Ltd, Newspapers
Jacob & Co, Biscuit Manufacturers
Jameson & Co, Jewellers

Kapp & Peterson, Tobacconists & Pipe Manufacturers
Kennedy & Co, Art Suppliers
Lafayette Ltd, Photographers
McDowell Bros, Jewellers
Mackey & Co, Seedsmen
John McNeill, Musicasl Instruments
Moran's Hotel
Mulvany Bros, Art Suppliers
Ormond Hotel,
Phoenix Assurance Co, Insurance Agents
Pigott & Co, Musical Instruments
Prescott & Co, Cleaners
John G Rathborne Ltd, Candle Manufacturers
E & W Seale, Shirtmakers
Stokes Bros, Accountants
Varian & Co, Brush Manufacturers
Wallace Ltd, Coal and Fuel Merchants
West & Son, Jewellers
Wynn's Hotel
Yeates & Son, Optician
Williams & Woods Ltd, Manufacturing Confectioners

APPENDIX XII
THIRD-LEVEL EDUCATION
(Seminaries & Religious Houses Excluded)

1320   **St Patrick's University** established by Archbishop Alexander de Bicknor with the approval of Pope John XXII. It gradually faded out due to lack of funds.

1475   **St Patrick's University** re-established by Bull of Pope Sixtus IV. Abolished by decree of Henry VIII in 1539. Unsuccessful attempts were made to revive it in 1568 and 1585.

1592   **Trinity College** founded by Queen Elizabeth I on the site of the old monastery of All Hallows. Its charter is dated 3rd March, 1592 and the foundation-stone was laid on 13th March of that year.

1667   **College of Physicians** granted charter by Charles II. New charter granted by William and Mary in 1692. Another new charter in 1890, granted by Victoria, makes it the Royal College of Physicians of Ireland.

1749   **Dublin Drawing Schools** taken over by the Dublin Society. Renamed as the Dublin Metropolitan School of Art in 1877, this became the National College of Art in 1936. Now located in the former premises of Power's distillery off Thomas Street, it is called the **National College of Art and Design**.

1784   **Royal College of Surgeons** founded. Having been based for some time at Mercer's Hospital and at Carmichael House, Aungier Street, it moved into its present premises on St Stephen's Green in 1810.

1795   **Royal College of St Patrick, Maynooth** founded. Affiliated to the Catholic University in 1854, it is now a recognised College of the National University of Ireland.

1800   **King's Inns** opened for the study of law. Gandon's design of 1795 was completed by Baker and extended by Francis Johnston in 1817.

1838   **Albert College** established in Glasnevin. Originally the Agricultural Model School, it eventually became part of the agricultural faculty of UCD. Taken over by the NIHE in 1980.

1843   **Incorporated Law Society** begins to hold classes. Moved into the former King's Hospital, Blackhall Place, in 1979.

1848   **Royal Irish Academy of Music** founded on Westland Row.

1854   **Catholic University** established by Catholic hierarchy at 85-86 St Stephen's Green. Cardinal Newman its first Rector. Its Medical School was on Cecilia Street.

1867   **Royal College of Science** founded as an off-shoot of Royal Dublin Society and as a development of the Museum of Irish Industry which had been founded in 1845.

1875   **St Patrick's Teacher Training College** founded on Drumcondra Road (facing down Clonliffe Road). Moved to its present location in 1883.

1877   **Carysfort Teacher Training College** founded in Baggot Street. Moved to Blackrock in 1884. Closure announced by Government, 1986. Its future uncertain at present.

1878   **Church of Ireland Training College** founded in Kildare Place. Now in Rathmines.

1881   **Royal University of Ireland** founded as examining and degree-granting body.

1882   **University College Dublin** (as the Catholic University has begun to be called) sends students for examinations and degrees to Royal University. The administration was handed over to the Jesuits in 1883: they ran it for twenty-five years.

1887   **Kevin Street College of Technology** begins life as a technical school.

1892   **College of Music** founded. Premises now in Chatham Street.

1904   **St Mary's College of Education** established in Marino. A teacher-training college for Christian Brothers until 1968 when laymen were admitted. Women students were admitted in 1975 when its association with Trinity College was formalized.

1905   **College of Commerce** founded in Rathmines. Originally a vocational school, it now has Schools of Business and Allied Studies, Management Studies and Professional Studies.

1908   **National University of Ireland** established. This replaces the Royal University of 1880. University Colleges in Dublin, Cork and Galway become constituent colleges; St Patrick's College, Maynooth, becomes a recognised college of the new university.

1908   **College of Marketing and Design**, now in Parnell Square, was formerly known as the School of Retail Distribution.

1911   **Bolton Street College of Technology** begins life as a technical school.

1929   **St Catherine's College of Education**, Sion Hill, opens. Originally specialized in Home Economics.

1933   **Montessori College**, Sion Hill, founded.

1936   **Froebel College**, Sion Hill, founded. Now associated with Trinity College.

1940   **Dublin Institute for Advanced Studies** founded. It now includes Dunsink Observatory which was founed in 1782.

1941   **Dublin College of Catering** established on Cathal Brugha Street.

1949   **College of Industrial Relations** holds its first classes in 35 Lower Leeson Street under the name of the Catholic Workers' College. Moved to its present location in Ranelagh in 1951.

1966   **Mater Dei Institute of Education** founded, Clonliffe Road.

1968   **Higher Education Authority** established.
       Milltown Institute for Theology and Philosophy founded at Milltown Park, formerly a Jesuit theologate.

1970   **St Nicholas Montessori College**, Dún Laoghaire, established by the Montessori Society. The College offered a three-year evening course from 1972 and started a two-year full-time course in 1984.
       Irish School of Ecumenics established at Milltown Park. Now associated with Trinity College, it has premises on Pembroke Park.

1972   **National Council for Education Awards** established. It became a statutory body in 1980.

1978   **Dublin Institute of Technology** founded. It embraces the Colleges of Technology on Bolton Street and Kevin Street, the College of Commerce, the College of Music, the College of Marketing and Design and the Dublin College of Catering.

1980   **National Institute for Higher Education** founded in Glasnevin on site of Albert College (see 1838).

APPENDIX XIII
DUBLIN HOSPITALS

Dublin's first hospital, St John's was established by Ailred the Palmer on Thomas Street, opposite the Augustinian Church, in 1180. (Ailred also owned land in Palmerstown). In 1188, Pope Clement III, assumed jurisdiction over the foundation: this was Dublin's first 'liberty' – the Liberty of Ailred. In 1260 the hospital was taken over by the Cruciferi, Augustinian hospitallers who wore a red cross over their red robes. The foundation was suppressed by Henry VIII in 1539.

Towards the end of the 12th century, the leper hospital of St Stephen was opened near St Stephen's Green. The site was occupied by Mercer's Hospital from 1734 to 1986. Early in the 13th century another leper asylum was founded on Lazars' (i.e. Lepers') Hill, now Townsend Street.

Other hospitals were attached to the many Dublin monasteries (qv). These were all suppressed at the time of the Reformation.

In 1593, George Carew opened a hospital 'for poor, sick and maimed soldiers' opposite the newly-established Trinity College, on the site of the present Bank of Ireland. This building was taken over by Viceroy Chichester (1604-15). It was not until 1680 that another military hospital was built in Kilmainham.

The establishment of a workhouse for the relief of the poor was first considered by the Corporation of Dublin in 1688. Due to the Williamite Wars, it was not until 1702 that 'a donation and grant of the walled grounds at the South West end of James's Street and fourteen acres adjoining' was made by the Corporation of Dublin. In 1727 a foundling hospital was attached to this workhouse. It became, in turn, the South Dublin Union, St Kevin's Hospital and St James's Hospital.

In 1772, on the initiative of the Protestant Bishop of Cloyne, Dr Richard Woodward, the Government passed an Act providing for the opening of 'Houses of Industry' in twenty-three different counties. The Dublin House of Industry was founded in the following year and led to the building of three hospitals (the Hardwicke, the Richmond and the Whitworth) named after the Viceroys who held office at the time of their construction. These now form St Laurence's Hospital (see 1803 1811, 1817).

Before these state hospitals opened, many doctors and concerned citizens had responded to the needs of the city. The following list gives the hospital dates in chronological order:

1680 **Royal Hospital**, Kilmainham. Designed by William Robinson for retired or wounded soldiers. Often (wrongly) said to have been designed by Christopher Wren. It pre-dates the Chelsea Hospital in London although it is often said to be modelled on it.

1718 **Charitable Infirmary**. Founded in Cook Street, by Doctors George Duany, Patrick Kelly, Nathaniel Handson, John Dowdall, Francis Duany, Peter Brennan. It moved to Inns Quay in 1728 and to **Jervis Street** in 1796.

1720 **Dr Steeven's Hospital** founded with money left by the Dublin doctor to his sister, Grizel. Formally opened in 1733. Designed by Thomas Burgh. Closure announced, 1987.

1727 **Foundling Hospital**, James's Street, opened in conjunction with the workhouse which was founded in 1702. Governors included Jonathan Swift, Arthur Guinness and Henry Grattan. Suppressed in 1830 by Government Order. (Several Courts of Inquiry had tried to discover why 41,524 of the 52,150 babies admitted between June 1796 and January 1826 had died). Premises then became the South Dublin Union (occupied by Eamonn Ceannt and Volunteers 1916). In 1922 it became a hospital proper (St Kevin's) and in 1971 the name was changed to **St James's**.

1734 **Mercer's Hospital**, founded by Mrs Mary Mercer on the site of the early thirteenth-century St Stephen's Leper Asylum. Closed 1986.

1743 **Hospital for Incurables**, Lazar's Hill. Started in Fleet Street, moved to Townsend Street in 1753 (under name of St Margaret of Cortona). Exchanged with Donnybrook Lock Hospital in 1792. Now called **Royal Hospital**.

1745 **St Patrick's Hospital**. Founded by bequest of Dean Swift. Formally opened in 1757. **Lying-in Hospital** opened in George's Lane (now South Great George's Street) by Dr Bartholomew Mosse. Although he established 'the Rotunda' in 1750, this hospital did not close till 1757.

1750 **Rotunda Hospital**. Originally called the Lying-in Hospital when Dr Mosse had it built as the first maternity hospital in the world. Designed by Richard Cassels (who for economy used his design for Leinster House and added a cupola). The Rotunda Hall (John Ensor) was added in 1764 for fund-raising activities (now the Ambassador Cinema). The New Assembly Rooms (Richard Johnston) were added for same purposes in 1784 (now the Gate Theatre). Thomas Plunkett Cairnes Wing added in 1895 through donation from the Drogheda brewer.

1753 **Meath Hospital** founded by Drs Alexander Cunningham, Redmond Boate, David McBride and Henry Hawkshaw, Surgeons of the Charitable Surgery in Spring Gardens, Dame Street. Originally on the Coombe, in 1774 it became 'the Meath Hospital & County Infirmary'. Moved to its present site, 'The Dean's Vineyard', in 1822. Genito-urinary unit opened in 1955. World-famous staff members included John Cheyne, Whitley and William Stokes, R J Graves, Richard Joynt and T J D Lane. **St Nicholas's Hospital**, Francis Street, opens.

1786 **Military Infirmary** , designed by James Gandon on Infirmary Road. Now GHQ of Irish Army. The Infirmary was moved across the road in 1896. Now known as **St Bricin's Hospital.**

1788 **Sir Patrick Dun's Hospital**, founded under the will of Sir Patrick Dun, a Scottish doctor who practised in Dublin. Started in what is now the presbytery of SS Michael & John's Church, off Essex Quay. Moved to Grand Canal Street in 1808 to a fine building by Sir Richard Morrison. Closed 1986.

1791 **Simpson's Hospital**, founded 'for reduced gentlemen, suffering from failing eyesight, gout or both'. Stood on Great Britain Street (now Parnell Street), facing down Jervis Street; moved to Dundrum in 1925.

1792 **Royal Hospital**, Donnybrook (see 1743).

1796 **Jervis Street Hospital** (see 1718). Rebuilt, 1877.

1803 **Hardwicke Hospital**. (Now part of St Laurence's).

1804 **Cork Street Fever Hospital**. **Cowpock Institution** (North Cope Street). Vaccinations against smallpox given in Dublin for the first time.

1810 **Bloomfield Hospital**, Donnybrook. Founded by Quakers in home of Robert Emmet's mother. It now caters for geriatrics. **Richmond National Institution for the Blind**.

1811 **Richmond Hospital** (Now part of St Laurence's).

1816 **Grangegorman Mental Hospital**. (Now **St Brendan's**). Originally called the Richmond Lunatic Asylum.

1817 **Whitworth Hospital**. (Now part of St Laurence's).

1821 **Institute for Sick Children**, Pitt Street. Became National Children's Hospital (Harcourt Street) in 1887.

1826 **Coombe Lying-in Hospital**. Founded by Mrs Margaret Boyle in premises of old 'Meath'. Moved to Dolphin's Barn Street in 1967. The old entrance is preserved on the Coombe (see 1753).

1832 **Royal City of Dublin Hospital**, Baggot Street. Enlarged 1895.

1834	**St Vincent's Hospital**, St Stephen's Green. Moved to Elm Park in 1970.
1837	**Monkstown Hospital**. Closed 1987.
1839	**Adelaide Hospital**, Bride Street. Closed in 1847. Re-opened in Peter Street, 1858.
1851	**Central Mental Hospital**, Dundrum. Originally known as the Criminal Lunatic Asylum.
1858	**St Mary's**. Home for adult blind and partially-sighted children, Merrion Road. Originally known as the Blind Asylum.
1861	**Mater Misericordiae Hospital**. Foundation-stone laid, 1852.
1861	**Bons Secours**, Glasnevin. In grounds of Delville, the home of Swift's friends, Dr and Mrs Delany, which had been built in 1722. The present building was erected in 1951.
1867	**Children's Hospital**, Buckingham Street. Moved to Temple Street in 1872.
1869	**Stewart's Hospital**, Palmerstown.
1876	**Orthopaedic Hospital**, founded by Dr Lafayette on Usher's Island. Moved (via Brunswick Street) to Merrion Square in 1902, and to its present location in Clontarf in 1941.
1879	**Hospice for the Dying**, now **Our Lady's Hospice**, Harold's Cross. Took over from the school established there (in Greenmount) by Mother Mary Aikenhead.
1879	**Dental Hospital of Ireland**, at 29 York Street. Dental School added in 1884. Moved to present site on Lincoln Place in 1895. Became Incorporated Dental Hospital 1899 and Dublin Dental Hospital in 1963.
1882	**St John of God** (Psychiatric) Hospital, Stillorgan.
1883	**Holles Street: South Dublin Lying-in Hospital**. Closed briefly but re-opened thanks to donation from RC Archbishop of Dublin in 1894. Received Royal Charter in 1903, and became the **National Maternity Hospital**. The Nurses' Home was formerly Antrim House, the town-house of Lord Antrim.
1887	**Harcourt Street Children's Hospital** (see 1821).
1897	**Royal Victoria Eye & Ear Hospital**. An amalgamation of the National Eye & Ear Infirmary, Molesworth Street, and St Mark's Ophthalmic & Aural Hospital, Lincoln Place (1844). Dr Wilde worked at St Mark's (which was the part of the Dental Hospital building called O'Hara's).
1899	**St Anne's Hospital**. Began in Beresford Place, moved to Pearse Street in 1904, to Holles Street in 1911, and finally to Northbrook Road in 1926.
1903	**St Ita's**, Portrane. Mental Hospital attached to St Brendan's.
1908	**St Mary's Orthopaedic Hospital**, Cappagh.
1911	**City of Dublin Skin & Cancer Hospital**, Hume Street. Established by Royal Charter.
1917	**Leopardstown Park Hospital**. For military veterans.
1919	**St Ultan's Infants' Hospital**, Charlemont Street. In 1987 this became a modern Private Clinic.
1922	**Garda Síochána Hospital**. In the Depot, Phoenix Park (18 beds).
1938	**Vergemount Hospital**, Clonskeagh. Originally a fever hospital, it began to cater for psychiatric patients in 1969 and for geriatrics in 1979.
1943	**St Joseph's Hospital**, Clonsilla.
1948	**St Mary's Hospital**, Phoenix Park. Originally a chest hospital, it became a geriatric hospital in 1962. (Built in 1766 as Royal Hibernian Military School).
1950	**St Loman's**, Palmerstown. Was a sanatorium till 1961.
1951	**St Gabriel's**, Cabinteely.
1952	**St Luke's**, Cancer Hospital, Terenure.
1952	**St Colmcille's Hospital**, Loughlinstown. Built as a Workhouse in 1841.
1953	**Cherry Orchard Hospital**, Ballyfermot.
1954	**St Mary's Orthopaedic Hospital**, Baldoyle.
1956	**Our Lady's Hospital for Sick Children**, Crumlin.

1956   **St Anthony's Hospital**, Herbert Avenue. Foundation stone laid, 1953.
1958   **Mount Carmel Hospital**, Braemor Park.
1958   **James Connolly Memorial Hospital**, Blanchardstown.
1958   **St Joseph's Hospital**, Raheny.
1966   **St Paul's Hospital**, Beaumont.
1967   **Coombe Hospital** (see 1826).
1970   **St Vincent's Hospital**, Elm Park (see 1834).
1971   **St James's Hospital** takes over from St Kevin's. Now the largest hospital in Ireland (see 1727).
1982   **Cheeverstown Hospital**, Templeogue. Replaces an old Convalescent Home.
1985   **Blackrock Clinic**, Merrion Road.
1986   **Mater Hospital**: New 'private' hospital opens, Eccles Street.
1987   **Beaumont Hospital**: due to open as we go to press.

BIBLIOGRAPHY

Andrews, C S. *Dublin Made Me*. Dublin & Cork: Mercier Press, 1979.

—*Man of No Property*. Dublin & Cork: Mercier Press, 1982.

Anon. *New City Pictorial Directory, 1850*. Dublin: Henry Shaw, 1850.

—*The Industries of Dublin*. London: Spencer Blackett, 1882.

Ball, F Elrington. *A History of County Dublin*. Dublin: Alex Thom & Co, 1906.

—*An Historical Sketch of the Pembroke Township*. Dublin: Alex Thom & Co., 1907.

Ballagh, Robert. *Dublin*. Dublin: Ward River Press, 1981.

Beckett, J C. *The Making of Modern Ireland*. London: Faber & Faber, 1966.

Bence-Jones, Mark. *Burke's Guide to Country Houses: Vol I: Ireland*. London: Burke's Peerage Ltd., 1978.

Bennison, George & Wright, Alan. *The Geological History of the British Isles*. London: Edward Arnold, 1969.

Bernard, J H. *The Cathedral Church of St Patrick*. Dublin: Talbot Press, 1940.

Bibby, Geoffrey. *Four Thousand Years Ago*. London: Collins, 1962.

Bieler, Ludwig. *Ireland – Harbinger of the Middle Ages*. Oxford: University Press, 1963.

Bolger, William & Share, Bernard. *And Nelson on his Pillar*. Dublin: Nonpareil, 1976.

Bottigheimer, Karl S. *Ireland and the Irish*. New York: Columbia University Press, 1982.

Boylan, Henry. *This Arrogant City: A Readers' and Collectors' Guide to Books about Dublin*. Dublin: A and A Farmer, 1983.

—*A Dictionary of Irish Biography*. Dublin: Gill & Macmillan, 1978.

Bradley, Bruce. *James Joyce's Schooldays*. Dublin: Gill & Macmillan, 1982.

Bradley, John (ed). *Viking Dublin Exposed*. Dublin: O'Brien Press, 1984.

Brady, Ciaran & Gillespie, Raymond (eds). *Natives and Newcomers: The Making of Irish Colonial Society 1534-1641*. Dublin: Irish Academic Press, 1986.

British Association. *Handbook to the Dublin District*. Dublin: Ponsonby & Gibbs, 1908.

Broad, Ian & Rosney, Bride. *Medieval Dublin: Two Historic Walks*. Dublin: O'Brien Press, 1982.

Brønsted, Johannes. *The Vikings*. (Translated by Estrid Bannister-Good). Harmondsworth: Penguin Books, 1960.

Brynn, Edward. *Crown & Castle: British Rule in Ireland 1800-1830*. Dublin: O'Brien Press, 1978.

Burke, Nuala. *Dublin's Wood Quay*. Navan: Civic Heritage Publications, 1977.

Burton, N J. *Letters from Harold's Cross, 1850*. Dublin: Carraig Books, 1979.

Byrne, Matthew. *Dublin and her People*. Dublin: Eason's, 1987.

Byrne, Patrick. *The Wildes of Merrion Square*. London: Staples Press, 1953.

—*Lord Edward FitzGerald*. Dublin: The Talbot Press, 1955.

Cahill, Susan and Thomas. *A Literary Guide to Ireland*. Dublin: Wolfhound Press, 1979.

Cairnduff, Maureen. *Who's Who in Ireland: 'the influential 1,000'*. Dún Laoghaire: Vesey Publications, 1984.

Caprani, Vincent. *A View from the DART*. Dublin: MO Books, 1986.

Charlesworth, J K. *Historical Geology of Ireland*. London: Oliver & Bond, 1963.

—*The Geology of Ireland: an Introduction*. London: Oliver & Bond, 1966.

Chart, D A. *Dublin*. London: J M Dent & Co., 1907.

Clarke, Austin. *Twice Round the Black Church: Early Memories of England and Ireland*. London: Routledge & Kegan Paul, 1962.

Clarke, Desmond. *Dublin*. London: Batsford Books, 1977.

Clarke, Howard B. *Dublin c.840-c.1540: The Medieval Town in the Modern City*. Map prepared for the Friends of Medieval Dublin. Dublin: Ordnance Survey, 1978.

Collins, James. *Life in Old Dublin*. Dublin: James Duffy & Co, 1913.

Comerford, R V. *The Fenians in Context*. Dublin: Wolfhound Press, 1985.

Conlin, Stephen. *Dublin: One Thousand Years of Wood Quay*. Belfast: Blackstaff Press, 1984.

—*Historic Dublin*. Dublin: O'Brien Press, 1986.

Connellan, Owen. *The Annals of Ireland translated from the Original Irish of the Four Masters*. Dublin: Bryan Geraghty, 1846.

Coogan, Tim Pat (ed). *Ireland and the Arts*. London: Namara Press, 1985.

Corcoran, T. *State Policy in Irish Education 1536-1816*. Dublin: Fallon Brothers, 1916.

Corish, Patrick J (ed). *A History of Irish Catholicism*. Dublin: M H Gill & Son, 1967.

Corkery, Tom. *Tom Corkery's Dublin*. Dublin: Anvil Press, 1980.

Cosgrave, Art. *Late Medieval Ireland*. Dublin: Helicon Ltd, 1981.

Cosgrave, Dillon. *North Dublin: City and Environs*. Dublin: C T S, 1909.

Cosgrave, E Mac Dowel & Strangways, Leonard R. *The Illustrated Dictionary of Dublin*. Dublin: Sealy, Bryers & Walker, 1895.

Cowell, John. *Where they lived in Dublin*. Dublin: O'Brien Press, 1980.

Craig, Maurice. *Dublin 1660-1860*. London: The Cresset Press, 1952, Reprinted, Dublin: Allen Figgis, 1980.

—*Architecture in Ireland*. Dublin: Dept of Foreign Affairs, 1978.

—*The Architecture of Ireland from the Earliest Times to 1880*. London: Batsford Books, 1982 & Dublin: Eason's, 1982.

Craig, Maurice & the Knight of Glin. *Ireland Observed: a Handbook to the Buildings and Antiquities*. Cork & Dublin: Mercier Press, 1980.

Cronin, Anthony. *Dead as Doornails*. Dublin: Dolmen Press, 1976.

Cronin, Sean. *Irish Nationalism: A History of its Roots and Ideology*. Dublin: The Academy Press, 1980.

Crosbie, Paddy. *Your Dinner's Poured Out*. Dublin: O'Brien Press, 1981.

Cullen, L M. *Princes & Pirates: The Dublin Chamber of Commerce 1783-1983*. Dublin: Chamber of Commerce, 1983.

Culliton, James. *The City Hall*. Dublin: Eason's, 1982.

Cunliffe, Barry. *The Celtic World*. London: The Bodley Head, 1979.

Curran, C P. *Dublin Decorative Plasterwork of the Seventeenth and Eighteenth Century*. London: Alec Tiranti, 1967.
—*Under the Receding Wave*. Dublin: Gill & Macmillan, 1970.

Curriculum Development Unit. *Viking Settlement to Medieval Dublin*. Dublin: O'Brien Educational, 1978.
—*Divided City*. Dublin: O'Brien Educational, 1978.

Curtis, Edmund. *A History of Ireland*. London: Methuen & Co, 1936.

Daiken, Leslie. *Out Goes She: Dublin Street Rhymes with a Commentary*. Dublin: Dolmen Press, 1963.

D'Alton, John. *The History of the County Dublin*. Dublin: Hodges & Smith, 1838, Reprinted, Cork: Tower Books, 1976.
—*The Memoirs of the Archbishops of Dublin*. Dublin: Hodges & Smith, 1838.

Daly, Mary E. *Dublin, the Deposed Capital: a Social and Economic History 1860-1914*. Cork: University Press, 1984.

de Breffny, Brian & Mott, George. *The Churches and Abbeys of Ireland*. London: Thames & Hudson, 1976.
—*Castles of Ireland*. London: Thames & Hudson, 1977.

de Buitléar, Eamonn (ed). *Irish Rivers*. Dublin: Country House, 1985.

de Courcy, Catherine. *The Foundation of the National Gallery of Ireland*. Dublin: National Gallery of Ireland, 1985.

de Paor, Liam. *Peoples of Ireland*. London: Hutchinson, 1986.

de Paor, Maire & Liam. *Early Christian Ireland*. London: Thames & Hudson, 1958.

Dickinson, P L. *The Dublin of Yesterday*. London: Methuen & Co, 1929.

Dillon, Myles & Chadwick, Nora. *The Celtic Realms*. London: Weidenfeld & Nicolson, 1967.

Donnelly, N. *Short History of Dublin Parishes*. Dublin: C T S, 1910-1915.

Dublin Corporation. *Official Guide to the City of Dublin*. Dublin: Irish & Overseas Publishing Co, 1965.

Dunbar, Janet. *Peg Woffington & her World*. London: Heinemann, 1968.

Elmes, Rosalind M. *Catalogue of Irish Topographical Prints and Original Drawings*. New Edition, revised & enlarged by Michael Hewson, Dublin: Malton Press for National Library of Ireland Society, 1975.

'Endymion'. *Dublin: What to do, where to go, what to see*. Dublin: Mount Salus Press, 1967.

Evans, Estyn. *Prehistoric & Early Christian Ireland*. London: Batsford Books, 1966.

Fagan, Patrick. *The Second City: Portrait of Dublin 1700-1760*. Dublin: Branar, 1986.

Ferguson, Lady. *The Irish before the Conquest*. Dublin: Sealy, Bryers & Walker, 1903.

Finlay, Ian & Bunn, Mike (phot.). *Dublin, with an Introductory Essay by James Plunkett*. Dublin: Dublin Corporation, 1976.

Finn, Mary. *The Adventure Guide to Dublin*. Dublin: Wolfhound Press, 1984, Revised ed 1987.

Fitzpatrick, Samuel A Ossory. *Dublin: A Historical and Topographical Account of the City*. London: Methuen & Co, 1907.

Fitzpatrick, William J. *The Sham Squire and the Informers of 1798*. Dublin: M H Gill & Son, 1895.
—*History of the Dublin Catholic Cemeteries*. Dublin: Cemeteries Offices, 1900.

Flanagan, Noel. *Malahide Past & Present*. Malahide, Co Dublin: Noel Flanagan, 1984.

Flynn, Arthur. *Famous Links with Bray*. Bray, Co Wicklow: Falcon Print, 1985.

Forde-Johnston, J. *Prehistoric Britain and Ireland*. London: J M Dent, 1976.

Garrett, Arthur. *In Ages Past: The Story of North Strand Church Sunday and Day Schools*. Dublin: North Strand Sunday and Day School Bi-Centenary Committee, 1985.

Gaughan, J Anthony (ed). *Mount Merrion: the Old and the New*. Dublin: Church of St Thérèse, Mount Merrion, 1981.

Georgian Society. *Records* (5 Vols). Dublin: University Press, 1909-1913.

Gilbert, Sir J T. *A History of the City of Dublin* (3 vols). Dublin: James Duffy, 1861, Reprinted, Dublin: Irish University Press, 1969, Dublin: Gill & Macmillan, 1978.

Gilbert, Sir J T (ed), and later Lady Gilbert. *Calendar of Ancient Records of Dublin* (19 vols). Dublin: Joseph Dollard, 1889-1944.

Gill, M H & Son (ed). *Guide to Catholic Dublin*. Dublin: Gill & Son, 1932.

Gillespie, Elgy (ed). *The Liberties of Dublin*. Dublin: O'Brien Press, 1973.

Goedheer, A J. *Irish and Norse Traditions about Gogarty, Oliver St John. As I was going down Sackville Street*. London: Rich & Cowan, 1937.

Gorham, Maurice. *Ireland Yesterday*. London: Batsford Books, 1971.
—*Dublin from Old Photographs*. London: Batsford Books, 1972.
—*Dublin Old and New*. Menston, Yorkshire: E P Publications, 1975.

Granville, Gary. *Divided City: Portrait of Dublin 1913*. Dublin: O'Brien Press, 1978, Reprinted as 'Dublin 1913' in 1982.

Guinness, Desmond. *Portrait of Dublin*. London: Batford Books, 1967.
—*Georgian Dublin*. London: Batsford Books, 1979.

Guinness, Desmond & Ryan, William. *Irish Houses and Castles*. London: Thames & Hudson, 1971.

Gwynn, Stephen. *The Famous Cities of Ireland*. Dublin & London: Maunsell & Co, 1915.
—*Dublin Old & New*. Dublin: Browne & Nolan, 1940.

Hackett, Francis. *The Story of the Irish Nation*. Dublin: The Talbot Press, 1924.

Haliday, Charles. *The Scandinavian Kingdom of Dublin*. Dublin: Alex Thom & Co, 1881. Reprinted, Dublin & Shannon: Irish University Press, 1969.

Hall, Mr & Mrs S C. *Ireland: Its Scenery, Character Etc*. (3 vols.) London: Virtue & Co, 1842.

Hamp, William. *If ever you go to Dublin Town*. Old Greenwich, Conn: The Devin-Adair Co, 1984.

Harbison, Peter. *National Monuments of Ireland*. Dublin: Gill & Macmillan, 1970.

—*The Archaeology of Ireland*. London: The Bodley Head, 1976.

Harbison, Peter, Potterton, Homan, & Sheehy, Jeanne. *Irish Art and Architecture*. London: Thames and Hudson, 1978.

Harrison, Wilmot. *Memorable Dublin Houses: a Handy Guide*. Dublin: W Leckie & Co, 1890. Reprinted by Menston, Yorkshire: S R Publications, 1971.

Hayward, Richard. *Leinster and the City of Dublin*. London: Arthur Barker, 1949.

Herman, David. *Hill Strolls around Dublin*. Dublin: David Herman, 1984.

Herries Davies, G L & Stephens, Nicholas. *The Geomorphology of the British Isles: Ireland*. London: Methuen & Co, 1978.

Hickey, Kieran. *Faithful Departed*. Dublin: Ward River Press, 1982.

Hogan, Jeremiah J. *The English Language in Ireland*. Dublin: The Educational Company of Ireland, 1927.

Hogan, Robert (ed). *Dictionary of Irish Literature*. London: Macmillan, 1980.

Hubert, Henri. *The Greatness & Decline of the Celts*. London: Kegan Paul, Trench, Trubner & Co Ltd, 1934.

Hughes, Kathleen. *The Church in Early Irish Society*. London: Hodder & Stoughton, 1972.

Humphreys, Alex. *New Dubliners*. London: Routledge & Kegan Paul, 1965.

Hunt, Hugh. *The Abbey: Ireland's National Theatre 1904-1978*. Dublin: Gill & Macmillan, 1979.

Hurley, Michael (ed). *Irish Anglicanism 1869-1969*. Dublin: Allen Figgis & Co, 1970.

Hurst, Michael. *Parnell and Irish Nationalism*. London: Routledge & Kegan Paul, 1968.

Hutton, Arthur Wollanston. *Arthur Young's Tour in Ireland 1776-1779*. London: G Bell & Sons, 1892.

Jeffrey, D W *et al* (ed). *North Bull Island, Dublin Bay: A Modern Coastal Natural History*. Dublin: Royal Dublin Society, 1977.

John, Brian. *The Ice Age*. London: Collins, 1977.

Johnson, Nevil. *Dublin: The People's City*. Dublin: The Academy Press, 1981.

Johnston, Máirín. *Around the Banks of Pimlico*. Dublin: Attic Press, 1985.

Joyce, P W. *Irish Names of Places* (3 vols). Dublin, Cork, Belfast: Phoenix Publishing Co, 1913.

Joyce, Weston St John. *The Neighbourhood of Dublin*. Dublin: Gill & Son, 1939.

Kearns, Kevin Corrigan. *Georgian Dublin: Ireland's Imperilled Arcchitectural Heritage*. London: David & Charles, 1983.

Kain, Richard M. *Dublin in the Age of William Butler Yeats and James Joyce*. Newton Abbot: David & Co, 1972.

Kee, Robert. *Ireland: A History*. London: Weidenfeld & Nicolson, 1980.

Kelleher, Terry. *The Essential Dublin*. Dublin: Gill & Macmillan, 1979.

Kelly, Deirdre. *Hands off Dublin*. Dublin: O'Brien Press, 1976.

Kennedy, P G. *An Irish Sanctuary: North Bull Island*. Dublin: Three Candles, 1953.

Kennedy, Tom (ed). *Dublin Handbook*. Dublin: Albertine Kennedy, 1978.

—*Victorian Dublin*. Dublin: Albertine Kennedy, 1980.

Kilroy, Jim. *Howth and her trams*. Dublin: Kilroy, 1986.

Lalor, Brian. *Dublin*. London: Routledge & Kegan Paul, 1981.

Leask, Harold G. *Irish Castles & Castellated Houses*. Dundalk: Dundalgan Press, 1941.

—*Irish Churches & Monastic Buildings*. Dundalk: Dundalgan Press, 1955.

Lehane, Brendan. *The Great Cities: Dublin*. Amsterdam: Time-Life International, 1978.

Le Harivel, Adrian (Compiler). *Illustrated Summary Catalogue of Drawings, Watercolours and Miniatures*. Dublin: The National Gallery of Ireland, 1983.

Lewis, Samuel. *A History and Topography of the City of Dublin*. Cork & Dublin: Mercier Press, 1980.

Liddy, Pat. *Dublin To-day*. Dublin: *The Irish Times*, 1984.

Little, George. *Dublin before the Vikings*. Dublin: M H Gill & Son, 1957.

Lord Mayor's *Book of Dublin*. Dublin: Cahill, 1942.

Lyons, F S L. *Charles Stewart Parnell*. London: Collins, 1977.

—*The Burden of our History*. Belfast: The Queen's University, 1978.

Macalister, R A S. *The Archaeology of Ireland*. London: Methuen & Co, 1928.

McBrierty, Vincent J. *The Howth Peninsula: Its History, Lore and Legend*. Dublin: North Dublin Round Table, 1981.

McCabe, Fergal. *Tallaght Village: A Visual and Environmental Study*. Tallaght: Chamber of Commerce, 1987.

McCarthy, Jack. *Joyce's Dublin: A Walking Guide to Ulysses*. Dublin: Wolfhound Press, 1986.

McCartney, Donal (ed). *The World of Daniel O'Connell*. Dublin & Cork: Mercier Press, 1980.

McCready, C T. *Dublin Street Names, Dated and Explained*. Dublin: Hodges Figgis, 1892.

MacGowan, Kenneth. *The Phoenix Park*. Dublin: Kamac Publications, 1966.

McGrath, Fergal. *Newman in Dublin*. Dublin: C T S, 1969.

—*Education in Ancient & Medieval Ireland*. Dublin: A 'Studies' Special Publication, 1979.

McIntyre, Dennis *The Meadow of the Bull: A History of Clontarf*. Dublin: McIntyre, 1987.

McIvor, Muriel. *Clontarf Past and Present*. Dublin: Eason's, 1976.

McHugh, Roger. *Dublin 1916*. London: Arlington Books, 1966.

MacLiammóir, Micheál. *All for Hecuba*. London: Methuen & Co, 1946.

Mac Liammóir, Micheál & Boland, Eavan. *W B Yeats and his World*. London: Thames & Hudson, 1971.

MacLoughlin, Adrian. *Guide to Historic Dublin*. Dublin: Gill & Macmillan, 1979.

—*Streets of Ireland*. Dublin: Swift Publications Ltd, 1981.

McNally, Robert. *Old Ireland*. Dublin: M H Gill & Son, 1965.

Mac Thomáis, Éamonn. *Me Jewel and Darlin' Dublin*. Dublin: O'Brien Press, 1974.

—*Gur Cake and Coal Blocks*. Dublin: O'Brien Press, 1976.

—*The Labour and the Royal.* Dublin: O'Brien Press, 1979.

Madden, Richard Robert. *History of Irish Periodical Literature* (2 vols). London: T C Newby, 1867.

Magnusson, Magnus. *Viking: Hammer of the North.* London: Orbis Publishing, 1976.

Maguire, J B. *Dublin Castle: Historical Background and Guide.* Dublin: Stationery Office, 1974.

Malone, J B & Martin, Liam. *Know your Dublin.* London: Sceptre, 1969.

Marks, Bernadette. *Born and Reared in Swords.* Dublin: Fingall Historical Societies, 1986.

Martin, Liam C. *Dublin Shopfronts and Street-scenes.* Dublin: Cobblestone Press, 1974.

—*Dublin Sketch Book.* Dublin: Dolmen Press, 1962.

—*A Visual Tour of Dublin Hospitals.* Dublin: Cobblestone Press, 1975.

Maxwell, Constantia. *Dublin under the Georges.* London: George Harrap & Co, 1946.

—*A History of Trinity College Dublin 1591-1892.* Dublin: The University Press, 1946.

—*The Stranger in Ireland from the Reign of Elizabeth to the Great Famine.* London: Jonathan Cape, 1954, Reprinted, Dublin: Gill & Macmillan, 1979.

Maxwell, N (ed). *Digging up Dublin: a Future for our Past.* Dublin: O'Brien Press, 1980.

Mitchell, Arthur & Ó Snodaigh, Pádraig. *Irish Political Documents 1916-1949.* Dublin: Irish Academic Press, 1985.

Moody, T W & Martin, F X (eds). *The Course of Irish History.* Cork: The Mercier Press, 1967.

—*A New History of Ireland.* (10 vols). Oxford, Clarendon Press, 1976-87.

Moore, D F. *Dublin: Baile Átha Cliath.* Dublin: Three Candles, 1965.

Moore, George. *Hail and Farewell* (3 vols). London: William Heinemann, 1911-14.

Moriarty, Christopher. *Dublin and North Wicklow.* Dublin: Gill & Macmillan, 1980.

Morrissey, Thomas. *Towards a National University: William Delaney SJ. An Era of Initiative in Irish Education.* Dublin: Wolfhound Press, 1983.

Morton, H V. *In Search of Ireland.* London: Methuen & Co, 1930.

Munster, Robert. *The History of the Irish Newspaper.* Cambridge: University Press, 1967.

Murphy, Denis (trans). *The Life of Hugh Roe O'Donnell from the Irish of Lughaidh O'Clery.* Dublin: Sealy, Bryers & Walker, 1893.

Murray, K A. *Ireland's First Railway.* Dublin: Irish Railway Record Society, 1981.

Neary, Bernard. *North of the Liffey: a Character Sketchbook.* Dublin: Lenhar Publications, 1984.

Nevill, W E. *Geology and Ireland.* Dublin: Allen Figgis, 1963.

Nolan, William (ed). *The Shaping of Ireland: the Geographical Perspective.* Cork & Dublin: Mercier Press, 1986.

Norman, E R & St Joseph, J K S. *The Early Development of Irish Society: The Evidence of Aerial Photography.* Cambridge: University Press, 1969.

Norris, David. *Joyce's Dublin.* Dublin: Eason's, 1982.

Ó Broin, Art & McMahon, Seán. *Faces of Old Leinster.* Belfast: Appletree Press, 1978.

Ó Broin, Leon. *Dublin Castle and the 1916 Rising.* London: Sidgwick & Jackson, 1966.

—*The Chief Secretary: Augustine Birrell in Ireland.* London: Chatto & Windus, 1969.

—*Fenian Fever: An Anglo-American Dilemma.* London: Chatto & Windus, 1971.

O'Broin, Sean. *The Book of Finglas.* Dublin: Kincora Press, 1980.

O'Connell, Derry. *The Antique Pavement: an Illustrated Guide to Dublin's Street Furniture.* Dublin: An Taisce, 1975.

O'Connor, Laurence. *Lost Ireland.* Dublin: Rainbow Publications, 1984.

O'Dwyer, Frederick. *Lost Dublin.* Dublin: Gill & Macmillan, 1981.

O'Meara, John J (trans). *The History and Topography of Ireland translated from the Latin of Giraldus Cambrensis.* Dundalk: Dundalgan Press, 1951.

Oram, Hugh. *Bewleys.* Dublin: Albertine Kennedy, 1980.

—*The Newspaper Book: A History of Newspapers in Ireland, 1649-1983.* Dublin: M O Books, 1983.

Ó Ríordáin, Seán. *Antiquities of the Irish Countryside.* London: Methuen & Co, 1942.

Otway-Ruthven, A J. *A History of Medieval Ireland.* London: Ernest Benn, 1968.

Pearl, Cyril. *Dublin in Bloomtime: the City James Joyce Knew.* London: Angus & Robertson, 1969.

Pearson, Peter. *Dun Laoghaire: Kingstown.* Dublin: O'Brien Press, 1981.

Peplow, Mary & Shirley, Debra. *Dublin for Free.* London: Grafton Books, 1987.

Pochin-Mould, Daphne D C. *Ireland from the Air.* Newton-Abbot: David & Charles, 1972.

Polsson, Hermann & Edwards, Paul (trans). *Orkneyinga Saga.* Harmondsworth: Penguin Books, 1978.

Popplewell, Seán. *The Irish Museums Guide.* Dublin: Ward River Press, 1983.

Powell, T G E. *The Celts.* London: Thames & Hudson, 1980.

Praeger, Robert Lloyd. *The Way that I Went.* Dublin: Allen Figgis, 1980.

Prendergast, John P. *The Cromwellian Settlement of Ireland.* London: Longman, Green & Co, 1865.

Pritchett, V S. *Dublin: a Portrait.* London: The Bodley Head, 1967.

Purcell, Mary. *Matt Talbot and his Times.* Alcester & Dublin: Goodliffe Neale, 1976.

Quinn, Edward. *James Joyce's Dublin.* London: Secker & Warbeck, 1974.

Raferty, Joseph. *Prehistoric Ireland.* London: Batsford, 1951.

Retler, Wolfgang. *Ireland Explored.* London: Thames & Hudson, 1966.

Reynolds, Mairead. *A History of the Irish Post Office.* Dublin: MacDonnell Whyte Ltd, 1983.

Robertson, Manning. *Dún Laoghaire: the History, Scenery & Development of the District.* Dún Laoghaire: Borough Corporation, 1936.

Robertson, Olivia. *Dublin Phoenix.* London: Jonathan Cape, 1957.

Ronan, Myles V. *The Reformation in Dublin 1536-1558.* London: Longmans, Green & Co Ltd, 1926.

Ryan, John SJ. *Irish Monasticism: Origins & Early Development.* Dublin & Cork: Talbot Press, 1931. Reprinted,

Dublin: Irish University Press, 1969.

Ryan, John. *Remembering How We Stood*. Dublin: Gill & Macmillan, 1975.

Sadleir, Thomas & Dickinson, Page L. *Georgian Mansions in Ireland*. Dublin: Ponsonby & Gibbs, 1915.

Sheehy, Terence J. *Ireland*. London: Colour Library International, 1979.

Simms, J. *Jacobite Ireland 1685-91*. London: Routledge & Kegan Paul, 1969.

Somerville-Large, Peter. *Irish Eccentrics*. London: Hamish Hamitlon, 1975.

—*Dublin*. London: Hamish Hamilton, 1979.

Stalley, R A. *Architecture and Sculpture in Ireland 1150-1350*. Dublin: Gill & Macmillan, 1971.

Stephens, James. *The Insurrection in Dublin*. Dublin: Maunsell & Co, 1916.

Shepherd, Ernie. *Behind the Scenes: the Story of Whitechurch District in South County Dublin*. Dublin: Whitechurch Publications, 1983.

Thackeray, W M. *The Irish Sketch-Book*. London: Chapman & Hall, 1843.

Thomas, Charles. *Britain and Ireland in Early Christian Times: A.D. 400-800*. London: Thames & Hudson, 1971.

Tinsley, M K. *The Bridges over the Liffey*. Dublin: M Tinsley, 1973.

Uris, Jill & Leon. *Ireland: A Terrible Beauty*. London: André Deutsch, 1976.

Wakeman, W F. *Handbook of Irish Antiquities*. Dublin: Hodges Figgis & London: John Murray, 1903.

Wall, Mervyn. *Forty Foot Gentlemen Only*. Dublin: Hodges Figgis, 1962.

Wall, Thomas. *The Sign of Doctor Hay's Head*. Dublin: M H Gill & Son, 1958.

Walpole, Charles. *The Kingdom of Ireland*. London: Kegan Paul, Trench & Co, 1885.

Walsh, John. *Rakes and Ruffians: the Underworld of Georgian Dublin*. Dublin: Four Courts Press, 1979.

Warburton, J, Whitelaw, J & Walsh, R. *History of the City of Dublin* (2 vols). London: T Cadel & W Davies, 1818.

Watt, J A, Morrall, J B & Martin, F X. *Medieval Studies, Presented to Aubrey Gwynn SJ*. Dublin: The Three Candles, 1961.

Webb, John J. *The Guilds of Dublin*. Dublin: Three Candles, 1929.

Wells, A K & Kirkaldy, J F. *Outline of Historical Geology*. London: Thomas Murby & Co, 1966.

Whelpton, Eric. *The Book of Dublin*. London: Rockliff, 1948.

Whitehead, Trevor. *Dublin Fire Fighters*. Dublin: Transport Research Associates, 1970.

Wilson, David. *The Vikings and their Origins*. London: Thames & Hudson, 1970.

Wrenn, Timmy. *The Villages of Dublin*. Dublin: Tamar Publishing, 1982.

Wright, Arnold. *Disturbed Dublin: the Story of the Great Strike 1913-14*. London: Longmans, Green & Co, 1914.

Wright, G N. *A Historical Guide to Ancient and Modern Dublin*. London: Cradock & Joy, 1821. Reprinted in Dublin: Four Courts Press, 1980.

Wyse Jackson, Peter. *The Story of the Botanic Gardens in Trinity College, Dublin*. Dublin: TCD, 1987.

Yee, Chiang. *The Silent Traveller in Dublin*. London: Methuen & Co, 1953.

Periodicals and Journals

Analectica Hibernica
Calendar of Ancient Records of Dublin
Calendar of the Patent Rolls, Ireland
Calendar of State Papers, Ireland
Collectanea Hibernica
Dublin Diocesan Historical Record
Dublin Historical Record
Dublin Opinion
Dublin Review
Freeman's Journal
Irish Builder, The
Irish Ecclesiastical Record
Irish Independent, The
Irish Historical Studies
Irish Monthly, The
Irish Press, The
Irish Times, The
Journal of the Irish House of Commons (1613-1800)
Journal of the Irish House of Lords (1634-1800)
Journal of the Royal Society of the Antiquaries of Ireland
Proceedings of the Royal Irish Academy
Reports on the Hospitals of the City of Dublin
Revue Celtique
Studies
Thom's Directory
Watson's Dublin Directory
Wilson's Directory

Maps of Dublin

John Speed, 1610
Sir Bernard de Gomme, 1673
Thomas Phillipps, 1685
Greenville Collins, 1686
Capt Pratt, 1708
Herman Moll, 1714
Charles Brooking, 1728
John Roque, 1754, 1756 & 1757
S J Neele, 1797
J Cooke, 1822
M Heffernan, 1861 & 1868
Ordnance Survey, 1837 on
Howard B Clarke, 1978

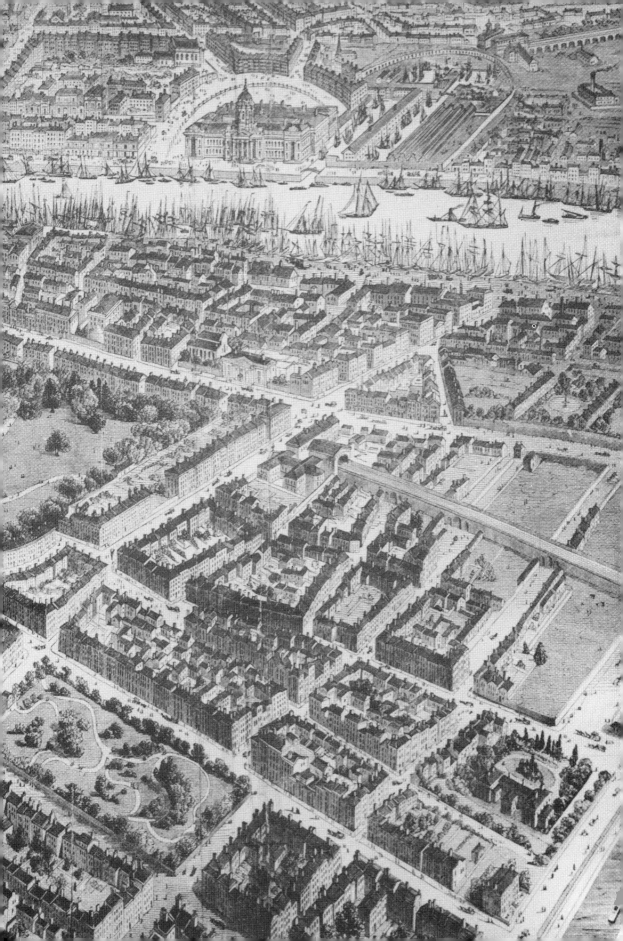